The Politics of Fear in South Sudan

About the author

Daniel Akech Thiong was born in 1980 in Sudan and started formal schooling at the Kakuma Refugee Camp in Kenya at the age of 19. The rudimentary knowledge of mathematics and English he gained allowed him to continue his studies and, within two years, he ranked among the top ten students in his eighth-grade class. After emigrating to the United States as one of the Lost Boys of Sudan in 2001, he continued to learn, passing his high school equivalency exam within three months of arrival and later obtaining a BA in theology and a BA in mathematics from the University of San Diego in California in 2007. He went on to obtain an MA in mathematics at the University of Colorado at Boulder in 2010. He has worked for a year as a full-time maths instructor at Pennsylvania State University and is currently a PhD candidate at the Institute of Mathematical Sciences at Claremont Graduate University with a research focus on matrix analysis and functional analysis. He is an adjunct maths instructor at the University of La Verne. He has applied the same methodological acumen required to solve math problems to understanding current affairs in South Sudan and has become a proficient writer on the topic. His analytical insights have been recognized by multiple economic, political and natural resource think tanks, and he published articles in top-ranked African journals, including the *Oxford Journal of African Affairs*. He is currently working as an independent consultant doing analysis on the political economy of public authority as it relates to violence in South Sudan.

Politics and Development in Contemporary Africa

Published by one of the world's leading publishers on African issues, 'Politics and Development in Contemporary Africa' seeks to provide accessible but in-depth analysis of key contemporary issues affecting countries within the continent. Featuring a wealth of empirical material and case study detail, and focusing on a diverse range of subject matter – from conflict to gender, development to the environment – the series is a platform for scholars to present original and often provocative arguments. Selected titles in the series are published in association with the International African Institute.

The principal aim of the International African Institute is to promote scholarly understanding of Africa, notably its changing societies, cultures and languages. Founded in 1926 and based in London, it supports a range of seminars and publications, including the journal Africa.

www.internationalafricaninstitute.org

Already published:

Forthcoming titles:

The Politics of Fear in South Sudan

Generating Chaos, Creating Conflict

Daniel Akech Thiong

ZED

Zed Books
Bloomsbury Publishing Plc
50 Bedford Square, London, WC1B 3DP, UK
1385 Broadway, New York, NY 10018, USA
29 Earlsfort Terrace, Dublin 2, Ireland

First published in Great Britain 2021
This paperback edition published in 2023

Series design by Burgess & Beech
Cover image © Roberto Schmidt/AFP/Getty Images

A catalogue record for this book is available from the British Library.

A catalog record for this book is available from the Library of Congress.

ISBN: HB: 978-1-7869-9678-7
PB: 978-1-7869-9679-4
ePDF: 978-1-7869-9680-0
eBook: 978-1-7869-9681-7

Series: Politics and Development in Contemporary Africa

Typeset by Newgen KnowledgeWorks Pvt. Ltd., Chennai, India

To find out more about our authors and books visit www.bloomsbury.com
and sign up for our newsletters.

To the late Commander William Nyuon Bany, a dedicated freedom fighter who shot one of the first bullets in Ayod in June 1983 and led to our independence, it is a blessing that you were the father to Nyadol and now a grandfather to my two angels: Angeth and Thiong, who are the silent thrust of my journey.

Contents

Preface

On the night of 15 December 2013, the manager of a hotel in Juba, who was terrified by the sounds of sustained gunfire, knocked on the door of the hotel owner, who was sleeping in the room next door.

'The shooting is not stopping,' he complained.

'It is not expected to stop,' the boss replied.

The South Sudanese Civil War had begun. The hotel owner exacerbated his already terrified employee's fear by telling him how he thought the days ahead would unfold. Provocations between competing political leaders – including President Salva Kiir, the chairman of the Sudan People's Liberation Movement (SPLM); Dr Riek Machar, the former vice president and deputy chairman of the SPLM; and Pagan Amum, the Secretary General of the SPLM – who had publicly criticized and threatened each other prior to the outbreak of the conflict, made it clear to many observers that the country was at the precipice of war. While the outbreak of civil war in December 2013 was not a surprise, 'the form it took of a government-orchestrated attack on Nuer civilians in Juba was'.[1]

Both the spread of conflict throughout the country and the online propagation of disinformation about the conflict quickly formed parallels that caused each other to grow. The shooting not only continued for days in Juba but also spread quickly to other major towns in the Upper Nile region, such as Bor, Bentiu and Malakal. During the initial months of the war, the Nuer dominated both sides of the conflict. To put it simply, the Nuer had the guns and the Dinka had the money – as the financial sectors were controlled by the Dinka in practice. Had the entire Nuer army fought on Riek's side, he could easily have gained control of the Upper Nile region. In Unity State, President Kiir relied on Generals Bapiny MonyTwil and Matthew Puljang, who were both from Nuer. In Upper Nile State, he relied on the 1st Division, which was largely composed of Nuer fighters who followed General Gony Biliu. When the 1st Division force was weakened, President Kiir had to turn to the Shilluk forces, who were under the command of General Johnson Olony. David Yau

Yau, from the Murle tribe, leading Cobra forces in his homeland in Pibor, was approached by the government and swiftly brought to Juba so that Dr Riek Machar could not recruit him to his side. A senior officer within the National Security has alleged that about six thousand Cobra forces were deployed in the frontlines to defend the government.[2] The total number of Cobra forces that were promised to be integrated into the national army was twelve thousand.[3] This dynamic shows that the war was more complex than journalists reported – as a tribal war that pitted Dinka against Nuer. This is not to deny the existence of a historical political divide along the Nuer–Dinka contours but to highlight that intra-group divisions have occurred at the start of the conflict, and more occurred later on as the conflict progressed.

South Sudan's political leaders' attitudes and behaviours triggered the civil war that has been ravaging the young nation since 2013. The same attitudes and behaviours have led to the collapse of the August 2015 peace agreement and the delay in implementing the September 2018 peace agreement, which promised a formation of the coalition government by the deadline of 12 November that was postponed because the warring leaders failed to resolve their disagreement over security arrangements and the number of states South Sudan should have.

The continuation of the war and repeated failures of the peace agreements have led to frustration among the international community as well as among the South Sudanese masses. For example, the US assistant secretary of state for African affairs, Tibor Nagy, has stated during his visit to South Sudan that 'the international community is sick and tired and fed up with providing the government services that the government of South Sudan should be providing for its own people'.[4] Unfortunately, this frustration came a little too late as John Young argued in his recent account of America's debacle in South Sudan.[5]

In South Sudan's dynamics of conflict, irrational behaviour is hardly a voluntary choice; it results from the manipulation of the elites. *South Sudan Imatong State Gov Tobiolo Oromo on SPLA-Civil Relations* noted in 2018 that 'our people need to be governed by laws and not by fear'.[6] This sentiment points to the use of fear as an instrument of governance or insurgency advance.

As a manifestation of their failure to achieve tangible results after the civil war, South Sudan's political leaders have continued to wrangle over liberation credits – determining who deserves to be recognized – which are used as a source of political legitimacy and for justifying the distribution of access to public resources amongst the elites. Although many things in South Sudan ought to be distributed to the country's political units, the procedures that the regulators employ tend to contribute to horizontal grievances (e.g. grievances between communities). A part of the problem is that many of the lucrative jobs in the country are predominantly government-based and require appointments by an appointing authority. This has led to an overcrowded political arena (in which there are those who understandably see themselves as losers both as individuals and/or as communities). The appointing authority picks individuals according to loyalty rather than knowledge or skill. Communities expect jobs to be awarded to community representatives in direct proportion to their past contributions to the liberation movements, as independence and the opportunities that have arisen as a consequence are considered to be the results of these efforts. During the civil war, communities contributed food items (e.g. farm products and livestock), youth fighters and transportation (such as boats to move ammunition from one place to another or men to carry ammunition boxes for days on end). The difficulty of coming up with an agreeable formula for sharing the 'national pie' ensures that conflicts fuelled by the perceived unfairness in dividing that share of the pie will continue to undermine the effective management of diversity. Compounding this issue is the notion that fairness is not something politicians view as a necessary component of an immediately successful future. Therefore, in fighting over liberation credits, South Sudan's political leaders have turned fear into instruments of political governance or insurgent advance, exacerbating the dilemma of security amongst competing sociopolitical groups.

The politics of fear has created fault lines that have dissected the country into two groups: those who perceive themselves as the marginalized masses whose bitterness is at its peak and those who are perceived to be the exploiters and are either genuinely ignorant or who feign ignorance about the levels of hatred that the conflict and its politics have generated. These designations may be unfair. For instance, all Dinka are considered to be exploiters, and there is no distinction between the Dinka and the government (regardless of their opinions and actions). Similarly, a majority of non-Dinka citizens are treated with suspicion, and there is no distinction between the non-Dinka and the armed opposition groups.

Oppositional elites point to the underrepresentation of their groups in institutions so that they can mobilize fighters, and the powerful government elites in Juba interfere in state politics, exacerbate the security dilemma and appoint government officials in a way that instils fear in those who view themselves as victims.

Whenever elites wish to outdo one another and disagree on a fair formula for sharing power and access to resources, they resort to the use of political fear so that they can manipulate the populace into supporting their policies, the success of which is aided by certain structural misfortunes, such as illiteracy, ignorance and poverty. Prior to the outbreak of the conflict, provocations by rivalling political leaders who publicly criticized and threatened each other made it clear to many observers that the country was at the precipice of war. Shockingly, the use of political fear amongst multiple parties with conflicting interests can generate a collective outcome that is vastly different from what any single party desires or expects. This sensitivity to foundational conditions is the main characteristic of chaos. While one party may escalate their threats in the hopes that the other party will back down and conflict will be avoided, the other party may feel that their security hinges on the success of a counter-attack. This generates a security dilemma, which exacerbates what may have been a dormant conflict and ultimately triggers chaos.

By weaving social, political and economic factors together into a comprehensive framework to explain how elite powers transform fear and animosity into violent and deadly conflict, this book unpacks the role that the politics of fear has played in the security dilemma framework. The powerful elite deploy politics of fear to manipulate and legitimate economic and security concerns across the globe. In South Sudan, the elites and their associates regularly reopen wounds from earlier episodes of their violent ethnic rivalry to promote hate and generate fear, creating a dynamic where elites fear each other and their rivals from other groups. As the warring parties target the masses along ethnic and regional lines, individuals are forced to assemble in ethnic or regional groups for security reasons. Nevertheless, in the effort to enhance security by arming several ethnic factions, South Sudan has become a land of fear.

'If there is a cattle camp, which doesn't have a cow belonging to you in it, nobody in that camp gives your children any milk, no son whose parents have cows from that cattle camp will ever marry your daughter, why should you call such a cattle camp "our cattle camp"?' Achuil Akoch, a former commissioner for Tonj North County in Warrap State and a former minister for finance, planning, trade and industry for the state government of Warrap, has asked this difficult question to almost every Dinka elite he has ever chatted with since 2013 or earlier. Then, Achuil turns this into a political question, asking why Dinka civilians in the villages who do not benefit from the government should be asked to contribute their sons to fight for the government in Juba. Achuil's arguments with others on this question could make an interesting PhD dissertation. He isn't an academic, but someone who deeply thinks about the political affairs of his country. The obvious answer to the question is that such a cattle camp shouldn't be called our camp by those who cannot benefit from it. Nevertheless, they do, which is basically a part of what this book has set out to find out why. This book will address the following two major research questions: (1) How were the masses persuaded to support mass violence? and (2) What key processes transformed the elite's rivalry over the control of state power and resources into a deadly conflict in South Sudan? The book tackles these research questions by applying the theoretical innovation of the politics of fear, which refers to the elite politicization of group identity, the decentralization of fear and the mobilization of perceptions of danger, insecurity, resentment and hatred to discredit and dominate rivals and to control populations. The three main channels through which the politics of fear serves as a manufacturer of group-based grievances include large-scale corruption (e.g. fear of domination), the propagation of fear/hate on social and mass media (e.g. smear campaigns) and fear-proving violence (e.g. rapes, extrajudicial killings, abductions, forced displacements, destruction of property and denials to humanitarian access) as political tactics, all of which have existed since the days of the civil war.

While existing studies have focused largely on contextual factors to explain the conflict, few have examined the role of psychological threats. As such, additional research is needed to understand how the manipulation of negative emotions plays a key role in driving ethnic conflicts.

It has been argued that the politics of fear has been effective in controlling the South Sudanese population. The elites' politicization of ethnic identity and their promotion of danger, insecurity, resentment and hatred have been successfully used to dominate rivals and control populations, suggesting that manufactured group-based grievances are more potent in determining the outbreak of an ethnic conflict than contextual factors. In South Sudan, group-based grievances have been manufactured through a patronage system of rewarding compliant supporters at the expense of others and through the dissemination of negative messages through mass media by the influential elites.

It has been specifically asserted that in 2013, the politics of fear reactivated the once-dormant conflict in South Sudan and continued to fuel hostility. South Sudanese political elites and their associates spread largely false narratives through the mass media, generating fear and hatred to manipulate community grievances.[7] The elites spread these narratives to discredit their rivals and their rivals' support bases so that they could gain – and later retain – control of power and the state apparatus. The result was increased suspicion and the victimization of South Sudan's various groups, as the crimes of the various rivals, real or imagined, were blamed on their communities. These hate-generating narratives pit communities against each other, trigger toxic exchanges, perpetuate deep enmity and damage the social fabric of South Sudanese society. These narratives are successful in amplifying social hostility – not because the stories are true – but because (1) they are repeated and re-disseminated by individuals through social media using the 'like' and 'share' buttons, (2) there are few counter-narratives to refute these misperceptions among different ethnic groups, both within and outside of South Sudan, as South Sudanese populations settle in communities that are defined by tribal lines and (3) the harmful social media narratives contain built-in appeals to ethnic resentments and hateful sentiments that are underpinned by earlier episodes of ethnic conflict.

Organization of the book

This book is organized as follows. Chapter 1 traces those features relevant to the instrumentation of fear, such as using violence to silence and control people, allowing power to flow in indeterministic ways and corruption with regards to meagre resources such as access to food aid that have recurred in post-2005 South Sudan. The author tries to avoid restating the history that has already been well documented but concentrates on rebuilding the history of fear from anecdotes shared by participants, which appear in print for the first time in this book.

Chapter 2 integrates existing approaches of the conflict's dynamics by grouping them into broader trends and by assembling these approaches under the general framework of the security dilemma model. It then presents the security dilemma model and explicates its applicability to the South Sudanese case. Existing works largely ignore the roles of agents who use the politics of fear to construct communal grievances and instead concentrate on contextual factors. This book proposes that such a strategy may be less potent in determining the outbreak of ethnic war. Rather, this chapter explains how the politics of fear generates chaos and contributes to the existing literature by examining the roles of actors and situational contexts from an integrative perspective. Literature on the ethnic conflict largely analyses this phenomenon from the perspectives of the security dilemma theory, which is derived from the realist paradigm of international relations theory, to identify the factors that increase the risk of violent conflict when imperial order breaks down.

Chapter 3 explains the internal dynamics of South Sudan's ruling elite, as well as those of the military and the ruling party, the SPLM, and shows how events that preceded the war can be explained through the prism of the security dilemma. In addition, it explains how the actions of certain leaders relied on or promoted politics of fear. It further proposes that the spread of violent conflict in South Sudan was a response to the provocations of influential elites – a process made possible through both social imitation and structural circumstances.

Chapter 4 advances the argument that the spread of corruption triggered fear of domination. When the benefits of corruption, which can include bribery, are perceived to be collective, the marginalized view it as a tool that the ruling group uses to express dominance. By comparison, the ruling group views any discourse about corruption as propaganda that the 'disgruntled' use to express their grievances. From either viewpoint, corruption enters into the dynamics of conflict as one of the tools that is used to manufacture group-based grievances and stoke fear, which, in turn, can trigger actions that may exacerbate the dilemma of security amongst competing groups.

Chapter 5 addresses the propagation of fear/hate through social media. It also analyses how South Sudanese political elites and their associates use social media to disseminate mostly false narratives, generating fear and hatred and manipulating community grievances by exploiting cultural biases to market fear and hatred. The result is increased suspicion and the victimization of South Sudan's various factions, as the real or imagined crimes of rivals are blamed on their communities.

Chapter 6 describes the role that coercion has played in the current conflict and analyses how rule by decree, cases of human rights abuses, destruction of properties, forceful displacements and unknown gunmen have contributed to the politics of fear and aimed to silence or force people to embrace uniform views that are favourable to the ruling elites.

Chapter 7 argues that external Western groups have failed in their efforts to intervene because their humanitarian and diplomatic efforts are susceptible to manipulation and have therefore been easily controlled by both the regime and insurgency leaders; it also addresses the role of external actors in the conflict.

Finally, Chapter 8 addresses the peace strategies, and the book concludes by deducing that the spread of violent conflict in South Sudan is a response to the provocations of elites, who make fear an instrument of political governance that results in humanitarian, economic and political chaos.

Acknowledgements

This book is the product of an adventurer in search of hands-on experience in various sectors of South Sudan – a journey through which I have met so many people who helped me to write about it. In 2007, I and a fellow South Sudanese friend, Mayak Deng Aruei, who graduated with me from the University of San Diego in 2007, convinced a few friends to start a transportation company called NileLine in Jonglei State. About seven of us pooled our meagre resources into $50,000 US dollars. Mayak and I flew to Kampala and headed to an auto shop. We bought three minibuses and headed to Nimule. The border personnel imposed harsh taxes on our goods, taking $6,000 from us. It looked like a robbery. We were blamed for not knowing how to speak Arabic and for failing to manipulate our receipts to lower the amount we had paid for the cars.

We avoided going to Juba, fearing that our American English would put us into more trouble. We drove from Nimule directly to Bor Town in Jonglei State, our home state. We were told that the Central Equatoria licence plates given to us at Nimule weren't allowed in Jonglei, and we had to pay for new ones. We chose a spot at Safari Hotel for our buses, and we attracted a number of passengers travelling to Juba or Panyagoor. Somebody reported us to the union of buses. We tried to resist, but we were forced to take our buses to the bus station. We were only given one spot for transportation to Juba once every few days. The buses of politicians, most of whom were former guerrilla commanders, were given top priority.

I realized the unsustainability of the venture and withdrew back to the United States, where I enrolled in a master's degree programme at the University of Colorado at Boulder in September 2008. I continued to travel in and out of South Sudan until 2012 when I approached Dr Majak D'Agoot, who was then the deputy minister of defence, to enquire about any possibility of a research job at the Central Bank. I booked myself into a hotel by the Nile behind Juba Stadium to wait for a response. A couple of days at the hotel, a fellow hotel resident, Deng Athuai Mawiir, was dragged out at night, beaten and sealed into a sack and tossed somewhere near the Nile. Due to the risk of staying and the hopelessness of spending the little money I had while waiting on a response that may never come, I booked a flight the next day heading to Nairobi.

Upon arriving in Nairobi, I received an email from a friend, Abraham Diing Akoi, working at the Ministry of Finance at the time, asking me to return to Juba to take up a research assistant job with General/Dr Malual Ayom Dor. I did not have that many options. So, I met with Gen. Malual, who asked me to accept a task that was befitting of a personal aide, which was to take notes and record and transcribe interviews, so that he could direct his efforts at more productive activities at the military headquarters and developing the theoretical framework for his PhD dissertation. I have benefitted more from him than he has benefitted from my research assistantship. I was able to have access to the SPLM/A's archive at South Sudan's Embassy in Nairobi; I have accompanied him to interviews with advisors of Dr John Garang, namely, Dr Mansour Khalid and Hon. Elijah Malok. I have also recorded his interview with Gen. Lazarus Sumbeiywo, the chief mediator of the Comprehensive Peace Agreement, as well as his interview with Hon. Michael Makuei Lueth. While my assignment ended after April 2013, we became friends. A cousin of mine, Chol Thiong, visited me at Nimule Resort on Sunday, 15 December 2013. Chol became unconscious, and we took him to the private hospital in Juba belonging to Dr Kameri Gribani, a surgeon who is a national hero in the armed struggle. I informed Gen. Malual, and he came to the hotel driving the car by himself without a bodyguard. I rode with him to the hospital to visit Chol in the evening. The doctor assured us that Chol would be well. While Gen. Malual was driving me back to Nimule Resorts, we heard gunshots. Gen. Kuol Manyang ordered all the generals not to respond to anything but to head straight to Bilpam, the military headquarters. The family members of the general began to call. He told one lady that he was with Daniel, and she asked if he was even a soldier, to which Gen. Malual essentially said that Daniel was more than a solider. I wanted to come to the military headquarters with him to watch the decision-making live, but Gen. Malual refused, and he quickly dropped me off at the hotel. I immediately began to compose short posts on Facebook about the situation. When the Americans were evacuated, I decided to stay until I left in August 2014. I was able to learn of the ongoing situation from other generals at lunch or at Gen. Malual's office.

Gen. Elijah Alier Ayom, Dr John Garang's most trusted officer when it comes to managing logistics, approached Gen. Malual to connect me with him after learning that my first two university degrees were in mathematics. He gave me a job in which I was in charge of actuaries, working for the SPLA Military Pension Fund, a unit of which he is the managing director. I worked with Bol Atem Manyuon, Yaak Deng Dut, Mading Abraham Mabior (who was killed by unknown gunmen in Juba on 8 March 2018) and others. I learned a great deal from Gen. Alier and his colleagues, who often visited the office just to converse about the past and the current affairs. Gen. Alier allowed me to join and participate in those conversations. Sometimes, we would go out for lunch and meet with a few others.

The place I chose to stay at, Nimule Resort, was the hub through which one could watch events unfolding. Among the people whose conversations I have benefitted from at Nimule Resort include former deputy minister of information and director of the Radio SPLA, Hon. Atem Yaak Atem; former advisor of John Garang, Dr Mansour Khalid; former minister of finance in Warrap state, Hon. Achuil Akoch; former governor of Lakes State and ambassador to Russia, Chol Tong Mayay; former minister of education, Dr John Gai Yoh; former deputy ambassador at the UN, Amb. Lumumba Di-Aping; former dean of the faculty of law at the University of Khartoum and head of Constitutional Review, Prof. Akolda Ma'an Tier; former minister of justice, Hon. Paulino Wanawilla Unango, and my friends Abraham Diing Akoi and Dr Yong Achuoth Deng.

I have learned a great deal from each one of the people I have mentioned – and others I have not mentioned – who shaped many ideas and anecdotes I have put in this book. I am indebted to all of them.

The book refers to songs in the Dinka language as well as interviews carried out in the Dinka language. I am grateful to those who have made such materials available, especially the director of the SBS Dinka Radio based in Australia, Ajak Deng Chiengkou, who has interviewed many actors in the Dinka language. I have the privilege of knowing the language.

All the stories I have included in this book are put out on some kind of forum – mostly Facebook – to corroborate them and for debate. The actual production of the materials took place on the author's Facebook wall where the readers were able to react on sensitive topics covered in this book. For instance, the author wrote a daily post on his observation about the conflict in South Sudan while he was on the ground in Juba. I thank my Facebook friends who have challenged me by providing angles I did not see – this book would not have been possible without their constructive reactions.

I thank Kon K. Madut, Majak D'Agoot, Alex de Waal, Zoe Cormack, Rebecca Lorins, Taku Mkencele, the editors and two anonymous reviewers of *African Affairs*, in which an article that provided the skeleton that grew into this book was published. I am indebted to colleagues from the Development Policy Forum whose reactions to and criticisms of the published article helped to shape the book.

I also thank an editor of the openDemocracy in which the original ideas on the politics of fear were published as an opinion article. I thank the editor of Gurtong, Jacob J. Akol, who edited and published my first piece on corruption. I am greatly indebted to the editor of African Arguments, James Wan, who has done amazing editorial work, leading to four wonderful pieces published in African Arguments, which are included in this book. I also thank two anonymous reviewers from Bloomsbury Publishing. I have benefitted greatly from informal conversations with Dr Lual Deng, Dr Malual Ayom Dor, Dr Majak D'Agoot, Kur Anyieth Kur, Achuil Akoch, Michele D' Arcy and Aluel M. B. Atem. I also thank my professors of the transformative diplomacy class at Claremont Graduate University, Amb. Dr Sallam Shaker and Dr David Drew, who provided valuable comments on some of the materials I have written in the class that have also been incorporated into the book. I also thank Kassem Al-Azem, a friend we share interests in both politics and mathematics. My email exchanges with Alex de Waal, Nicki Kindersly and Luke Patey were helpful as well as many other exchanges I have had via Messenger, WhatsApp and Twitter with a number of people, of whom I would like to mention Yotam Gidron, Lauren Blanchard, Reath Muoch Tang, Dr Luka Biong, Matthew LeRiche and Jane Kani Edward. I am indebted to all of the others I have not mentioned. All of the errors of fact and interpretation in this book remain my sole responsibility.

The role of historical legacy in South Sudan's conflict dynamics

The work of scholars of South Sudan has pointed to the appropriate historical legacy in understanding the existing conflict dynamics in South Sudan. Such an analytical inquiry is supported by literature elsewhere, particularly in natural sciences, where it is called hysteresis – the dependence of the state of a system on its history.

The South Sudanese people, who had experienced fear-provoking violence since the opening of the Nile basin for exploration between 1839 and 1862, voted overwhelmingly to separate from Sudan in 2011. The political-economic history of South Sudan reads as a story of resistance against foreign interventions before 2005, and post 2005 it reads like a chapter in the world annals of organized crime, with the former rebel commanders and political elite in South Sudan playing the roles of junior accomplices in a tale of massive and protracted robbery.[1] Though true, this interpretation does not adequately reveal the never-ending violent negotiation of power relations among competing groups.

The most dominant elite groups before the British and Egypt jointly took control of Southern Sudan in January 1899 hailed from sedentary communities. All of the Southern Sudanese social groups resisted foreign powers for years, but a few groups, mainly those with centralized political systems, realized quiet earlier to take the option of negotiating relations peacefully. The largest Nilotic groups, the Dinka and the Nuer, who are pastoralists, remained impervious to external influence. The Church took over education in Southern Sudan (1900–26), and the pastoralists were initially discriminated against by the education system established.[2] There were notable exceptions, such as the elementary school at Malek among the Dinka of Bor District, opened in 1905, and a secondary school at Rumbek among the Agar Dinka opened in the 1940s.[3] As a consequence of this uneven access to education, from 1899 to 1955, known as the Anglo-Egyptian colonial period, the educated class was dominated by the non-Dinka and non-Nuer. This infrastructure played a role in how the existing political structures, shaped by the civil wars, came into existence.

Exclusionary politics from Khartoum sparked the First Sudanese Civil War (1955–72) led by the Anya-Nya guerrilla movement that was badly disunited until 1969. When Israel entered South Sudan in 1969–71 to support the rebels to address its regional agenda sparked by the politics following the Six-Day War of 1967, they viewed education as the criteria for selecting people to work with. They chose Joseph Lagu, from Equatoria. With the military resources from Israel, Joseph Lagu unified the Anya-Nya guerilla forces under his overall command. He formed the Southern Sudan Liberation Movement (SSLM), which would negotiate the Addis Ababa Peace Agreement in 1972 with Khartoum and ended the war.[4] The period from 1969 to 1983 saw a fierce competition between political leaders from the Equatoria region and Dinka group. This being said with the understanding that Equatoria is a region with more than thirty-six groups with varying political interests, and it is unfair to compare it to Dinka, which is a single ethnic group. Nevertheless, the South Sudanese political relations since 1982 began to be discussed in incomparable groupings into the Dinka, the Nuer and the non-Nuer plus the non-Dinka. The non-Nuer plus the non-Dinka are predominantly in the Equatoria region with some in Bahr el Ghazal and Upper Nile regions. The Dinka is mostly in Bahr el Ghazal, and the Nuer being dominant in Upper Nile (where Dinka comes second).

The politics between 1972 and 1983 was marked by the rivalry between the Dinka group and the Equatoria region. Abel Alier, a Dinka from Upper Nile, led the Southern autonomous regional government twice in 1972–7 and in 1980–1; Joseph Lagu, a Madi from Equatoria in 1977–9; and Joseph Tombura, an Azande from Equatoria, in 1982–3; while Joseph Lagu became the Vice President of Sudan in 1982. So, Equatoria was the dominant group in South Sudanese politics by May 1983.

The origin of the SPLM/A

In 1983, the president of Sudan, Nimeiri, dissolved the Southern Regional Government and divided the region into three provinces in violation of the Addis Ababa Peace Agreement of 1972. Fearing revolts, the government ordered the transferring of the Anya-Nya guerrilla forces to the North contrary to the clause in the Addis Ababa Agreement that stipulated that they were to serve only in the South. The former Anya-Nya forces revolted in protest and the SPLM/A was born, which would wage the Second Sudanese Civil War from 1983 to 2005. Col. John Garang, head of the Staff College in Omdurman, who was sent by the government to negotiate with Southern officers who had refused orders to be transferred away from their bases in the Upper Nile region, ended up joining the mutineers. The rebels fled to Ethiopian border areas of Gambella where they met with another group that had previously rejected the Addis Ababa Peace Agreement. The SPLM/A was dominated by the Nuer, and the Equatoria region was largely absent by July 1983. Various independent groups converged in the Itang camp at the Ethiopian border with the Upper Nile. Wrangling over leadership ensued.[5]

By July 1983, before the Muor Muor and Koryom divisions, which were dominated by Dinka youths, joined the SPLA, it was up to Nuer officers to decide who should win the leadership of the SPLM/A between Dr John Garang, a Dinka, and Samuel Gai Tut, their fellow Nuer. Samuel Gai Tut did not contest the leadership of his group for himself. His approach was to propose Akuot Atem, a 58-year-old Dinka, from the same Bor District with Garang, to be the political leader while Tut was hoping to lead the military wing. Tut took his time in the decision and planned carefully. The last thing he would expect was for officers from his Nuer support base to stand against him in support of Garang when he needed a unified front. William Nyuon Bany, a Nuer with the largest army among Garang's initial allies, chose to side with Garang against his fellow Nuer, Samuel Gai Tut. Nyuon decided that either his national identity as a South Sudanese was tied to his primacy or his decision was motivated by revenge, having been demoted by Tut from the rank of a captain to the rank of a sergeant major in the 1970s before his rank was restored by the Khartoum government.[6] Garang exploited the frustration of the Ethiopian government with the group of Samuel Gai Tut and Akuot Atem, one of the guerrilla leaders operating from Ethiopia who did not accept the Addis Ababa Agreement of 1972, might not have been performing to the expectation of the Ethiopian government that was fighting a proxy war with the government of Sudan. The Ethiopian government helped the South Sudanese leaders to form the liberation movement with a military wing by June 1983.[7] But the unity fell through, and Garang moved to frame issues in a way that appealed to the Ethiopian backers. His group won with him as he became the chairman and commander-in-chief of the SPLM/A, followed by Kerubino Kuanyin Bol, William Nyuon Bany, Salva Kiir Mayardit and Arok Thon Arok, in that order. All but William Nyuon Bany, a Nuer, were Dinka.

The military aspect of the movement became more important than the political aspect, and consequently, politicians were marginalized.[8] What became the Dinka elite domination of the government of South Sudan could be traced back to the wrangling over leadership at Itang Refugee Camp. A fault line was created that would be exacerbated by the split in the movement in 1991, and the wounds created between the two groups would reopen in 2013. While leadership wrangling has always been at the heart of leadership failure in South Sudanese history, critics of the SPLM/A and its leader Dr John Garang blame the deterioration of relationships on ideological orientations that the SPLM/A chose at the beginning. The SPLM/A's ideology was to fight for a united secular socialist Sudan under new terms.

The backing of the Ethiopian government made the leader of the SPLM/A, John Garang, and his group to be a bit reckless with political orientations just as the donor money from the West would make Salva Kiir's government in Juba to behave recklessly with their domestic resources. There was more hope from outside than from within.

For example, Sudan was predominantly a Muslim country, and yet the SPLM Manifesto released in July 1983 called for a secular Sudan, and the SPLM/A expected everyone to rally to their cause. The general public in Sudan might have been prepared for a secular state over a strictly religious state, but when a group of non-Muslims and outsiders to the elite club in Khartoum were the ones commanding such a change, suspicions were bound to inform the reactions of the majority of Muslims. A few Muslims who joined the SPLM/A might have been drawn there in search for a political space that might not have been available for them in Khartoum. The SPLM/A's compensation for this shortcoming was to call for a united Sudan under new terms rather than separation, which, in fact, neutralized some Arab countries such as Libya and Yemen, who lent support to the SPLM/A.

The SPLM/A leaders, having fought in the Anya-Nya movement, knew that self-determination was a popular demand of the South Sudanese people, and yet the Manifesto called for a united Sudan. Though necessitated by the circumstances, both positions were unsustainable in the long run as the events would prove, but the SPLM/A were mostly preoccupied with capturing power, and they would sing songs of any supplier of military resources. A strong defence of the SPLM/A is contained in the last section of this chapter. Gen. Malual Ayom Dor aptly noted in his PhD's dissertation the contradiction:

> During the civil war, the SPLM/A encompassed socialist and liberal ideas in search of ideological allies to achieve this New Sudan, shifting its ideological preferences from East to West at the end of the Cold War. As a result, given the absence of a clear political ideology, the SPLM/A remained a military movement during the conflict while its political organisation was never properly institutionalised. The SPLM, as a movement was really only used as an institutional cover for diplomatic initiatives, for mobilisation throughout Sudan and abroad, and for humanitarian assistance in the liberated areas but not as an ideological vehicle.[9]

Indeed, when the SPLM/A lost the support of the Ethiopian government in 1991, it made a transformation in both rhetoric and symbols to win the support of the West.[10] The red star in the SPLM/A's flag was changed to yellow, and pronouncements of democratic changes were announced at Chukudum in 1994.

Initially committed to an ideological orientation backed by a powerful foreign patron, the SPLM/A overlooked internal issues such as diversity in the composition of its ranks and file, and it was already too late when moves were made to correct this in the 1990s.

The manner in which the SPLM/A came into existence created problems of ethnic representations in the military, particularly the marginalization of the Equatoria region in the ranks and file of the national army, which would resurface in the independent South Sudan. The second civil war broke out at the time when Joseph James Tombura, a South Sudanese politician and member of the Sudan African National Union from Azande, was in charge as the president of the High Executive Council of the Southern Sudan Autonomous Region, serving from 23 June 1982 to 5 June 1983. Just as some Azande view the current government in Juba as the Dinka government, some Dinka viewed the government at that time as the Azande government.

President Nimeiri took advantage of the leadership rivalries in Juba, and on 5 June 1983, he abruptly announced his Republican Order Number One over primetime national television, which held that the Southern Region be divided into the three provinces of Bahr el Ghazal, Equatoria and the Upper Nile. This was viewed as the final stage for the dismantling of the Addis Ababa Agreement of 1972 between the North and the South, but it was also viewed as a win for those politicians who supported the Kokora (a Bari language for fair division). As such, those who supported the Kokora in Khartoum were viewed as allies to Southern Sudan's archenemy.[11] In a pattern that is common to South Sudan's conflict dynamics, where the sins of the elites are linked to their communities, blame for these politicians' crimes (largely from Equatoria) was pinned on their communities, a narrative which alienated many Equatorians from joining the SPLM/A in the early 1980s. Some SPLA soldiers exacerbated hostilities by committing violent acts against civilians in Equatoria.[12]

When news of the SPLA rebellion spread, it was viewed as a move against the Azande's rule. In turn, patriotic Azande leaders who could have joined the SPLA at the initial stages of the rebellion avoided the conflict or fled to neighbouring countries in an effort to circumvent ending up on the wrong side of the Azande's history by joining a rebellion that was led by a group that opposed James Tombura and the Kokora. Even in places where mutinies broke out, such as Bor, Ayod, Pibor and Pochalla, any Azande who might have continued with the rebels to Ethiopia were those who were trapped or had no way to escape. All the Equatorian soldiers who were part of the 105 who fought in Bor under Kerubino Kuanyin Bol later surrendered to the government after Bol's forces were expelled from Bor.[13]

Another historical fact that explains the apparent underrepresentation of the Azande in the military came from the SPLA's telegraphs in 1985. The SPLA had a system in which messages and orders were sent 'to all units', and some of these included responses from field commanders. These messages were archived, and a number of files containing these correspondences can currently be found at the Embassy of South Sudan in Nairobi. The director of Radio SPLA (based in Addis Ababa) at the time, Atem Yaak Atem, and his staff started a programme where they broadcasted local South Sudanese languages alongside Arabic and English. The leader of the SPLM/A, Dr John Garang, was impressed with the impact of both the Dinka and Nuer language programmes and motioned for the Azande language to be added to the list. On failing to find an Azande within their ranks to be a presenter, Atem asked Garang to find one, who then sent a 'to all units' message asking the field commanders to find an Azande among their soldiers. None of the commanders but William Nyuon reported any Azande. Nyuon claimed that he had one Azande soldier who had fought in Ayod with him, but he had gone to Ethiopia with his soldiers and was later killed while fighting under Kerubino Kuanyin Bol.

Although Azande soldiers joined the SPLA later, most people who became officers attended their officers' trainings at a time when the SPLA had already graduated at least seven officer grades known as the 'cadet shields'. In fact, it was the officers of Shield Seven who went to the Azande territories to recruit new fighters in 1990. There were enormous disparities between those who became officers in 1983 and those who became officers in the 1990s, especially if they received equal educations. This explains why the military leadership in Juba was not entirely accountable for the underrepresentation of certain groups, like the Azande, at the highest levels of military leadership at two to four stars, but this cannot be an excuse for not correcting the image of SPLM/A both internally and externally. In fact, John Garang attempted to correct this, but it was a little too late. Between 1992 and 2005, Garang drew up a timetable for selecting highly competent young officers from communities that were underrepresented in the armed sectors, having them jump a number of grades, sending them for training and deploying and monitoring them. Those that performed according to the described criteria would jump an additional number of grades until the top echelon of the armed sectors was diverse and made up of competent leaders. If the strategy were to succeed, it would reduce the domination of a few groups in the top echelon of the armed sectors and do so in a sustainable and peaceful manner. This approach ended in 2005.[14]

How the SPLM/A actually operated

On 26 March 1998, *The Economist* summed up the prevalent impression of the
SPLM/A during the period (1983–91) as follows:

> The rebels have always, in theory, been a political movement as well as an
> army. In practice, the army was the movement. Led by John Garang, a former
> colonel in the national armed forces and a man with strong dictatorial
> tendencies, it has, at its worst, been little more than an armed gang of Dinkas
> (Mr Garang's ethnic group), killing, looting and raping. Its indifference,
> even animosity, towards the people it was supposed to be 'liberating' was
> all too clear.[15]

The Economist further noted, 'In the bad old days, criticism of Mr Garang
was punishable by imprisonment in a pit for several months.'[16] Indeed, even the
insiders agreed with this criticism of the SPLM/A as anyone publicly criticizing
SPLM/A's policies or performance of its leaders (not just Mr Garang) 'ran the
risk of being branded quisling'.[17] Obviously, this sensitivity to criticism among
the SPLM/A leaders did not die with Dr John Garang.

In what may be compared to the national security in the independent South
Sudan, it has been noted that 'independent and liberal political opinion was
throttled by the security apparatus – the "Combat Intelligence" '[18] during the
civil war. A number of people were imprisoned in appalling circumstances,
others died mysteriously in prison or outside of prison and some were executed
publicly.[19] Lakurnyang Lado, the chairman of the Front for the Liberation of
South Sudan, was detained and publicly killed. Section 35 of the 1984 SPLM/A
laws established the chairman and commander in chief of the SPLM/A as the
confirming authority for the enforcement of the death sentences passed by
the general court martial; the law required that the case be submitted to the
chairman in order to uphold or alter the decision, but logistical difficulties
militated against strict adherence to the law.[20] Although Garang as the leader
of the movement bore full responsibility and should be held accountable for
the wrongs of the organization he led, what is not often noted in the history
of the brutality of the SPLM/A is the role of the other actors who either applied
the extreme versions of the law derived from the Manifesto of July 1983 and
the 1984 SPLM/A laws or who simply acted on their own to settle rivalry in

their favour. In May 2017, the SBS Dinka Radio interviewed Commander Majur Nhial Makol, who identified some of the actors usually unknown for human rights violations outside of the SPLM/A's circle:

> When I left Bor in 1983, as a postgraduate of Cambridge University, I had the rank of Lt Colonel in police services. I became the second ambassador after Lual Diing Wol to Libya. I helped in setting up the first SPLM/A radio in Libya which used to broadcast for one hour. In the SPLA, I was arrested 7 times, sentenced to death three times but I am alive today because Dr. John Garang de Mabior intervened. Most of this arrest was done by Lam Akol, Salva Kiir, Kerubino Kuanyin, and William Nyuon. My last arrest in Pageri was done by Salva Kiir in which I was sentenced for firing squad but someone again leaked the news to Garang. I never met Garang after every release but I have been told that there is an order to release you. I was arrested by Lam Akol at Abuong for 1 year and then transferred to Bilpam. I walked while shackled from Abuong to Bilpam. I was kept in the same prison with Paul Malong Awan. Sometime later, Malong went on hunger strike for days. At that point, I manage to sneak out of prison and helped to communicate the message to Dr. John Garang on the radio that one of his officers was almost dying in prison on hunger strike. Dr. John Garang immediately ordered the review of cases within 72 hours and that was how we survived the Bilpam prison.[21]

Some crimes were committed on John Garang's behalf as some commanders arrested or killed people purportedly acting on orders from above.[22] Fresh charges were then drawn up against the dead man.

This means coercive means weren't controlled by Garang alone. The exact same scenarios have repeated themselves in South Sudan. For example, the director of special programmes in the office of the president, Akot Lual, was arrested in July 2020. The family told the author that they were told that 'the order to arrest him came from the office of the President',[23] but the *Sudan Tribune* reported later that President Salva Kiir himself learned of the arrest from his relatives and body guards.[24] This could be explained away by noting that the Office of the President might be lying, which would still mean that the president is not actually in control.

The SPLM/A was also blamed for adopting the military practices of Colonel Mengistu Haile Mariam, president of Ethiopia, such as forced conscription needed to generate large numbers needed for fighting in human waves.[25]

John Prendergast, in his 1997 book *Crisis Response: Humanitarian Band-Aids in Sudan and Somalia*, described the SPLA as having 'attained possession of adequate means of coercion and has terrorized the southern population into passive compliance. The predominant instruments of the movement since 1983 have been and still are coercion and corruption'.[26]

The former director of the Radio SPLA, who had served as the speech-writer of Dr John Garang, and former deputy minister of information in South Sudan, Atem Yaak Atem, agreed with the corruption portion of Prendergast's assessment stating that 'SPLA officials stole booty in the form of vehicles and cash after capturing government garrisons and accumulated illegal wealth'.[27] The ruling SPLM/A's leaders after 2005 would treat South Sudan exactly like a garrison captured from the enemy. Corruption lived on too after the Second Sudanese Civil War ended in 2005. Prendergast would become the champion of advocacy to combat corruption in South Sudan as the organization he co-founded, the Sentry, has made the case that the key catalyst of South Sudan's civil war has been competition between rival kleptocratic networks for control over state assets and the country's abundant natural resources.[28]

A few anecdotes also illustrate Prendergast's claim of terror against civilians. The victims of the SPLM/A's brutality weren't distinguishable by ethnic categorizations.

In Yirol, of the current Eastern Lakes State and a number of other areas, artists tried to push back by calling officers out for their crimes against civilians around unfair revolutionary taxes. Songs are a popular platform that are used to express opinions that contest the views of the elites, informing listeners of the painful history of the struggle against the elites, their adoption of criminal methods and their attempts to suppress individual freedom.

In the 1980s, a singer from Lakes State composed a song that lamented the corruption of the SPLM/A officers after their soldiers had denuded Yirol of goats:

Akur amääl duk ber lɔ ŋɛŋ eei kɔc acuet ee ruɔ̈n.

Kuanyin ë Bol ku Arok Thɔn Arok!

Jenyë tarir jeny ë Maluk ë Mɔ̈u.

Marial ë Canuɔɔŋ ariŋ ë tɔŋ Buɔna.

Awet eei, kёckё thök thöl.

Awet Aköt wek cё thök thöl.[29]

White sheep don't cry because animals are being devoured this year.

Kuanyin Bol and Arok Thon Arok!

The liberation army of Maluk Mou!

Marial Chanuong has dashed off to take the news of the whereabouts of goats and sheep to Bona Bang.

Oh Awet, you have denuded the land of goats and sheep.

Awet Akot, you have denuded the land of goats and sheep.

Daniel Awet Akot was one of the eleven alternate members of the SPLM/A Political-Military High Command. At one point during the 1980s, Akot became the overall commander of the SPLA forces in the Bahr el Ghazal region. Bona Bang Dhol, also mentioned in the song, was one of his deputy commanders and was in charge of the SPLA forces in the areas around Yirol, Rumbek and Tonj by the end of 1985. Maluk Mou, who came from Yirol, was a first lieutenant who was later killed while trying to take a government outpost in Central Equatoria. Marial Chanuong, along with Bona Bang, was one of many students from Yirol East who trekked to Ethiopia and was later deployed there with Bang as a second lieutenant. In the piece above, the singer was complaining about the forces commanded by these officers and calling out to Kerubino Kuanyin Bol and Arok Thon Arok, who was fifth in the overall hierarchy of the SPLM/A command chain and was in charge of the Timsah Battalion during the initial years of the civil war (Arok's deputy was Bona Bang).

The singer was later forced by one of the SPLA officers, allegedly Daniel Awet Akot, to change the line 'Awet eei, you have denuded the land of goats' to 'Awet eei, you have liberated/captured the land'. The song is sung in this corrected version to this day.

In the chorus of another song by Marol Garang from Jonglei State, Garang berated SPLA soldiers who had commandeered his personal ox and killed it for food:

Lönhdiёn cё dönpiny ku rё ka cïn miɔɔr bï ye yup török dεεr. Aŋö cïn ye leer ba löth reem Anya-Nya. Piny acï riääk aakɔc acuet miɔɔr ё yum ё löth török dεεr.

My bell that has been left behind after the killing of my ox will go unused.

Why don't you take it to go and cook it and eat it too, oh you the Anya-Nya?

The civil population did not distinguish between the SPLA, SPLM/A and Anya-Nya, all of which they referred to in the Dinka language as 'kɔc roor' – the jungle people. For people to dare to eat a personal ox could only mean the collapse of the world order. Although Garang had always been disqualified from military service due to his tall height, which was deemed unsuitable for the guerrilla manoeuvres required of fighters, he was still made to pay for composing the song. Some artists were forced to edit their songs and to make them flattering instead of condemning of armed men.

The SPLM/A also copied forced conscription from the government of Ethiopia. For example, executing the orders given him by the Chairman and Commander in Chief Dr John Garang, Alternate Commander Jok Reng Magot ordered parents to give up their children for conscription into the SPLA in Bor District, and those who did not comply were ordered to dive and stay down in a pool or else he would shoot them should they attempt to surface. He also ordered the SPLA soldiers to burn and prick the chiefs' and subchiefs' genitals with molten plastic and a needle and drown innocent children in water.[30] Commander Reng did not spare anyone, including people from his own village. Some of the correspondents recalled his quarrels with some chiefs. In one such incidence, Chief Manyok Kuol told the commander that he (Manyok) had given all the youth to the SPLM/A. Jok retorted by saying that the chief was lying because a certain Ayuen Anyuon who had gotten into a dispute with Jok in a local court over a cow, a couple of years back, wasn't among the youth who had showed up.[31]

There are countless tales of graphic punishment of criminals. For example, Machor Makuek, a soldier based in Panyagoor in the 1990s, whose dad came from the Dieng section of Ciec Dinka (in Eastern Lakes) and whose mother hailed from the Pakeer section of Twic Dinka in the present Jonglei, overheard a conversation from his friend Akech-Makal (a man from the Ador section of Ciec Dinka, who had killed someone and escaped to join the SPLM/A forces in Panyagoor). It was a rainy day. Akech-Makal told a group of soldiers in the Dinka language: 'Yeŋö jɔl raan guɔ̈p lɔ ŋou-ŋoou kalë, na ye Pandɛɛntui ke ɣɛn duur anyin teem në raan', meaning, 'On a gloomy day like this, I would have killed someone if I were back home.'[32] Machor asked him if he had ever killed someone for such a reason. Akech-Makal started confessing, and one of his victims turned out to be from Dieng. Machor slipped out and informed alternative commanders Wuor Mabior Ayiik and Deng Garang Beny. Akech-Makal was immediately arrested and transferred to Eastern Lakes, and Machor was the soldier who was tasked to transport him. Akech-Makal was related to a famous chief in the Adior village (of the Ador section of Ciec Dinka) who was known for his spiritual powers. After handing over Akech-Makal to the authorities in Eastern Lakes, Machor returned. It was said that the spiritual leader of Ador grew mad at Machor. Some months later, Machor accidentally shot his uncle Lual-Bok d' Ayiei in the leg (at a fishing camp in the Sudd). People blamed Machor for exposing a criminal related to a spiritual leader. In the 1990s, criminal activities, such as the ones committed by Akech-Makal, increased in the Lakes region. The chairman and the commander in chief of the SPLM/A, Dr John Garang, sent Marial Nuor Jok to the area to instil discipline and punish criminals. Marial introduced graphic punishments in the lands of Agaar Dinka, Atuot and Ciec Dinka. A popular legend in the area has it that Marial Nuor Jok became infamous for putting criminals to death using pangas to chop them to death to instil fear in others.[33]

Besides the violent capturing of food from civilians and violence, the SPLM/A also created a culture of lying. 'This is Radio SPLA. The voice of the Sudanese revolutionary armed struggle.'[34] These were approximately the words with which the 'Rebel Radio', designed in the same way as the Radio Rebelde of the Cuban rebels (from Sierra Maestra), of the insurgents from Southern Sudan opened its broadcasting. Everything reported was always exaggerated: the size of the enemy, the number killed or captured from the enemy, the damage suffered by the enemy in terms of military resources lost and the importance of the town captured. The enemy was to be characterized in dehumanizing words. Truth didn't matter. Lies were not objectionable as long as they hurt the opponents. Nyaba amply described the SPLM/A: 'Much of what filtered out of the SPLM/A propaganda machinery, notably Radio SPLA, was about 90% disinformation or things concerned with the military combat, mainly news about the fighting which were always efficaciously exaggerated.'[35]

The former head of Radio SPLA, editor of the SPLM/A newsletter, speech-writer of Dr John Garang and his distant relative agreed with Nyaba's assessment:

> Despite the fact that I was the chief editor of news (as well as director) of Radio SPLA, I never saw the original reports from the warfront before any details of top secret had been removed. More often than not, casualty figures were subjected to alteration, with enemy losses increased and the SPLA's kia (killed in action) or wounded either missing or greatly reduced.[36]

The Radio SPLA operated for only a few years in the 1980s at its base in Ethiopia, but it has changed the future of how media would work in South Sudan. Every media house in South Sudan or a significant source of news within the South Sudanese social media network is modelled in the likeness of the Radio SPLA. Any communication (a message or a document) from a South Sudanese media outlet ought to be considered hesitantly.

The SPLM/A system was chaotic in the sense that power flowed in indeterministic ways. During the civil war era, titles didn't equate to power; some believe that it was one's proximity to the chairman that determined the power one was permitted to exercise. One implication is that there can never be any genuine representation in a system in which power flows in a very indeterministic way, which leads to communal grievances. The same practices would be recycled in the independent South Sudan.

Junior officers were also deployed to spy on the senior commanders as John Garang used surveillance as a form of control. Three examples illustrate this.

Brig. Gen. Makuei Mathai Ruei, then a junior SPLA officer in the intelligent unit, was assigned to monitor the activities of Commander Anthony Bol Madut in the 1990s. At that time, Commander Bol was in charge of Tonj-Wau-Raja SPLA forces as the independent area commander. Ruei filled his notebook with corruption charges against Bol. Someone stole the notebook and gave it to Commander Bol. Infuriated, the commander locked up Ruei, waiting to be sentenced to death. One of the charges was that the commander had robbed a cow (in Dinka 'wɛŋ rɔ̈l', meaning tawny and white blotchy cow) from a civilian. The author of the note was countercharged with the same crime among a host of others, including a charge that he had two pistols. Gen. Paul Malong Awan rescued the junior officer some years later. The junior officer today has the nickname of 'wɛŋ rɔ̈l', which Gen. Malong gave to him as a joke about one of his bogus charges for simply trying to do his job.[37]

Although the monitoring of the commanders was made to look like anti-corruption measures, it was dictatorial, as it meant that the SPLM/A leader John Garang intended to control the movement tightly. The composition of those assigned to do the monitoring also raised the question of ethnic bias by John Garang in favour of the people from Bor District. Especially among the Bahr el Ghazal people, some felt as though their leaders were targeted and that the SPLA officers working in the intelligent gathering were predominantly from Bor District. There was favouritism, but it was partly built into the societal structure, especially the way education was received in South Sudan. One of the legacies of the British rule in Sudan was uneven access to education. The Nuer and Dinka were overtly marginalized when it came to accessing education compared to the tribes in Equatoria and Western Bahr el Ghazal.[38] Fortunately for the Dinka of Bor District, an elementary school was opened in Malek in 1905. Because the population spacing in Bor District is dense compared to the population density in the Aweil, Gogrial and Tonj Districts (where one school in such a district won't make much of a difference because the population is very sparse), Malek School impacted the access to education in Bor District. The displacement caused by flooding in 1961 and 1962 also triggered the migration of people from Bor District to places where they had access to education. A merit-based recruitment into the officers' corps at the training camps among those who showed up at the Bilpam and Bonga training camps was bound to create imbalance. At each training camp, a batch comprising high school graduates, university dropouts and primary dropouts was given a written test, and the scores determined the hierarchy and whether one would be placed in the intelligent unit or not. Gen. Makuei Mathai Ruei was batch number one in his class. The mistake John Garang made was that the test measured only one aspect of intelligence, namely, analytical intelligence, but it did not test creativity and practical intelligence, which are equally important. In this case, a more comprehensive test that did not exacerbate an already existing injustice would have been appropriate to balance the scale and to have a more diversified recruitment into the officers' corps. As a consequence, both the cadet shields I and II were dominated by the members from Bor District and this has created one of the biggest challenges for President Kiir and his security advisors in the absence of sustainable retirement benefits.

The proximity to John Garang did not spare a commander from feeling the fear under which the movement operated. Commander Garang Ngang Abui used to be cautious around one junior officer under his command, who was called Haramdan Mathiang. He wore pens on his shirt pocket, and Garang took him for someone monitoring his activities. One day, the mail came. Commander Abui asked the officer to read them out loud. The officer said he didn't know how to read. Commander Abui was shocked and angry at himself for living in so much fear, thinking the officer was keeping a journal of everything going on. To the officer, Abui allegedly said something like, 'You have terrorized me for too long.' Commander Abui behaved as though he were actually being monitored. He might have been monitored but by someone else he didn't suspect.[39] This anecdote illustrates the use of fear as an instrument of control during the civil war.

Usually, the frustration with the manner in which the movement was managed was heard from Garang's opponents, but Garang's hardcore supporters did have their frustrations.

In 2014, the author went out for lunch with Brig. Gen. Elijah Alier Ayom, who, together with Commander Abdel Aziz El Hilu, was in charge of logistical needs of the SPLM/A in the 1990s. Gen. Alier was also the managing director of the Military Pension Fund. We met a former bodyguard of Dr John Garang named Akoon Yol (a Dinka from Aweil). Unfortunately, Akoon didn't cope well after Dr John Garang died in a helicopter crash in 2005. While seated, Akoon approached us, and he started conversing about the past. He asked where comrade Deng Alier was. Gen. Alier asked him, 'So, you still remember Deng Alier?' Akoon responded by telling a story to demonstrate that he hadn't forgotten any moment of the struggle. In New Site, Akoon used to be sent into the community from Dr John Garang's office to go and listen to people's conversations. One day, he listened to elders talking. He realized that Deng Alier was critical of the way the movement was being run. He heard other elders telling Deng: 'Muk yi piou', or 'Hold your heart', to which Deng responded, 'Yen e pione, aca doc muk aka ce dong anyin ben xeen poc cin', meaning, 'I have been holding my heart for too long; it is about to slip through my hands.'

The dictatorial manner in which the SPLM/A was handled by John Garang was cited as one of the reasons that led to the split within its rank and file in 1991, fitting John Garang and some of his closest aides, who were mostly former Anya-Nya fighters during the First Sudanese Civil War on one hand versus coup makers Dr Riek Machar and Dr Lam Akol, who were engineering lecturers at the University of Khartoum.[40] The split created fault lines that the future conflicts would follow. External shocks, particularly the loss of the support from Ethiopia in 1991, left the SPLM/A in a vulnerable position. John Garang began to visit Western countries. A three-person team comprising Oyay Deng Ajak, Elijah Malok and John Garang himself visited France to seek support after the split. Elijah Malok told the author that the ideological standing of the SPLM/A was questioned by an associate of the French President Francois Mitterrand. The United States came to the rescue of the SPLM/A as a way of dealing with the National Islamic Front in Khartoum,[41] but its support had to be implemented by the neighbouring countries such as the Ethiopia, Eritrea and Uganda just as the Israeli support of the Anya-Nya in the 1960s was tied to Israeli's interests in Ethiopia and Kenya. The SPLM/A reunified in 2002, but an internal crisis resurfaced in 2004. This tension fitting Salva Kiir versus John Garang was calmed by a meeting in Rumbek in which criticisms of the SPLM/A's leader were legitimized as the commanders poured their hearts out in recounting the sins of the movement. The reconciliation of the SPLM/A at Rumbek paved the way for peace.

The Comprehensive Peace Agreement (CPA) signed in Nairobi in 2005 ended the war. Dr John Garang, a Dinka, became the first vice president in Khartoum and head of regional government in Juba. At the same time, Salva Kiir, a Dinka, was the deputy of the regional government in Juba. This looked like a repeat of 1982 when Joseph Tombura, from Equatoria, became the leader of the regional government in Juba while Joseph Lagu, from Equatoria, became the vice president of Sudan. The critics of the SPLM/A's leadership tend to ignore any mention of positive attributes of its chairman and commander-in-chief. We end this chapter with a few words on John Garang.

John Garang: Positive attributes of the man and his ideas

Born in Wangulei in the former Bor District in 1945 and educated in Tonj, Bussere and Rumbek, all in the former Bahr el Ghazal Province, John Garang left the country before completing his secondary education. Before joining the Anya-Nya, he attended school in what was then Tanganyika. He later on studied for his degrees – bachelor's, master's and doctorate – in the United States. It turned out that Garang went to the wrong schools because a prerequisite for being accepted into the elite club in Southern Sudanese politics as well as the politics in Khartoum was for one to attend Loka Intermediate, Rumbek Secondary School or the University of Khartoum.[42] Garang's classical Arabic was wanting, which was viewed as a weakness by his 'bitterest critics who dismiss the man as devoid of leadership qualities'.[43] He was dismissed in Sudanese circles as a secret advocate of separatism.[44] While in the Western circles, the SPLM/A was characterized as divided, poorly organized and without a clear common strategy for achieving power and what to do should they achieve it. Some aspects of such criticisms hold true. However, hardworking and possessing analytical, creative and practical intelligence, Garang had some positive leadership qualities. For example, his patience allowed him 'to put up with the most frustrating situations and very irritating people including a few among his colleagues'.[45] Dr Mansour Khalid, the former advisor of Garang and a personal friend, had elsewhere told Atem Yaak Atem, the former speech-writer of John Garang and director of the Radio SPLA, that 'what was great about John Garang was that he always led from the front and that was the reason why people respected him'.[46] Garang did not often practise nepotism as he 'was often reluctant to appoint persons related to him by blood or regional affiliations to positions seen to offer power and perks'.[47] For example, George Garang Deng Chol, Chol Kuany Deng and Chau Mayol Juuk, all from Bor District, were initially rejected to work at the Radio SPLA despite their impressive educational backgrounds and experiences in journalism.[48] Garang was witty. He once asked his personal friend and advisor, Dr Mansour Khalid, who represented the SPLM at a talk in Ethiopia in 1998, what he thought of President Omar Al Bashir. 'He is an idiot,' Mansour said. 'Given how messed up Sudan is, don't you think it is fit to be ruled by an idiot?' Garang wittingly asked.[49]

It was the messed-up Sudan that he was fighting to fix while remaining in one piece. One shortcoming with critics of the SPLM/A and its Chairman/Commander-in-Chief Dr John Garang is failure to acknowledge positive attributes. Despite its failure to instil discipline in the soldiers, the multi-prong strategy of drawing in as much support to win the war did actually work.

The South Sudanese liberation movements that fought for the independence of South Sudan ended up settling down with a united Sudan while only the SPLM/A, which fought for a united Sudan under new terms, eventually achieved the independence of South Sudan and won South Sudan many friends both regionally and internationally. Atem Yaak Atem, former head of the Radio SPLA and editor of the SPLM/A newsletter, asked the SPLM/A leader Dr John Garang, 'Why do you insist on unity when it is unpopular in your constituency, Southern Sudan?'

Garang responded by saying that calling for separation does not bring independence. Atem paraphrased Garang:

> The Anya-Nya programme was separatist, yet its leader Joseph Lagu ended by signing an agreement based on unity, he argued, adding that Dr Riek Machar called his organization South Sudan Independence Movement. Riek Machar's Khartoum peace agreement affirmed unity, not separation, Garang concluded.[50]

The strategy of the SPLM/A was designed to draw in any support the rebels could get from various groups that wouldn't normally work for a common cause. Ethiopia[51] and Uganda were drawn into supporting the SPLM/A to exact revenge because Khartoum was supporting Eritrean rebels and Ugandan rebels, respectively. Some Arab countries such as Libya and Yemen supported the SPLM/A on ideological grounds as the SPLM/A declared itself to be fighting for a united socialist Sudan under new terms. Though not demanded by the Ethiopian government, the SPLM/A voluntarily chose to sing the songs of communism, which earned the movement support from Cuba, including taking children to study in Cuba. The SPLM/A used the Church to attract the attention of Christians in the West.

The South Sudanese have obtained what they had tried to get since the 1960s through the methods laid out by Dr John Garang. However, the legacies built during the protracted war have recycled themselves in the independent South Sudan as the next chapter shows.

Dr John Garang died in a helicopter crash on 30 July 2005, while travelling from Uganda to his base in South Sudan. The SPLM Leadership Council appointed Salva Kiir in John Garang's place in August 2005, and Dr Riek Machar became his deputy. Limited by educational background and international experience, Salva Kiir Mayardit could not fill the shoes of his predecessor; he chose to wear new shoes.

This chapter has shown that the existing political structures, externally constructed and internally maintained, have failed to ensure a peaceful negotiation of power relations among groups. For example, all of the internal conflicts within the SPLM/A (1983–2005) and in post-2005 South Sudan, as will be shown, are attempts to redistribute political and military power among competing groups, that is, to negotiate power relations using violence. Before diving into post-2005 South Sudan's affairs of governance, the next chapter grounds that coming analysis in a theoretical framework.

2

Integrating existing approaches

This chapter integrates existing approaches on conflict dynamics by grouping them into broader trends and assembling these approaches under the general framework of the security dilemma model. It presents the security dilemma model and explicates its applicability to the South Sudanese case. Existing works largely ignore the roles of agents who use the politics of fear to construct communal grievances and instead concentrate on contextual factors. This book proposes that such a strategy may be less potent in determining the outbreak of ethnic war. Rather, this chapter explains how the politics of fear generates chaos, and it contributes to the existing literature by examining the roles of actors and situational contexts using an integrative approach. The literature on ethnic conflict largely analyses this phenomenon from the perspective of the security dilemma theory, which is derived from the realist paradigm of international relations theory to identify the factors that increase the risk of violent conflict when imperial order breaks down.

Security dilemma model

The concept of the security dilemma is derived from the realist paradigm of the international relations theory to identify the factors that increase the risk of violent conflict when imperial order disintegrates.[1] In particular, the concept of the security dilemma rests upon the impossibility of knowing the true intentions of the 'enemy/opposition', wherein both sides are tempted to prepare for the worst while acknowledging that this proclivity will most likely lead to conflict.

Barry Posen, who first applied the model to conflicts that were based on ethnicity, stated that the security dilemma model accurately captures 'the special conditions that arise when proximate groups of people suddenly find themselves newly responsible for their own security'.[2] Adopting Posen's approach, Chaim Kaufmann argued that 'regardless of the origins of ethnic strife, once violence reaches the point that ethnic communities cannot rely on the state to protect them, each community must mobilize to take responsibility for its own security'.[3] Posen's and Kaufmann's works suggest that a durable solution to ethnic conflict may be achieved only by going beyond the partitioning of splintered states and physically separating ethnic groups to minimize threatening perceptions and maximize their capacity for self-defence, thus eliminating the security dilemma facing both sides.[4] However, the cases of Sudan and South Sudan have indicated that the separation of groups may only shift the axis of political struggle from the centre to the periphery and can exacerbate border disputes that might otherwise remain dormant.

While state behaviours can generate uncertainty and fear in some groups – aggravating the security dilemma and potentially leading to war – not all wars are caused by security dilemmas.[5] The security dilemma theory is restrictive and suffers from certain limitations in its original form; it assumes that actors survive and interact in an anarchic political structure that is characterized by uncertainty. For all cases of ethnic conflict to which the security dilemma theory has been applied (research that was started by Posen), the existence of a central authority has been assumed prior to disintegration.

Shiping Tang's reformulation predicts that a security dilemma can result in four different outcomes:

1. The security dilemma is brought under control because the central authority is restored quickly, or both sides take effective measures to alleviate the security dilemma.
2. The two sides of the security dilemma are unable to take effective measures to alleviate it, but neither side takes measures to exacerbate the security dilemma because they do not harbour malign intentions towards each other.
3. The security dilemma is exacerbated because some elites on one or both sides – although they harbour no malign intentions against the other group – strive to gain power or to avoid losing power by encouraging ethnic tension and hatred.
4. One or both sides harbour true malign intentions. The security dilemma is real only at the very beginning of the process. As soon as one or both

sides begin to harbour malign intentions against the other side, the security dilemma ceases to operate and becomes a genuine security threat. Such situations almost inevitably result in mass violence or war unless international bodies intervene in a timely manner.[6]

When applied to the Sudanese case, Tang's reformulation of the integrative theory of ethnic conflict contends that 'the security dilemma can emerge when the central authority is captured or dominated by one group, thus becoming a de facto intra-elite group while the other group has to provide their own security'.[7] The blossoming of non-state actors in South Sudan speaks to the inability of the central authority to mitigate fear and points to the accumulation of power, a necessary condition of a genuine security dilemma.[8] Ole Frahm noted that non-state actors who fill the void of a government presence, such as localized militias, are generally sources of insecurity themselves.[9] Jok Madut agreed, remarking that 'nowhere did it become more evident than in South Sudan that a society where everyone is armed on the pretext of self-defence is a society where no one can be assured of safety'.[10] This assertion confirms Posen's thesis that 'the actions taken by groups to enhance their security produce reactions that in the end can make them less secure'.[11] The conflict in South Sudan arose from the use of fear as an instrument of governance or insurgent advancement by political leaders who had established control mechanisms that relied on coercion and threats through mass media, aiding this process as lines of transmission. Because fear allows one group to dominate another, and group polarization and identity all affect risk assessment, the security dilemma concept is important and necessary for understanding the role that political elites play in transforming fear and politicizing anger into deadly conflict. The next section integrates existing approaches that explain the conflict dynamics in South Sudan by grouping them into broader trends and by assembling them under the security dilemma framework.

Greed, neopatrimonialism and identity

Mainstream literature about the factors that influence social conflicts classifies these factors into macro-level (e.g. sociopolitical and economic) and micro-level factors (which include relevant agents, such as the government, rebels and the masses). By applying these categorizations, existing approaches that have been used to study the dynamics of conflict in South Sudan can be further grouped into three subcategories: greed, neopatrimonialism and identity, all of which are integrated into the security dilemma model.

In a series of quantitative studies on the causes of civil wars, Paul Collier and his colleagues produced a number of theories that focused largely on macro-level factors, with rebels as the primary agents of study. In 1998, Collier and Hoeffler argued that civil wars are primarily caused by the greed – not the grievances – of rebel groups who aim to produce economic returns.[12] In 2004, Collier and Hoeffler modified some of their previous theoretical claims, adding a grievance-based explanation that proposed that objective social exclusion can explain the impetus behind civil war.[13] In 2009, Collier and his colleagues offered the feasibility hypothesis, which proposed that rebellion is more likely to occur when it is financially and militarily feasible.[14] They argued that a combination of certain structural features, such as the abundance of resource rent, low secondary-school enrolment among potential youth fighters, the availability of weapons (e.g. from a prior war), a geography that provides a safe haven to rebels and a state that is ineffective at maintaining a monopoly on legitimate violence, can make circumstances ripe for conflict.

To elucidate why a conflict occurs when it does, additional explanations are necessary. Despite the presence of the same structural features that Collier et al. mentioned in South Sudan, the conflict did not occur until 2013. The feasibility hypothesis ignores the effects of the role of the ruling elite. The greed versus grievance paradigm assumes that rebels are rational actors who perform a cost-benefit analysis before engaging in violent behaviours, an assumption that Collier himself doubted in a later work.[15] Notably, the greed-grievance paradigm neither accounts for the types of intermittent violence that occurred in South Sudan in 2013 and 2016 nor for the risks associated with the group identities or grievances that were engineered by the elites. This is the very oversight for which the Collier–Hoeffler framework has received serious criticism. Aleksi Ylonen argued that the Collier–Hoeffler framework does not sufficiently explain Sudanese conflicts because it cannot quantify culturally and regionally defined political grievances or the socio-economic consequences that result from these two factors.[16] Justin Leach argued that southern rebel groups do not develop along 'any single economic-rationalist model' but rather around 'deeper concerns about security and culture'.[17] Finally, David Keen maintained that Collier and Hoeffler considered only vertical inequalities between individuals and neglected horizontal inequalities that occur between the communities or cultural groups within a country.[18]

Since the 1980s, several scholars have used the concept of neopatrimonialism in an effort to account for these factors and to explain the forms of political dominion in the African states.[19] Neopatrimonialism is the vertical distribution of resources that engender patron-client networks centred around a powerful individual or party. Early accounts defined it as 'the distinctive institutional hallmark of African regimes'.[20] Recent studies have increased the relevance of the model by expanding its scope and using the rebranded framework to explore the link between armed conflicts and neopatrimonial systems. For example, Paul D. Williams argued that neopatrimonial systems of governance do not automatically lead to armed conflicts because they can vary considerably, taking more or less severe forms, and because some rulers have been adept at managing factionalized politics, effectively stifling opportunities for rebellion.[21] Williams argued that risks can be acute when neopatrimonial systems experience a crisis that the ruling authorities are unable to contain.[22] Such crises tend to occur when external resources are exhausted, when outrageous behaviours test the limits of the systems' legitimacy or when other factors develop that make armed rebellion feasible for marginalized segments of the population.[23]

This account resembles Alex De Waal's political market model, wherein a ruler must secure enough money before they can operate the political machine, and lacking legitimate sources of funds, turns to corruption to compensate.[24] De Waal argued that although widespread corruption in Sudan was economically inefficient, it enabled the ruling elites to consolidate domestic control and to minimize internal strife. This gambit made it extremely expensive and difficult for the Sudanese government to sabotage Kiir's political goal of independence. Regardless, once an independent state had been achieved and the funds had diminished, Kiir did not possess the political business skills to maintain a centralized, neopatrimonial system of government.[25] Using resources to bribe pivotal groups was not the only measure preventing internal war during the interim period (2005–11); the political elites relentlessly exploited historical group-based grievances and invoked fear that an external aggressor, based in Khartoum (with the support of southern allies), could undermine the referendum exercise on self-determination for what was then Southern Sudan (2011). The elites' promotion of fear not only moderated the masses' expectations during the interim period but also crucially forced cohesion within the country's elites, as its members largely began to focus on the common goal of becoming an independent country. The successful outcome of the referendum that resulted in the creation of the Republic of South Sudan in 2011 eradicated fears of an external aggressor and rendered this form of manipulation ineffective. The prospect of establishing a democratic state and delivering services threatened the political survival of the ruling elites. The immediate response by these elite factions was to engage in the politics of fear and to outmanoeuvre each other, transforming ethnic politics into outright ethnic war.

One criticism of the political marketplace has pointed out that the framework has commoditized social interactions without considering the social context of the phenomena it studies. The political market framework is explained in the language of markets and capital without explicitly and consciously critiquing it. As Edward Thomas's (2019) report for the Rift Valley Institute demonstrated, markets and cash economies are not part of every dealing in South Sudan, implying that every relationship that is monetized is both empirically wrong and morally unsound. What is troubling goes beyond the mere assertion that cash and patronage are important to specific contexts and classes. Rather, this concept of 'payroll peace' is ultimately wrong and unpleasant due to its lack of nuance and complexity.[26] Political relationships can be managed through either market or social norms. In South Sudan, once some leaders (or the circumstances) have cultivated strong social connections between them and their support bases, they occupy a space where they cannot be easily replaced during their lifetimes. Dr Riek Machar in South Sudan has successfully cultivated political relationships with his core support based on social norms.

Many scholars have attributed the conflict in South Sudan to the struggle within the dominant class over power and resources. Clémence Pinaud argued that the conflict must be understood within a system of class domination that is based on wartime predation, from which a dominant class emerges to occupy most of the country's wealth and can make decisions about how to allocate state resources.[27] The South Sudanese elites secured their positions by establishing a regime through a system of patronage that rewarded close supporters and punished opponents, thereby producing grievances that increased the risk of war.[28]

Literature on the role of corruption has focused largely on structural circumstances as the dominant explanatory variables for corruption and its link to violence. The literature has contended that the structure of government institutions and the nature of the political process determine the level of corruption in a given polity. In particular, weak governments that do not control their agencies are said to experience significantly high levels of corruption. The absence of deterrence lowers the risk of getting caught; conversely, bureaucratic corruption leads to structural and institutional distortions by limiting the government's fiscal capacity to efficiently raise sufficient taxes. The correlation between rent-seeking and unaccountable public servants is viewed as one of the primary causes of corruption. Jain summarized this issue into three factors, arguing that the existence of corruption requires discretionary regulatory power, economic rents linked to power and sufficiently low thresholds for punishment.[29] Regardless, these publications were dominated by economic analyses and did not focus on social factors that influence agents by examining how individuals/institutions who engage in corrupt practices affect those around them or how the aggregate behaviours of society impact the behaviours of individual decision makers.

Mohamed Suliman asserted that the war in the south is best understood as the consequence of marrying opposing political approaches to the reality of diminishing resources.[30] Some scholars have challenged this interpretation because a violent appropriation of resources can emerge as part of a larger set of political strategies predating rent-seeking opportunities rather than as a cause of conflict in the first place.[31] Shiping Tang, Yihan Xiong and Hui Li revealed that oil does not cause war. Rather, it is the location of oil and not rent, income or relative distribution/concentration that connects oil with the onset of ethnic war.[32] They argued that when the core territory of a subordinate minority group holds a significant amount of mineral resources (e.g. oil, gas, diamond and other mineral resources), that group is more likely to rebel, especially if the group has been marginalized or dominated by the central state. Consequently, any state with significant mineral resources that is located within the core territories of subordinate minority groups is more likely to experience ethnic conflict. In contrast, oil does not contribute to a higher risk of ethnic war when it is located within the core territory of a dominant majority group or in a country with a fairly even distribution of ethnic groups where no group can lay exclusive claim to the oil.

To dissect the components of bad governance in South Sudan, it is necessary to look back at the past that may be relevant to the present. In this vein, Jok attributed the conflict to the cumulative impact of the long march to independence that burdened the conscience of South Sudan.[33] Douglas Johnson traced the root causes of the conflict to 'unresolved tensions following the split in the SPLA in the 1990s, and the incomplete reintegration of anti-SPLA forces into the SPLA after 2005'.[34] In a similar vein, Øystein H. Rolandsen attributed the conflict to 'the combination of neo-patrimonial politics, a weak state structure and legacies of violence from the previous civil war'.[35] Rolandsen and M. W. Daly viewed the conflict as an outcome of historical processes restricted to and shaped by external and institutional processes.[36] This literature that points to the relevance of historical legacy in understanding the conflict dynamics in South Sudan is supported by a literature elsewhere, particularly in natural sciences, where it is called hysteresis – the dependence of the state of a system on its history. For example, if one looks at the governance style of the ruling SPLM party as a system, some of the practices from 2005 to 2020 may be traced back in time to the days of Sudan People's Liberation Movement/Army (SPLM/A) as shown in Chapter 1. With the Nile River functioning as the Nile Valley region's natural highway, most important administrative centres in South Sudan were established in towns near the Nile River (e.g. Juba, Bor, Mongalla, Malakal). The indigenous people in these towns felt marginalized during the formation of the state, and the SPLM viewed this cultural marginalization as an effort by Khartoum governments to pull the Nile Valley's indigenous people off the rails of history.[37] Ironically, the administrative grievances for which the North was blamed have lived on today. For example, Juba's interference in each state's administrative issues and the politics of uneven administrative developments exacerbated communal grievances in the Upper Nile and ultimately pit the Shilluk against the Padang Dinka. The Murle cited administrative grievances to justify David Yau Yau's rebellion in Jonglei State.

The legacy of the civil war, together with the divide and conquer policy copied from previous systems, has affected a number of communities. Among the Dinka of the former Bor District, a palpable tension has been made visible online. Due to their dominant diaspora population, these communities have chosen to express their grievances using online platforms and tools, like live videos. In addition, this text examines Western Equatoria due to the grievance of military marginalization that triggered conflict there, which could be blamed on the politics of 1982–83 and the manner in which the SPLM/A was formed.

Existing works have largely overlooked how political elites who use the politics of fear to construct communal grievances have contributed to the conflict in South Sudan and have instead focused predominantly on contextual factors, which may be less potent in determining the outbreak of ethnic war.[38] The three main channels through which the politics of fear has served as the manufacturers of group-based grievances include corruption, the propagation of fear and politicized anger through mass media and the use of physical and psychological violence as a political tactic. This chapter contributes to existing literature by examining the roles of actors and the various situational contexts that have taken place during the conflict.

The neopatrimonialism paradigm highlights a limited number of macro-level factors, such as 'historical legacies', 'historical grievances' and 'economic shocks', with little consideration for communal grievances or internal shocks that the powerful elites have fabricated through deliberate, painful reminders of the past. The paradigm focuses on the risk management skills of the powerful elites at the expense of addressing the impact of their manipulative tactics. Like the Collier–Hoeffler framework, in which fractionalization is attributed to the level of a society's heterogeneity,[39] the neopatrimonialism paradigm views the fractionalization of society as a structural problem that is produced by neopatrimonialism.[40] Both approaches fail to consider the role that elites play in manufacturing fractionalization. When fractionalization is viewed as a characteristic of certain societies, these arguments do not adequately explain the events that transpired because they do not consider that the elites were capable of creating and designing their societies' textures.

In spite of these limitations, both approaches can provide insight and depth into the security dilemma framework. The core insight into the framework is that the fear of unknown intentions inexorably leads to conflict. The ability of a sovereign power to centralize and mitigate the fears of all people under its jurisdiction is the currency of its political legitimacy.[41]

According to Ole Frahm:

> Not only is the South Sudanese state not physically present in much of its territory, it also does not properly represent its citizens. South Sudan is therefore a non-performing state whose legitimacy is fragile and presently on the wane. The South Sudanese state is either not present at all and delegates tasks to NGOs or traditional authorities or, where it is present, does not fulfil its nominal tasks in, say, health care or education. The army, the country's most established and well-endowed institution, is unable to police the state, and the other branches of the state that receive a much smaller share of the budget also do not fulfil their functions.[42]

In sub-Saharan Africa, many governments attempt to mitigate fear in the sectors of society that are pivotal to maintaining the status quo of power; however, those ethnic groups that are excluded from this state protection rarely view the central authority as a legitimate power, generating rival non-state actors in response. Often, the actions non-state actors take to enhance their security ultimately make them less secure.[43]

The neopatrimonialism paradigm offers the following criterion for evaluating how the security dilemma progresses: armed conflict is highly likely to occur when ruling elites are 'no longer able to assert their dominance over local strongmen in their patronage network'.[44] In such cases, the political landscape enters a mode of crisis instability – the perception that there is a danger for war due to each side's fear that the other is about to attack.[45] According to David A. Lake and Donald Rothchild, 'intense ethnic conflict is most often caused by collective fears of the future'.[46]

The media regularly characterizes the dynamics of conflict in South Sudan to be motivated by an ancient history of ethnic or tribal hatred between the country's various groups. A piece appearing in *African Arguments* noted that 'in South Sudan, few doubt the political and military saliency of ethnicity'.[47] Ole Frahm asserted that 'both ethnic group identities and politicised ethnicity play a large role in South Sudan. There is a widespread belief that the Dinka dominate the army and the government and that jobs and positions in the administration are tied to membership in the "correct" ethnic group'.[48]

While South Sudan's Auditor General, Stephen Wondu, argued that 'ethnicity became the defining factor in the allocation of public offices',[49] Francis Deng characterized the Sudanese conflict as an event that came as the result of competing visions of multiple identities.[50]

Although the role that ethnic identity has played cannot be dismissed in an analysis of the conflict in South Sudan, political actors should consider changing how ethnic identity is used to label various groups. One person can identify with multiple groups, and their circumstances will determine which one of the country's multitude of identities is most relevant to them. Ole Frahm succinctly summarized this phenomenon as follows:

> More often than not, it is not the supra ethnic identity that matters most to the individual and his or her political mobilisation but a group that is either smaller or bigger. The Dinka and Nuer, the country's two largest ethnic groups, not only do not know a centralised authority but are split amongst themselves in a substantial number of clans (for instance Jikany and Lou for the Nuer and Ngok and Bor for the Dinka) which is where the real loyalties lie – if not in even smaller sub-units that comprise for instance the extended family or the cattle camp. On the other hand, in Equatoria ethnic identities are crucial for the individual and the family but when it comes to political organization and representation, the regional identity as Equatorians is more important, not least because otherwise each Equatorian group on its own would be too insignificant in size to have much clout. Moreover, if survey results can be trusted, ethnic identification does not stand in the way of attachment to the nation of South Sudan. The relevance of ethnic loyalties thus appears very much tied to situational circumstances which applies with added force to the politics of autochthony and other exclusionary practices in the country.[51]

During the last two weeks of December 2013 and the first four months of 2014, officers from Nuer denied Dr Riek Machar what would have been easy military governance over Malakal and Bentiu. During the initial phase of South Sudan's conflict dynamics, while the Dinka elites controlled access to money, the Nuer elites had greater access to combat-ready forces. Also, the Shilluk militia force of Johnson Olony fought alongside the government forces in Malakal against the opposition forces despite the fact that the main grievance raised was about land dispute with Dinka Padang. Similarly, the Murle militia led by David Yau Yau, who cited marginalization against his people by the Dinka in Jonglei State, fought alongside the government forces. These factors did not dismiss the presence of an ethnic dimension in the conflict.

While ethnic competition may be encoded into our DNA, 'research has shown that when leaders in a community do the right thing, this can set a tone for others, eventually encouraging everyone to behave more fairly'.[52] Two types of leadership approaches that have exacerbated the impact of ethnic competition include the following: (1) leaders seeking political power to settle long-held personal or communal grievances and (2) leaders refusing to transcend their predefined political territories even when doing so would make them appear to be wonderful leaders and win them admiration beyond the contours of their villages.

While the role of ethnicity in the conflict cannot be dismissed, ethnicity itself does not explain why the conflict occurred. Rather, its exploitation by political actors for political and economic gain illustrates the conflict as ethnic in nature.[53] Although ethnic differences may have provided leaders with the rhetoric for mobilization,[54] South Sudanese scholars have dismissed explanations that have focused exclusively on ethnicity – without sufficiently incorporating other contributing factors – as simplistic,[55] claiming that these arguments have disguised the complex historical relationships within and between the ethnic groups.[56] In addition, some political alliances across ethnic lines have endured despite the prevalence of ethnically targeted violence.[57] The politicization of group identity can also take place at the micro level, where the political elites redefine the previous identities of their supporters so that they can exclude their rivals' constituencies due to their clanship (as in the Lakes and the Warrap states, where elite-fuelled conflicts between various clans within the Dinka ethnic group have been raging) or the memory of past alliances (as in the Unity state, where a deadly rivalry has pitted members of the Nuer clans against one another).

While ethnicity is not a driving force behind the conflict per se, the politicization of ethnic identity is a crucial process in propelling ethnic politics towards ethnic war.[58] As Ann Laudati argued, 'Any investigations into conflict must explore how identity has been mobilized for social and political purposes, as well as strategies to access material (natural resource) gains.'[59] Elites generate support and antagonize rural communities by appealing to ethnic sentiment and invoking the memory of past factional violence to disguise the fact that local grievances are, in fact, caused by failures of governance, development and security and by high levels of corruption.[60] The success of this approach pivots on politicized ethnic discourses of fear and ethnically based grievances and by targeting civilians along ethnic lines[61] through the conscious manipulation of ethnic loyalties by the elites.[62] The relevance of the manipulation of identity politics to this book's conceptual framework has been noted by Syed Mansoob Murshed and Mohammad Zulfan Tadjoeddin, who posited that grievances are based on 'identity and group formation'.[63]

In summary, existing approaches have primarily concentrated on macro-level factors, often ignoring the roles that powerful political agents, who can (and do) construct communal grievances via the politics of fear, have played in South Sudanese conflict. In order to explain the outbreak of ethnic war, an analysis of these actors is necessary.[64] The following section will present the empirical work on the conflict and evaluate existing data using the analytical framework. The chapter will also discuss the internal dynamics of South Sudan's ruling elite and the way in which the events that preceded the war can be explained through the prism of the security dilemma paradigm. In addition, the text will explain how the actions of certain leaders relied on or promoted the politics of fear and show how the spread of violent conflict occurred in response to the provocations of the competing political elites in South Sudan.

3

Internal dynamics of South Sudan's ruling elite

The Nuer's definition of government or ruling elite, as 'a small group of people that possesses means of coercions, which it uses to facilitate robbing of the masses',[1] resonates to this day. The ruling elite in South Sudan was constructed through chieftainship, preferential education and liberation movements. The amalgamation of these processes is perhaps what Dr Majak D'Agoot had described as the interaction between warlords, guns, ethnicities and classes, which gave rise to corporatist governing elites, which he grouped under the rubric of a *gun class* – a fusion of the predatory warlord class that uses ethnicity and violence to control or contest state power, exploit public resources, extract livelihoods or achieve upward social mobility.[2]

Until South Sudan separated from the rest of Sudan in 2011, South Sudanese leaders blamed governance failures and all of the atrocities committed against South Sudan's population on the government in Khartoum. Citizens and friends of South Sudan abroad almost believed this narrative to be the entire truth. The role that the deadly rivalries played in the power struggle between the South Sudanese rebels and political leaders was ignored until after December 2013. This chapter explains the internal dynamics of South Sudan's ruling elite, as well as those of the ruling party, the Sudan People's Liberation Movement (SPLM), and it shows how events that preceded the war can be explained through the prism of the security dilemma model. In addition, it explains how the actions of certain leaders relied on or promoted the politics of fear. It further proposes that the spread of violent conflict in South Sudan was a response to the provocations of influential elites.

Salva Kiir and Riek Machar: Fighting each other through targeting each other's fans

Although the South Sudanese masses hardly have avenues for airing out their grievances due to the fear of repression, a culture copied over from the days of civil war as shown in Chapter 1, the author was privileged to have had access to a wide number of citizens in places that are hardly visited by other researchers. While playing chess with many youths in various estates in Juba, the author realized that upon taking a pawn from an opponent, most players would pause and announce a justification for their move to the fans watching the game: 'Käk aa keek ëbën ya yï Kiir', meaning, 'These pawns (if not taken off the board) could advance to become yet another Kiir.'

Although this statement could be interpreted as an acknowledgement of President Kiir's humble background, other interpretations centred around frustrations with his ineffective administering of the country are also plausible. So, what are the dominant characteristics of President Kiir's governance style?

Salva Kiir

President Kiir led the autonomous government of South Sudan from 2005 to 2011, and he continues to lead independent South Sudan to this day.[3] Kiir was granted the capacity to arbitrarily impose sanctions on individuals and institutions, remove and reappoint governors, state assemblies or the vice president, by the Transitional Constitution of Republic of South Sudan, 2011.[4] Having fired his vice president, Dr Riek Machar, in July 2013, Kiir approached the parliamentarians in August 2013 and introduced Dr James Wani as his nominee for vice president, threatening to 'dissolve the parliament and make the lawmakers roam in the streets' unless his nomination was confirmed.[5] As demanded by the Transitional Constitution, Kiir sought to ensure approval by a two-thirds majority from all members of the National Legislative Assembly. Kiir's approach – installing compliant supporters in key positions, rewarding supporters at the expense of others and punishing opponents – drove the country into 'crisis instability'.[6] When asked by a journalist whether he would consider stepping down after the conflict resumed in July 2016, Kiir warned, 'My exit could spark genocide'.[7] Kiir intentionally drew upon the threat of terror as a self-preservation tactic that aimed to spread fear and mobilize perceptions of danger so that he could gain control over populations and maintain his hold on power.[8]

The single most crucial survival skill that served President Kiir better than it served his colleagues was not to fake it until he made it or to be so powerful and so smart that he scared the hell out of his opponents; rather, it was his ability to give his rivals sufficient reasons to underestimate him. By using this powerful trick, President Kiir managed to reduce many of his rivals to nothing.[9] Indeed, the ploy was so effective that his rivals continued to underestimate him even after their defeat. President Kiir even tricked the mighty US government when he convinced the Obama administration and the regional governments in Eastern Africa, in a move that was unheard of in international politics, to jail his arch-rival Dr Riek Machar in South Africa. The US government's support of the appointment of Taban Deng as a replacement for Machar and Machar's eventual marginalization proved to be badly mistaken.[10] Nearly every political leader with a significant following from Kiir's Dinka ethnic group who opposed him has since returned to Juba to serve him with the exception of Gen. Malong Awan, whom he had rendered powerless through isolation and using divide and conquer tactics. A number of leaders who had joined Malong had returned to Juba, and even some of his family members as well as his close former aides had returned to Juba. If that is not a demonstration of the power Kiir has amassed, then nothing else demonstrated such a power he has over his support base than one obvious lie: 'Kiir is a great leader who is surrounded by bad advisors'. This has been sung repeatedly by a number of Kiir's supporters. This is nothing short of a startling display of power over subordinates as the act of 'being made to repeat an obvious lie makes it clear that you're powerless'.[11] This tactic has ensured that positive actions of Kiir are credited to him while negative actions are blamed on his advisors, some of whom have denied having misled Kiir.[12]

Kiir's ability to control everyone is due to several factors: (1) his control of resource revenues, which allows him to settle competitions against rivals in his favour; (2) his positive liberation credit during the 1983–2005 civil war, which he uses against rivals with blemished records of liberation; and (3) his social ties to numerically strong Dinka. As things stand, any attempt to try to overthrow Kiir is equitable to a suicide because the preceding factors allow Kiir to deploy the divide and conquer strategy effectively.

Despite his credit of having successfully led his country into independence against serious challenges and having effectively subdued his rivals, Kiir's legacy has already been badly tainted within the short span of his governance over South Sudan. Kiir is running a government where all of his political rivals' clans and friends are marginalized and whose domain of influence and legitimacy are shrinking to a few bases of support. Like other African leaders who govern through presidential decrees, who permit elections and ambush the voters to rob votes, who boldly edit their country's constitutions to prolong their stay in power and who use coercion to grab any resource that sustains life to force the poor to kneel and pledge allegiance, Kiir invokes fear to divert attention away from his failures in governance, which are far too many. President Kiir took the country to war with Khartoum over Heglig in 2012, which resulted in an instant loss of 98 per cent of the government's revenue in oil and forced Juba to borrow money at exorbitant rates from the Qatar National Bank. In turn, this resulted in the letters-of-credit saga where close to $1 billion was stolen by companies connected to the ruling elites.

President Kiir fired his entire cabinet in July 2013 and threatened members of the National Legislative Assembly with expulsions if they did not approve his choices for replacing those he fired in August 2013. Instead of supporting agriculture with $2 billion, President Kiir authorized a disastrous plan to give billions of dollars to businessmen to import dura in 2008, a corrupt venture that led to outright theft and came to be known as the dura saga. President Kiir created the Crisis Management Committee, which mishandled the money during the first ninety days of the conflict in December 2013, and the committee's members, who took advantage of the arrangement to enrich themselves amidst death and confusion, faced no consequences. President Kiir authorized the devaluation of currency at a dangerous time, which resulted in an immediate liquidity crisis and an instantly high inflation that caused the money market to implode. In violation of the Transitional Constitution, President Kiir also authorized the division of states into smaller regions, which threatened to completely dismantle the communities and the country as a whole. Surprisingly, while this increase in the number of states from ten to twenty-eight violated a peace accord that had been signed in August 2015, foreign diplomats failed to 'denounce creation of the 28 states as egregious violation of the Agreement on the resolution of the conflict in the Republic of South Sudan (ARCISS)'.[13] The demand to reverse the inflation of the number of states became the main hurdle in the process of implementing the September 2018 peace accord, but the international pressure eventually forced Kiir to revert the country back to the ten-states system with additional independent administrative areas, which are Abyei, Ruweng and Pibor. Kiir's decision allowed the formation of the government of unity in February 2020.

Kiir has allowed his advisors to ground him to Juba so that he does not have to see the suffering of his people. In addition, he has never visited a site of conflict or one of many of the displaced camps during the civil war. While there are more than two million refugees who have sought safe harbour in Uganda, Kenya, Ethiopia and Sudan, Kiir and his advisors have blamed social media and propaganda from 'rebels' rather than the war for this growing number.

In keeping up with the tradition of the SPLM/A during the civil war, President Kiir does not take criticism without protest. At a meeting of the Council of Ministers in 2013, Prof. Elias Nyamlell Wakoson, the deputy minister of foreign affairs at the time, boldly said, 'This government is rotten from the top to the bottom.'

'Why are you still in the same system if it is rotten to its core?' President Kiir retorted. Nyamlell was fired for his 'repulsive remark'.[14]

In a speech he delivered at Nyakuron Cultural Centre on 15 December 2013, Kiir contested his comrades who had come out to challenge his executive decisions. In a clear attack on Machar's previous split with the SPLM in 1991 in a speech broadcasted on the afternoon of 15 December 2013, Kiir said, 'Since I took up arms in the 1960s, I have never betrayed the cause of my people.'[15] This came after he had already made explicit his target in his opening lines: 'Inevitably, the path of struggle was very difficult. Along the way some comrades abandoned the struggle and others even joined the enemy.'[16] The attacks weren't surprising given that the leaders had been attacking each other publicly in the media. But what was surprising was the reaction of Kiir's supporters who stood up and sang old SPLA war songs with drums beating.

Kiir's inner circle is predominantly made up of men with rudimentary educations and an outdated knowledge of the outside world. This style of promoting people based on the reputations of their fathers rather than their ability to deliver has crippled his government, but Dr John Garang did not do any better on this either. Another style of governance Kiir has adopted from Garang is the chaotic manner in which information flows. Power is centred at Kiir and it emanates out in concentric circles with those in the smaller circles, meaning those closer to Kiir through anthropological links held the most power regardless of their hierarchies in the government's institutions.

Riek Machar

Within the dynamics of the conflict, one of President Kiir's arch-rivals is Dr Riek Machar. The former deputy president of South Sudan turned rebel leader Dr Riek Machar had engaged in destroying aspiring leaders within his support base to ensure his position was safe from ambitious in-group leaders. Riek Machar built his political leverage as a rebel commander during the 1983–2005 civil war and as vice president from 2005 to 2011, a position which he held until he was fired by President Kiir in July 2013. At the start of the war in December 2013, Machar had no serious rivals within his Nuer ethnic base. Kiir had attempted to find Machar's replacement within the Nuer community, but all the potential candidates were hesitant to oppose him. Although those who had worked with Machar as undersecretaries or as cabinet ministers believed that he was a hardworking man, they pointed out that his politics were weak in the area of distinguishing between public and private resources, which is a pandemic issue among South Sudanese ruling elites. Machar also proved incapable of controlling his supporters, failing to intervene when they abused helpless bystanders during episodes of conflict. In addition, when Machar worked with President Kiir from 2005 to 2011, he did not work towards South Sudan's collective success, but rather, bided his time in the hopes that Kiir's failing government would result in the public demand for Kiir to be removed from office, leaving Machar as the best candidate to be installed in Kiir's place. His experience in managing two separate rebel movements in 1991 through 2002 and in 2013 through 2019 illustrates his poor organizational skills. In 2013 and 2014, Machar's external backers quickly realized the high risk of investing in his utterly disorganized armed revolution and withdrew or offered very rudimentary support to his army, which was largely composed of untrained and armed youths who were fighting to avenge loved ones who had been killed in Juba by government forces.[17] Indeed, Machar made a number of blunders that politically and militarily weakened him. First, his use of the White Army to fight both the Uganda People's Defence Force (UPDF), the armed forces of Uganda that came to Juba to allegedly help Kiir to defeat the rebels and the SPLA along the Bor–Juba road led to catastrophic losses. Yes, the young men were visibly beaming with the intent to avenge their loved ones, but they lacked the military resources needed to achieve the task that faced them. Dr Machar could have joined the White Army, taken them to the Ethiopian border, trained them and used them as leverage to negotiate a lucrative peace deal that would have reinstated him into his position. Instead, his army was decimated, and he was forced to sign an accord in 2015 with comparatively smaller forces at his disposal.

Second, upon making it to Khartoum after the conflict broke out in July 2016, Riek could have denounced violence and avoided being forced into exile to South Africa. Instead, he declared war in Khartoum, which prompted the US government to intervene and settle the conflict between Kiir and Machar in Kiir's favour. In turn, Machar was detained in South Africa under house arrest, and the international and regional communities followed the US government, recognizing Gen. Taban Deng Gai as Riek Machar's replacement. The fact that Machar remained in full control of the SPLM-IO while he was under house arrest in South Africa as well as having lost support from both Sudan and Ethiopia during his detention made it clear that he was indeed holding power in opposition. Contrary to his usual posing as an apostle of democratic ideals, 'Machar is undermining the political and military capacity of the SPLM-IO by opposing institutionalization, democratic accountability, and the formalization of policy, which he fears would threaten his overwhelming dominance of the organization'.[18] Just it has been noted of both Garang's and Kiir's style of governance, power flowed in indeterministic ways in Riek's camp. For example, Dr Peter Adwok Nyaba pointed to how Gen. Taban Deng Gai led the advance team in the presence of SPLM/A-IO Deputy Chairman Alfred Lado-Gore.[19]

Although Machar still enjoyed overwhelming support from his ethnic base, this did not translate into a military advantage that would reverse the military power that favoured Kiir since 2014. Machar's human resources of able and courageous young men had been liquidated, and his support base had increasingly disintegrated. While Machar lacks Raila Odinga's calculative skills, he is not a completely worthless quantity among the South Sudanese political leaders. With all the blunders he has committed, he still lacks a serious replacement amongst the Nuer, just as Kiir lacks a legitimate replacement amongst the Dinka.

Fear is what has kept both Salva Kiir and Riek Machar in power amidst the chaos into which they have wrangled to maintain or grab power, plunging their country into chaos. The Nuer are afraid of Salva Kiir and the Dinka are afraid of Riek Machar. The rest of this chapter discusses two parallel conflicts within the army and within the party.

Competition within the SPLA

In an interview with the SBS Dinka Radio on 21 July 2020, the former chief of the SPLA, Gen. Paul Malong Awan, declared that none among the top former and present military leaders of the SPLA knew the parade of the SPLA. He went on to elaborate that the size of an army is determined by law, and neither the SPLM/A leadership under John Garang nor the SPLM-led government in Juba has figured out what that number should be.[20] In the same interview, Gen. Malong hinted at the competition within the SPLA that led to his ousting while Gen. Akol Koor Kuch became the most powerful armed man. This section traces the history of rivalry within the SPLA. The author uses private armies to refer to militias that had been reintegrated or integrated into the SPLA on paper while they remained loyal to their former militia leaders. Organized armed youth are usually co-opted by politicians and turn into private armies that are used to help politicians to negotiate access to power. This had happened to the Arrow Boys, the White Army, Pandang armed youth, Cobra, Agwelek, Gel-weng and Tiit-weng, among others that are not as well known.

In July 2005, following the death of John Garang, the leader of the Sudan People's Liberation Movement/Army (SPLM/A), Kiir became the chairman of the SPLM, the commander-in-chief of the SPLA and the leader of the autonomous government of Southern Sudan. A group of loyalists began to position themselves to make decisions about the distribution of influence and wealth. In addition to the group's political and economic interests, it aimed to settle wartime grievances against its rivals. The competition for access to resources and power resulted in a slow expulsion of certain elites from the centre of power and the consequential rise in power for others.[21]

The competition made it clear that guns were going to play some roles, but South Sudan had established a military that was dominated by few social groups, mainly the Nuer and the Dinka.

During the liberation, the SPLM/A created a fast-track option for officers from minority groups joining the SPLM/A late. The scheme was to find the most competent officers and to design a gradual promotional avenue that would see them jumping several grades and gaining extra training. If they made enough progress, then they would be promoted once again. A number of officers who joined the SPLM in the 1990s were able to catch up with university graduates who had joined the movement in 1983. The first chairman of the SPLM, Dr John Garang, planned to continue this process. Following the signing of the Comprehensive Peace Agreement (CPA) between Omar Al Bashir's National Congress Party and the SPLM/A in 2005, which ended the second civil war in Sudan, John Garang began to reorganize the SPLA. He retired every SPLA commander who ranked above Commander Oyay Deng Ajak and promoted only one three-star general (Gen. Ajak himself) and fifteen two-star generals.

After Garang died in the helicopter crash in July 2005, President Salva Kiir took over and began to use promotions as his sole means for controlling threats to the agreement from other armed groups and the ambitions of various armed actors within the SPLA. This prevented large-scale conflict within South Sudan and ensured a level of stability prior to the CPA-mandated referendum on self-determination in 2011.[22] However, this policy created incentives for armed rebellion, inhibited efforts to transform the military and left the army vulnerable to fragment along factional lines during periods of heightened political competition.[23] The immediate result was a bloated army at the top, and internal competition ensued. For instance, in 2006, Gen. Dominic Dim wanted to be the chief of the general staff for the SPLA, which prompted President Kiir to ask Gen. Oyay to take up the position of the minister of the SPLA affairs. Gen. Oyay refused. So, Gen. Dim was appointed to that post. Unhappy, Gen. Dim sought revenge against Gen. Oyay. This raised tension within the SPLA headquarters as each leader mobilized officers loyal to him. Gen. Mathok Geng, then the deputy chief of general staff in charge of administration, also wanted the position of Gen. Oyay.[24]

While tensions were brewing within the SPLA, the SPLA increasingly became the primary vehicle for political-military accommodation in South Sudan.[25] However, the co-opting of warlords into the SPLA led to the increasing privatization of security, which further created fear and grievances among the competing elites. The conflict between South Sudan and Sudan over Heglig exposed the lack of an army in South Sudan. This marked the beginning of a process that led to the privatization of South Sudan's army, when President Kiir asked all of the country's ten governors to recruit young people for training. Gen. Malong Awan, the governor of Northern Bahr el Ghazal at that time, took advantage of this order and recruited the infamous Mathiang Anyoor, the first militia to be used in the early 2013 government campaign against the warlord David Yau Yau, who had also built a private army in Pibor. In Jonglei State, the government's uneven disarmament exacerbated the security dilemma between the Murle and the Nuer[26] and uneven administrative development that favoured the Bor Dinka for the headquarters of Jonglei State. That this occurred when South Sudan had only ten states created grievances between the Murle and the Bor Dinka. David Yau Yau, who rebelled after losing his election, took advantage of these grievances within his community to anchor his rebellion. By doing so, he managed to build a private army that was ready to contract its services to any willing buyer.

In the Upper Nile, Johnson Olony built a private army known as the Agwelek, which the government contracted to rout the SPLA-in-Opposition (IO) forces from the east bank of the White Nile. The Padang Dinka elites built a private army, which the government also contracted to fight against Olony when he defected to join Riek Machar. In 2014, a number of private Dinka armies from Northern Bahr el Ghazal and Warrap, including the Mathiang Anyoor, Gel-Weng, Tit-weng, were contracted by the government to deploy to the Upper Nile. In Unity State, Generals Bapiny MonyTwil and Matthew Puljang shared a powerful private army. The president himself was no exception, the ability of the republican guard "to draw on SPLA funds while reporting direct to Salva Kiir meant that the republican guard had begun to look more and more like a private army, subject to almost no control or oversight."[27]

While President Kiir used the resources available to him to collect intelligence on opposition groups in the region and to manage these private armies, buying the most powerful ones and fighting the weaker ones, it remained a challenge for him to manage strong and ambitious military allies whose needs were too expensive to meet. This was exacerbated by the country's trinity of setbacks – an oil shutdown, a drastic fall in global crude oil prices and civil war – and ultimately presented Kiir with one of the most difficult tasks that he faced throughout his governing period. Each of Kiir's strong military allies was managing a separate network of clientele, which resulted in unchecked and competitive corruption amongst various military networks. The determination of military actors to continue stealing from rapidly emptying coffers led to an immediate collapse in the clearing house at the Central Bank and threatened a violent dismantling of the system. When the oil-dependent economy boomed from 2006 to 2012, military allies used their positions and access to resources to plunder the national economy through graft, corruption and extortion and participated in private business activities where they awarded themselves and their associates with large contracts. However, as the revenues for crude oil prices fell in the global economy, oil outputs decreased from 350,000 barrels per day in 2012 to less than 160,000 barrels per day in 2013. Resources became dangerously limited and the patterns of corruption became disrupted, the consequences of which included an economic collapse and the violent breakdown of the ruling club. This was a system of integrative corruption when the economy boomed, linking various warlords 'into lasting networks of exchange and shared interest',[28] which became a system of disintegrative corruption when the economy failed, leading the elites to turn against one another.

In May 2013, President Kiir publicly admitted at a military parade in Bilpam that he was aware that 'the current SPLA consisted of cousins and nephews of generals who are in uniforms only as a means of employment and who cannot perform any duties required of a soldier'.[29] He then accused the country's forces of corruption, saying they had squandered resources through dubious activities and citing ghost names in the payroll system as the culprits.[30] While nearly 40 per cent of the national budget had been allocated to the SPLA, much of this had ended up in the hands of a few powerful men who were in charge of the private armies, leaving most of the armed forces neglected and barely capable of making ends meet.[31]

The number of soldiers who are recruited after a peace agreement or other similar arrangement is not necessarily verified by an outside party to ensure its accuracy. Without having to provide proof, a commander can assert that he has X number of men in county Y and so on. No one is going to check that his reports are true. It is easy to inflate this number, and there is an economic incentive to do so. In 2006, the Juba agreement between Paulino Matip and President Salva Kiir invited Matip and his South Sudan Defence Forces (SSDF), which was estimated to be between thirty-five thousand and fifty thousand units strong and to have had enlisted seventeen two-star generals, most of whom were from Nuer, to join the SPLA. The government of Sudan had inflated the ranks of the leaders of its southern proxies as a way of buying their loyalty. Before this reintegration, the SPLA had just one three-star general and fifteen two-star generals. This created a panic, and the president was pressured to urgently promote more SPLA officers in response. The officers that Paulino Matip brought to Juba represented a power-sharing bargain that was not proportional to the actual force he led. Because salaries were paid in cash for commanders to distribute to their soldiers without any centralized roster, it became clear to many commanders that the more forces they reported to be under their command, the more money they would receive. Subsequent reintegrations into the SPLA followed similar trajectories, wherein the number of soldiers who were reintegrated into the SPLA was based on what rebel commanders had successfully negotiated with President Kiir.

When violence erupted in Juba in December 2013, each side assembled their respectively available armed forces. Riek Machar and the SPLA-IO relied more heavily on the White Army than anything else. In fact, the SPLA was outnumbered by the White Army in Malakal and Jonglei, which were home to some of the largest-scale clashes during the conflict. Kiir had to rely again on Mathiang Anyoor's Lion Division because he lacked SPLA soldiers and a host of other private armies, such as Generals Bapiny's and Puljang's forces, which had decisively backed Kiir in Bentiu. While Kiir's conclusive win in Malakal of the Upper Nile can be attributed to Olony's private army, not many of the soldiers on Kiir's payroll could be called into battle. During the December 2013 conflict, Machar's military strength came from a militia known as the White Army instead of the Nuer men in the SPLA. For President Salva Kiir, it was mainly a collection of independent private armies. In other words, the

SPLA was largely an army in name only between 2006 and 2013, and what we call the South Sudan conflict was nothing more than a clash between various private armed forces. A senior SPLM leader agrees with the observation that the 'SPLA has never been a robust united force since we started to incorporate militia into it in appalling numbers'.[32]

The co-opting of warlords into the national military has led to increased security privatization in South Sudan. Whenever these groups are backed by the state, fear and grievances increase amongst competitors. In a typical case of the security dilemma, the counter-insurgency of outsourcing military services to private armies to counter the fear of Nuer soldiers, who have dominated the SPLA since 2006, has led to the over-representation of Nuer groups in the ranks of the SPLA. The SPLA commanders who made their names during the liberation struggle have found themselves neglected under President Kiir's policy to direct resources to the funding of private armies. Some of these commanders have since opened discussion about seeding power away from the commander-in-chief, who alienated them in a system they built with their toil.

Following the outbreak of conflict in Juba in December 2013, a number of powerful former-SPLA commanders were accused of plotting a coup and were rounded up and detained. While in their cells, one of them, who had no military background, asked his colleagues to explain how it was possible that members of the ruling SPLM party and the SPLA's most powerful commanders, who had been in charge of the army, security and foreign affairs, had found themselves in jail. One of the other inmates provided an honest answer, which was echoed by several of the others: 'We have never worked as a team.'[33]

The government's accusations turned out to be false, as the court dismissed all the cases brought against the alleged plotters for a lack of evidence. Nevertheless, at least one popular narrative within Kiir's camp held these accusations to be true. This account held that the initial plan was for the press conferences to trigger a mass protest in Juba. Following this, Gen. James Hoth Mai, a sympathizer of the SPLM leaders who would be detained following the outbreak of the war, would move in to establish a Transitional Military Council for twelve to eighteen months, and elections would be held without the participation of the remaining members of the former-SPLM/SPLA political-military high command (e.g. without Salva Kiir, Riek Machar, James

Wani Igga, Daniel Awet Akot or Kuol Manyang). This narrative concluded that Gen. Hoth withdrew from the plan when he saw the tension at the Nyakuron Cultural Centre on 13 December 2013 and Dinka's reaction to the conflict with SPLA-led songs of war.[34]

Though evidence for this narrative is shaky because 'nobody while still serving under Kiir will accept or agree that he was planning to reign over Kiir by military means',[35] it remains difficult to rule out that certain SPLA officers did not wish to strip Kiir of his power, as Kiir had increasingly alienated the top SPLA commanders whom Dr Garang had chosen to lead the SPLA. Since Kiir took over, fear of a coup had clouded the political atmosphere. One of his former security advisors claimed that 'Kiir had those fears since 2005 although I kept assuring him that the phenomenon is fast dying out given the AU position on military takeovers and the fact that "Southern Sudan" was a subnational entity on transition'.[36] Despite such assurances, numerous rumours of an internal coup have continued to spread, which, according to the account of one insider, are intended to instil fear in the president and manipulate him into making unconsidered decisions against those holding lucrative positions.[37]

In October 2006, Generals Dominic Dim and Salva Mathok accused Gen. Oyay of hatching a plot to stage a coup. This turned out to be a false alarm. In reality, the three generals had competing interests, and both Dim and Mathok desired Oyay's position as the chief of general staff for the SPLA. Career politics were to blame for this rumour. In the beginning of this dispute, Dim wanted to be the chief of general staff. However, when President Kiir asked Oyay to take the position of minister of SPLA affairs and Oyay declined, suspecting that he was being pushed out of the SPLA, which was his true political constituent, Kiir appointed Dim as the minister of SPLA affairs as a compromise. In turn, Dim sought revenge against Oyay, and the two began to mobilize support within the SPLA leadership. Mathok, who also desired Oyay's position, became a natural ally to Dim.

In 2009, Generals Malong and Gregory accused Dr Majok D'Agoot (also a general) of planning a coup. This turned out to be one of the four false accusations of insurgency that occurred between 2009 and 2013. Very little literature has examined the preceding narrative on the tensions within the army but instead predominantly focused on the tensions within the ruling party.

Although it is difficult to separate the SPLA and the SPLM, the contradictions within both institutions are similar.

The explosion of organized armed youth, who are usually co-opted by opportunistic elites as private forces, points to the failure of the central authority to fulfil its basic duty to provide security. Ingrid Marie Breidlid and Michael J. Arensen noted that 'the mass mobilisations of Nuer civilians in the Greater Upper Nile region at the onset of the ongoing conflict illustrated the complete breakdown of trust in government, particularly its ability and willingness to provide security, protection and justice for all citizens'.[38] Among Western Equatorians, the SPLA's failure to respond to the Lord's Resistance Army's (LRA) threat confirmed long-held perceptions of marginalization by the Juba government and triggered the formation of a private army known as the Arrow Boys.[39] The Gelweng and Titweng Dinka militias from the Warrap and Lakes States formed Kiir's most loyal troops and effectively constituted the president's private army during the civil war.[40] The incorporation of the Titweng into the SPLA marked a shift in the status of non-state security actors from their traditional roles of protecting cattle and communities to the responsibility of protecting the national government's elite.[41] Violence in Jonglei is closely linked to the prevailing security vacuum in rural areas.[42] In March 2017, youth from Hol, Nyarweng, Twic and Bor Dinka mobilized and attacked Murle,[43] an action that prompted South Sudanese commentators to point to increasing anarchy: 'If not a failed dysfunctional and abnormal state, how else would you describe a country in which citizens armed themselves and mobilized on a tribal basis to wipe out members of another tribe, yet the government remains dead silent without responding to such lawlessness?'[44] Some concluded that 'we don't have a government in Juba, but a militia warlord'.[45] Ole Frahm noted that non-state actors, such as localized militias that fill the void of government presence, are generally sources of insecurity themselves.[46] Jok Madut agreed, noting that 'nowhere did it become more evident than in South Sudan that a society where everyone is armed on the pretext of self-defence is a society where no one can be assured of safety'.[47] This sentiment confirmed Barry Posen's thesis, which proposed that 'the actions taken by groups to enhance their security produce reactions that in the end can make them less secure'.[48] In acknowledgement of the relevance of Barry Posen's application of the security dilemma framework to the Sudanese conflict, Hilde Johnson also invoked the security dilemma to explain the almost spontaneous ethnic response to the Nuer killings in Juba in 2013.[49]

The SPLA increasingly became a collection of private armies that consisted of armed combatants who owed their allegiance to individuals before the state and who contracted their military services to the state in exchange for cash, uniforms and weapons. In turn, this triggered destructive competition in the business of raising private armies and led to the inflation of army payrolls and competitive corruption. It also created serious indiscipline in the army. In early 2013, a brigadier general complained to his nephew, a friend of the author, about how his rank was not sufficiently recognized by certain junior officers at the SPLA's headquarters. These officers refused to salute him because they saw his rank as inflated, as he had been reintegrated into the SPLA from a private army and jumped above his old comrades by several grades.

Forming a private army has become little more than a risky entrepreneurial adventure. Like other aspects of governance within the state of South Sudan, one dangerous consequence that feeds into the environment of fear is that the privatization of the armed sector translates into the privatization of security. As an example, Ole Frahm noted that 'South Sudan in its current state is a privatised state in which corruption and privatisation of state resources for personal benefit are very common as even the president himself admitted'.[50] Frahm correctly confirmed that 'privatization is only in part done with the purpose of sustaining a neo-patrimonial web of dependent and dependable clients to maintain control of the state'.[51] A host of anecdotes collected over the course of researching this book supports this thesis of privatization. Businesspeople interviewed for this book had all agreed that it is nearly impossible to do business in Juba without the protection of a powerful general.

Competition within the SPLM

Internal struggles within the SPLM leadership led to a security dilemma during the SPLM convention in 2008, when Kiir urged attendees to endorse

James Wani Igga as deputy chairman (to replace Machar) and Taban Deng as secretary general (to replace Amum).[52] Members were concerned about the adverse consequences of this decision, particularly at a time when unity within the SPLM rank and file was thought to be necessary to withstand the machinations of an external aggressor in Khartoum (who could ostensibly undermine the exercise of a referendum). With the help of elders, Abel Alier and Joseph Lagu, amongst others from Warrap, were able to avert the efforts to dismiss Riek Machar and Pagan Amum, and the status quo was maintained to avoid the disintegration of the party.[53] The crucial element in preventing this crisis was that the rivals did not make their grievances public or wage a war of words.

The intra-party power struggle re-emerged in early 2012. While dining with Thabo Mbeki, the former president of South Africa, and two other former African presidents in early 2012, President Kiir said he was looking forward to retirement.[54] As if this was long-awaited news, some SPLM leaders at the dinner shared this information with their colleagues, which immediately triggered a scramble for succession. Riek Machar, Pa'gan Amum and Rebecca Garang declared their intentions to run for the party nomination in the 2015 elections. James Wani Igga also hinted that he would run if Kiir indeed would not contest. Whether Kiir was pressured by his support base to recant his words, or he was just entertaining his guests who were all retired African presidents, this incident sowed a deep distrust between Kiir and certain senior leaders of the SPLM.

In a move that was seen to weaken any remaining trust between Kiir and his senior cadres, President Kiir went public on 3 May 2012 and accused seventy-five of his officials and several business persons of the gross embezzlement of public funds, which he estimated to be $4 billion. The move was viewed as 'an attempt by the president to use corruption at a broad-brush to implicate political rivals'.[55]

In July 2012, the SPLM dispatched leaders to various towns in South Sudan. The SPLM leadership wanted to thank the population for its overwhelming votes for independence in July 2011, thank grassroots organizations for their support during the civil war era and receive feedback on how the SPLM was doing. The SPLM leaders were expecting the grassroots organizations to come out and sing 'we've made it' in celebration of the SPLM party's achievements.

They were in for a shock when they were presented with a comprehensive internal report that surveyed grassroots communities to evaluate the performances of the SPLM after the end of the civil war in 2005, as 'the feedback from these opinion surveys was unsympathetic as leadership was labelled as visionless, corrupt, and incompetent'.[56] The report, which became public in 2012, coincided with the time when the secretary general of the SPLM became aware of how poorly his party had governed the country. In other words, the SPLM leaders were unaware of how badly they had governed South Sudan until after the survey was released.

Instead of addressing the public grievances caused by the SPLM's style of governance, the leaders attempted to outdo each other by trading blame for the failures of the SPLM (mainly among the three principal leaders: President Salva Kiir, Riek Machar and Secretary General Pagan Amum). In February 2013, Riek Machar tailored his campaign to address these concerns, using these collective failures as a kind of secure platform for staging his ascent to power.

Secretary General Pagan Amum and vice chairman of the SPLM Riek Machar deflected blame for the failure of the SPLM onto the chairman and president, Salva Kiir, attempting to position themselves as viable alternatives. Upon failing to quell the tension internally, the president, vice president and secretary general began to use the mass media as a platform to trade accusations and to air their grievances. The SPLM trisected itself into hostile power centres. Pagan Amum led a camp of former SPLA commanders who perceived themselves to have an ideological fidelity to the founding chairman of the SPLM, John Garang. Riek Machar led another camp, consisting largely of the former fighters who had aligned with him during the 1991 split with the SPLA. Kiir created a faction consisting of former SPLA commanders, who were loyal during an internal crisis within the SPLA in 2004 that pitted him against John Garang, and several politicians who were aligned with Khartoum during the civil war and other senior SPLM leaders.

With no external intervention and weakening communications between Kiir's camp and the other two camps, the public statements that the ruling elite transmitted through mass media and social gatherings created a 'fear contagion effect' across the country and triggered considerable uncertainty among the rival camps. While the heightened criticism that the vice president and secretary general allayed at the president was viewed as a pre-emptive strike, the president's removal of those he deemed disloyal and the anti-corruption measures he took to target his opponents exacerbated tensions. On 16 April 2013, President Kiir stripped his long-serving vice president, Riek Machar, of his vital executive functions. In May 2013, the governors of Bahr el Ghazal resolved to support Kiir.[57] Identity politics soon began to shape internal power struggles in the party, and a security dilemma occurred in classic fashion.

To purge rivals, the president removed Governor Taban Deng of Unity State, which Machar protested openly as unconstitutional, giving interviews to the BBC and *The Guardian* in the beginning of July 2013. This angered President Kiir. The two camps, which were led separately by the now fired Riek Machar and Pagan Amum, aimed to politically depose Kiir and engaged in a highly risky confrontation in a country with an army that lacked cohesion.[58] On 6 December 2013, senior SPLM leaders held a press conference at the party's headquarters in Juba and decried Kiir's dictatorial tendencies. According to Rolandsen, 'The reference they made to a possible chaotic future was interpreted both as a concern and a threat.'[59]

On 8 December 2013, a faction loyal to President Kiir held their own press conference in the same venue and described the dissidents 'as disgruntled, power-hungry malcontents'.[60] On 14 December 2013, President Kiir convened the National Liberation Council, and 'he denounced Riek Machar in strident terms, turning Juba into a powder keg, and any spark was enough to set off a pyre'.[61]

During the rally at the Nyakuron Cultural Centre, Kiir charged that 'some comrades challenged my executive position' and that 'this takes us back to 1991'.[62] He also warned, 'I will not allow this to happen again.' He then acknowledged the purge he had been carrying out since his dissolution of the cabinet in July 2013, stating that he was 'determined to combat these evils'. Machar and a group of thirteen other leaders left in protest of Kiir's hostile statements. At one point, Kiir's supporters started singing SPLA songs of war in the Dinka language, and one woman invited Kiir to join her in singing the chorus: 'Aɲuën ë thou' – 'Better death.'

Research has shown that memories of fear can change upon their retrieval.[63] This process is referred to as memory reconsolidation. In normal settings, our brains are able to update their stored representations of content, strengths and/or expectations through the memory reconsolidation process. Thus, a reactivated memory enters into a transient labile state (destabilisation), followed by a restabilization phase so that the memory may persist (memory reconsolidation). During his speeches at the Nyakuron Cultural Centre on 14 December, one day prior to the beginning of the conflict, Kiir reactivated his supporters' traumatic and fearful memories of his arch-rival Machar, leaving them more fearful of Machar than before. By describing Machar as a 'prophet of doom' and insisting that he 'will not allow the incidents of 1991 to repeat themselves', Kiir evocatively reminded his support base of perhaps the worst violence to occur between the Dinka and the Nuer during the civil war.

The crux of the security dilemma is that through efforts to enhance their own security, actors provoked fear and enacted countermeasures, which reduced rather than increased security. This is precisely the trajectory that occurred at the end of 2012 and into early 2013. According to Tang, the security dilemma was exacerbated because certain elites on one or both sides – although they harboured no aggressive desire to launch a conflict – strove to gain power or to avoid losing power by inciting ethnic tensions and hatred. One former commander of the SPLA wrote:

> When our Archbishop spoke in Nyakoron Hall in the evening of the 14th December 2013, followed by Bishop Paride on 15th evening, they both raised concern about the dangerous stage people were passing through and both of them appealed to the President before all to take some practical steps to ease the tension.[64]

Unfortunately, such warnings came a little too late as the situation had already switched from a security dilemma to a security threat by the second week of December. The three-person competition that set the president, vice president and secretary general against each other is best captured by one of Tang's categories, wherein 'the leaders set an aggressive goal, usually domination over another group, not because their constituents demand it, but because the leaders expect that once they have succeeded in provoking violent conflict they can count on a "rally around the flag" effect, which will bolster their power and de-legitimise their political opponents'.[65] However, the marked increase in fear and hatred quickly transformed the situation from a security dilemma into a genuine security threat by the second week of December. Tang noted that this type of phase typically takes place when one or both sides harbour truly malign intentions. He also predicted that unless international society intervened in a timely manner, the situation would almost inevitably end in mass violence or war.[66]

Following the Equatoria Conference in February 2013, the Bahr el Ghazal Conference in May 2013 and the SPLM Leaders' Conference on 6 December 2013 (led by Riek Machar and Pagan Amum, who were both from the Upper Nile), political alliances began to take on regional and ethnic contours. By December 2013, the Dinka group had split into two factions: the moderate elites and the hardliners. The Nuer group was also split into moderate elites and hardliners, who were further divided into two more groups due to internal politics in the Nuer community and Kiir's exploitation of this dynamic. As in the case of the Dinka group, the Equatoria regional group had two actors.

While the moderate Dinka leaders who opposed Kiir's policies were framed in the mass media as traitors and thieves, Kiir and the hardliners framed themselves as the protectors of Dinka's interests.[67] Both Minister of Information Michael Makuei and Presidential Spokesperson Ateny Wek launched a media campaign that depicted Gen. Paul Malong as a thief.[68] In an effort to frustrate Deng Alor to the point of resignation, junior employees and President Kiir harassed and accused him of working against the government as a traitor.[69] Young people in Jonglei composed a song that trended on social media, depicting Majak D'Agoot, a former deputy defence minister who had fallen out with President Kiir in 2013, as a traitor. A coercive strategy called *loony chok* – meaning to unleash hunger – was deployed against internal dissenters. The *loony chok* strategy was effective because the system was centrally controlled by Kiir so that those who did not express loyalty were denied jobs, even in the private sector. Moderates who did not harbour real hatred were forced either to cooperate or be replaced by hardliners who expressed genuine loathing for out-groups (or at least pretended to do so).[70] In this atmosphere, strategies to remain in any influential position in the government became nothing short of efforts to adopt extreme views or to play-act extremism. While those who acted deceptively by pretending to hold extreme views did not go to jail, those who were uncooperative became part of the group known as the 'former detainees'. In addition, some moderates survived in the system by pretending to profess ethnic hatred, which forced them to put these beliefs into practice.[71]

In 2013, a group of elites from the Dinka group emerged under the name of the Dinka Council of Elders (JCE). The group appeared to have adopted an already existing body. 'In the beginning of 2004 the Dinka community in Sudan has formed a JCE, to function as a kind of Dinka language academy, where linguistic matters like orthographies and lexical expansion can be discussed and decided upon'.[72] While speaking at an event organized by a group of students to celebrate their graduation at St Paul's University in Kenya (the author of this book also spoke there as the keynote speaker), the Right Reverend Moses Deng Bol, the archbishop of the internal province of the Northern Bahr el Ghazal (Aweil, Wau and Warrap), explained why he disagreed with the JCE to a Dinka audience.

The archbishop began by declaring that while there was nothing wrong with having an organization like the JCE, its members crossed the boundaries of their proper domain of duties and what was expected of them. Instead of legislating cultural issues, such as high dowries that affect young people, helping to settle internal disputes within the Dinka or seek reconciliation with elders from non-Dinka communities so that tribes could coexist peacefully, the JCE wrote threatening press releases to the United Nations (UN) and Intergovernmental Authority on Development (IGAD). Who did these elders think they were to write to the UN – a unity of nations and not tribes – using our collective name of Dinka? The extent to which this madness has been permitted to continue makes us look stupid to the world when there are many wise people among us. The archbishop cited an ancient law: 'Do unto others as you would have them do unto you', asking the Dinka representatives how they would feel if a non-Dinka became president the next day, and a council of his tribal men interfered with his governance. He also asked if they would allow their members to do what they would not allow others to do to them.

From the audience's reaction, it was clear that the archbishop's logic was greatly appreciated. Indeed, this internal dialogue/debate within the Dinka is important.

Through the productive manipulation of fear, animosity and ethnic and regional identities, the Dinka hardliners, led by the JCE, mustered support through ethnic solidarity to optimize the success of the collective political and military actions of its supporters. The assurance of in-group solidarity and a collective response to the ethnic conflict strengthened the security dilemma.[73] Driven by the desire to centralize grassroots power,[74] Kiir issued a decree that divided South Sudan's ten states into twenty-eight new ones, modifying an initial proposal by the JCE. Motivated by the same calculations, Riek Machar also considered the politics of redrawing boundaries to optimize his political influence.[75]

Although the original twenty-eight states were created as a part of political calculations, people's biases were exploited to make it appear like the population had demanded the creation of additional states. Increasing the number of states from ten to twenty-eight led to immediate economic losses for certain types of businesses and was particularly harmful to the former headquarters of the original ten states. Hospitality and housing sectors also suffered immediate losses. In places like Bor Town, a majority of the business owners in the service sector were Bor Dinka, and it was this sector of the former Jonglei State that suffered the heaviest losses as a result of executive order number 36. Surprisingly, this same sector was vocal in backing the executive order, supporting a policy that was clearly harmful to their own interests. The South Sudanese political leaders did not allow people to view the policies they proposed from different angles. Although safety depends on increased interactions between neighbouring communities rather than isolation, the South Sudanese political elite framed isolation as the main solution to insecurity and the threats posed by hostile neighbours. This did little to improve security. As one observer noted:

> With the recent creation of more states decrees, General Kiir has not only successfully brought the fight to our doorsteps but also smartly switched the war to be fought in our own families, between us and our uncles, fathers-in-law, brothers, sisters and cousins while at the same time he has secured his tight grip on power and to use the resources of this country as he wishes.[76]

Indeed, rather than remove the security dilemma, this ethnic balkanization exacerbated it. Douglas Johnson illustrated that in colonial times, establishing effective instruments of law minimized security dilemmas in most of what was formerly Sudan because they included hostile or competing neighbours within the same districts or provinces so that they could better regulate them and more easily resolve their disputes. To prove this, Johnson highlighted an instance where an attempt at segregation was abandoned.[77]

Indeed, as it will be shown, the separation of communities based on ethnic or clan linkages into administrative units (states or counties) immediately led to the exposing of dormant communal cracks and polarized discourses on the political affairs along clans or ethnic lines. In Jonglei State, people celebrated the division of the state into tribally based mini states for the Nuer, Dinka and Murle. The same old communal grievances had resurfaced within each group.

The architects of the division of South Sudan into thirty-two states thought the Dinka could relate better and that their differences would be easier to manage once the Dinka were encircled into their own states, a sentiment which history has proven wrong. Some mistakenly thought that if Bor and Twic were separated into separate states, the noise would calm. They were wrong again. A new noise that is even louder would surface in each group. Separation is hardly a solution because it's merely an avoidance. Reintegration is actually the only approach suitable for fragmentary societies (societies in which a separatist keeps dividing the community until it's him versus his sibling from his dad's other wife). A way to make the reintegration approach effective is 'eating together'. If one creates common experiences around shared economic gains and get the communities to work together, one will cement their unity.

The other consequence of the division of the states is the decentralization of violence. Some of the deadly intra/inter-communal conflicts related to the politics of administrative structures in South Sudan were triggered by the following questions: (1) Which community owned the shared administrative centre or a strategic land (e.g. an island)? (2) What should a shared administrative centre be called? (3) What should a new county be called? (4) Where should the headquarters of a new county be located? I am certain there are more reasons. The four I have mentioned have already triggered communal conflicts in the former Jonglei, Warrap and Upper Nile states and potentially other areas. We have increasingly seen neighbouring communities of the same ethnic group raiding cattle between each other, fighting each other with big weapons like rocket-propelled grenades (RPG) – and the deaths related to inter-/intra-communal conflicts being far too many.

In the early days of the conflict, some hardliners fanned the flames of fear so that they could reject any notion of peaceful settlement. Telar Deng, the president's legal advisor, sowed dread about the opposition's ambitions for leadership by opining as follows: 'I think peace is difficult to be achieved especially at this time because Riek Machar's ambition for the presidency is increasing.'[78] Deng also blamed Pagan Amum's group of ten former detainees, claiming that 'to be frank, this group was the one that ignited the ongoing war because it incited Machar to do so'.[79]

After reluctantly signing the August 2015 Peace Agreement, Kiir and the hardliners in his camp publicly impugned it. As an example, Chief General Malong Awan of the SPLA stated, 'We will not reward those who have rebelled with positions in the army'.[80] Information Minister Michael Makuei echoed similar resistance: 'We strongly believe that this document [the August 2015 Peace Agreement] cannot serve the people of South Sudan; it is a sell out and we cannot accept it'.[81] Makuei later softened his stance: 'As of now, let us change the language: if you are a supporter of the government, don't write any other unhealthy language. We don't want any further hostile propaganda. We don't want hate speech on the radios'.[82] While speaking at the SPLM House, President Kiir stoked fears about the dangers of implementing the August 2015 Peace Agreement by welcoming back opposition members: 'If they find you unorganized, you will all be bought. The information I have about this peace agreement is that our brothers are told by their own friends to keep destabilising South Sudan permanently so that South Sudanese do not see development'.[83]

Joshua Dau, the deputy chair of the JCE, termed the idea of deploying the regional protection force – as stipulated in the peace accord – as a 'strategy to advance their regime change objective'.[84] Ambrose Riiny, the chairman of the JCE, described the suggestion as 'a declaration of war and invasion of the country'.[85] Following reports that Dinka members had been targeted on the highways in Equatoria, Aldo Ajou Deng, a JCE member, spread panic by claiming, 'We know that there is hidden boiling hatred against the Dinka community in Central Equatoria'.[86]

Fighting for equitable representation among the elites was a key motivator for the non-Dinka elites in this conflict. Anti-government militias sought to exploit insecurity and tribal tensions to mobilize and to engage in military operations so that they could advance their local political aspirations.[87] Like the Dinka elites, some non-Dinka elites contributed to the manipulation of certain ethnic groups' psychological responses. Similar to a phenomenon Edward L. Glaeser noted elsewhere,[88] non-Dinka elites supplied stories that created hate for the non-Dinka masses in attempts to discredit the government. While Riek Machar was rarely seen fomenting ethnic hatred/fear through mass media himself, some top opposition military leaders, who spoke in native Nuer, along with spokespersons and other social media users associated with Riek Machar, deployed various messages across the media to fan ethnic hatred. This followed the pattern noted in Tang's framework by (a) attributing the government's crimes to the Dinka ethnic group; (b) mythologizing such crimes against Nuer civilians as part of the collective memory; (c) painting the Nuer as innocent victims while demonizing the Dinka as unforgivable perpetrators and; (d) painting the Nuer as heroic, powerful and glorious 'freedom fighters' and the Dinka as treacherous, weak and inglorious 'genocidal forces'.[89] 'Pagak is now fully under the SPLA-IO. The forces of the genocidal regime have been eliminated and defeated',[90] said Major General James Ochan Puot, who later defected from the SPLM-IO and rejoined the 'genocidal regime' less than two months ahead of the formation of the transitional government scheduled for 22 November. According to General Puot, his defection was due to the 'deliberate attack, killings and displacement of innocent Cie-waw and Gajaak civilians in Adar State (Maiwut); where over seventy-nine thousand four hundred and fifty (79,450) civilians were looted and displaced from their homes by the forces loyal to Dr. Riek Machar from July 31, 2019 to Date'.[91]

All Nuer members who had remained in the government were stigmatized as 'Nuer whew' – the Nuer who were bought with jobs or money – even though many Nuer leaders occupied their positions long before the conflict began.

On the offensive side of things, the chief aim was demonization – a special kind of moral mandate that identifies an out-group as evil and justifies any measures taken against them, including violence.

In a regional conference held in Juba in 2013, Governor Bakosoro stirred regional fear/hatred by claiming that the Equatoria region had been innocently victimized by the Dinka-dominated government, declaring that 'most of the time, Equatorians are being suspected, jailed and accused'.[92] Josephine Lagu, the daughter of the prominent South Sudanese revolutionary leader Gen. Joseph Lagu (who hailed from Equatoria), was accused of embezzling public funds in 2012. Governor Clement Wani framed the imprisonment of Josephine Lagu as a punishment for all of Equatoria and alleged that the funds likely ended 'up in the hands of one community (Dinka) and families who are not even in schools'.[93]

Thomas Cirilo, a former deputy SPLA chief who resigned and announced the formation of a new movement, hinged his military mobilization on the Dinka political-military elites' alleged implementation of the JCE's agenda of 'ethnic cleansing', 'forceful displacement of people from their ancestral lands' and 'ethnic domination'.[94] Cirilo invoked 'ethnic cleansing' to appeal to the ethnic Nuers. His mention of 'the forceful displacement of people from their ancestral lands' was aimed at the Shilluk and the Fertit of Western Bahr el Ghazal, where a conflict had been raging over this particular issue of land. The fear of 'ethnic domination' in vital government organs by the Dinka has been a constant fear in Greater Equatoria.

Complaints in the literature about the lack of representation from the top leadership of the military among certain Equatorian groups have omitted important historical processes due to either a lack of knowledge or because these publications have been used by Equatorian leadership to sow fear as an instrument for their insurgency advance. In either case, a narrative has been promoted that may become a genuine communal grievance to justify war. As an example, a piece by the Small Arms Survey on the Conflict in Western Equatoria shared the following anecdote by an important community leader:

> According to the paramount chief of the Azande, Wilson Hassan Peni, the Azande did not have an officer at the rank of major general at the beginning of 2015. The Azande are one of several ethnic groups claiming to be the third-largest in South Sudan behind the Dinka and Nuer.[95]

The government has since failed to close the gaps in representation through proven strategies, such as those used in Uganda and Ethiopia and the initiative by Dr John Garang, the first Chairman of the SPLA, who recruited young and competent officers from communities that were underrepresented and fast-tracked their promotion by integrating superior training so as not to create any disorder in the rank and file. Instead of taking options like these, the government rewarded warlords, which led to the privatization of the army and to communities increasing their military representation by backing leaders who used violence as a bargaining chip. Even upon its widespread implementation, this process did not result in the promotion of any competent army leaders. The government rewarded warlords, such as Johnson Olony and David Yau Yau, but not the leaders of the Arrow Boys, like Fatuyo and Welebe. While in an effort to appeal to the grievances arising from the Azande's military underrepresentation, Riek Machar eventually promoted both Fatuyo and Welebe to the rank of major general, which was ultimately Machar's way of using the politics of fear to recruit and amass another private army to his already worthy collection.

The scale in which David Yau Yau mobilized Murle youths in 2012 and early 2013 demonstrated the elites' success in exploiting the Murle population's feelings of resentment, distrust and marginalization, especially in the wake of an abusive and uneven SPLA disarmament campaign.[96] The collective demonization of the Dinka due to the behaviour of a handful of their elites led to the attacks against Dinka civilians on South Sudanese roads, in Equatoria and in other towns, as well.[97]

The main source of fear amongst the elites was their rivals' undergoing a consolidation of power,[98] and the elites succeeded in translating their individual fears into tribal ones.[99] Jok explained that contests for state power turned violent because political leaders drew upon local communities and turned their individual quests for power into matters of survival for their communities.[100] The politicization of group identity and the manipulation of psychological responses mobilized young people on both sides of the conflict. For their part, the political elites mobilized the least privileged people across all ethnicities to defend themselves against their rivals.[101] To mobilize the masses in the Dinka, Nuer and Equatorian areas, the political elites exploited the historical hostilities of the past,[102] which included conjuring memories of ethnically charged killings, economic disenfranchisement and ethnic marginalization.[103]

Acute illiteracy and poverty caused the South Sudanese people to be more prone to manipulation.[104] The youth fighters' incentives to take arms stemmed from their socio-economic grievances, which, as has been argued, were often constructed by the manipulative elites. During previous civil wars, Southern Sudanese young people were largely drawn into armed conflict to protect themselves and their communities against the military.[105]

The rebels successfully incorporated the government's indiscriminate violence into their appeals to recruit supporters.[106] In the days following 15 December 2013, the systematic targeting of Nuer civilians in Juba and the resulting anger and desire for revenge were critical to mobilizing the Nuer to join the opposition.[107] As Tang observed, the malicious elite on one or both sides of a struggle who mobilized even a fraction of the population could inflict so much devastation to the other side that the response was sure to be one of hatred and rage.[108] When this reaction was achieved, those from the side that initiated the violence feared becoming the target of revenge. Consequently, the people on both sides felt 'rationally' compelled to support mass violence and ethnic war.[109]

The hardliners sought to generate politicized anger and to then divert this resentment towards outer-group leaders. Presenting themselves as the victims of power-hungry opponents who were solely responsible for all the chaos absolved hardliners of the responsibility for what occurred around them. It excused them for their failures, allowed them to blame everything on their rivals and enabled them to use political fear to motivate their support bases to endorse self-destructive policies. The elites' machinations hardly stood against basic cultural logic. Nevertheless, the politics of fear still encouraged individuals to publicly lie about their privately held political beliefs due to the perceived political, economic, security and social sanctions in their centrally controlled system.[110] Despite the conspicuous wealth that was accumulated by officials in Kiir's government[111] and the apparent mismanagement of the economy under his rule,[112] President Kiir has continued to receive active support from sizeable shares of his impoverished ethnic Dinka base.

In a TV interview in South Sudan, Hon. Deng Alor Kuol, a prominent leader of the Former Political Detainees of the SPLM who had been a cabinet minister leading foreign and cabinet affairs ministries during multiple time periods, shared his views on how an internal conflict within the ruling SPLM party led to war in South Sudan in December 2013:

> The problem [conflict] started with reforms within the party [the ruling SPLM]. We, the SPLM leaders, differed and could not tolerate our differences. As a result of that the war broke out. Something we didn't imagine. We thought it was not going to lead to that because differences are normal in politics. Unfortunately, we took up arms against one another and brought this misery to our people.[113]

Characterizing the internal conflict within the ruling SPLM by those who vied for reform versus those who resisted it is a misdiagnosis of the root cause of the internal conflict. The SPLM leaders seemed oblivious to the brewing discontentment throughout the country. Although internal peace within the ruling party was maintained through a tacit agreement that allowed Salva Kiir to maintain the presidency and the chairmanship of the party, other influential actors within the ruling party maintained free access to the public treasury.[114] All this and more played a role in delaying the conflict among the elites. By allowing leaders to be corrupt as long as they remained loyal, many others began to threaten defection or the use of outright violence to bargain for access to resources. This led to an increase in the number of actors seeking access to finite resources, which became sharply less available after oil production was shut down in 2012. It became clear that while the corruption could not be sustained, any radical shift to how things had been done since 2005 would be seen as an outright violation of the tacit agreement that allowed actors to be corrupt as long as they did not challenge their ruler. Corruption may have served a political purpose for the ruling elites, but it inhibited the government's capacity to deliver services to the people it was supposed to serve.

Advocating for reform and resistance to reform were little more than political tactics to deal with rivals within the SPLM party. It is important to point out that South Sudan's resources were vanishing when the internal conflict reached a boiling point in 2013. South Sudan's net oil revenue had dropped from a monthly average of $556.3 million during the first six months of independence on 9 July 2011 to $0 when South Sudan halted oil production over a dispute with Sudan over transportation fees in January 2012. Although oil production had resumed by March 2013, the net oil revenues, which then made up nearly 98 per cent of the government's total revenue, were rapidly declining. The disagreement among the SPLM leaders had nothing to do with genuine reform. As one local observer noted:

> There has always been a competing interest against public good since the SPLM took over the affairs of the South during the interim period. The oil monies are like the manna from the sky – no one has to toil for them. This is precisely why the other sectors of the economy have

basically been abandoned because no one wants to put in work. The competition for public funds that are essentially up for grabs precipitates the present crisis. The elites therefore define a 'public enemy' in relation to themselves – your opponent in this reckless competition for power becomes the enemy of the state. The masses are then mobilised to fight that defined enemy.[115]

The leaders disagreed on a fair formula for sharing power and access to resources. To outdo one another, they resorted to using political fear to manipulate the masses into supporting their side.

Nevertheless, due to their significantly conflicting interests, the use of political fear resulted in a vastly different outcome than anyone expected. The war of words that preceded the conflict in December 2013 was intended to cause the rivals to back down and resist the temptation to pick up arms. After it became clear that the SPLM leaders were publicly threatening each other, Danial Awet, a prominent SPLM leader who was allied to President Salva Kiir during the period of internal strife within the SPLM, was asked by a local businessman during breakfast at a restaurant in Juba: 'What if those who may feel bullied by the speech of the President resort to war?'[116] Awet shrugged this off by replying, 'Nobody will dare to leave behind his V8 and head to the bush to lead a guerrilla life again.'[117] The war broke out two days later.

Surprisingly, South Sudan's leaders ended up in a position they had not expected, or as Deng Alor characterized, 'something we didn't imagine.'[118] One party escalated their threatening gestures in the hopes that the opposing party would cooperate to avoid conflict, but the other party felt that its security hinged on the launch of a counter-attack. This generated a security dilemma, which exacerbated what might have been a dormant conflict and ultimately triggered chaos.

4

Governing through fearful means

Kiir's regime style of governance has been characterized by coercion of the country's institutions, granting him almost complete control of its flow of resources and dividing the political class into allies versus enemies. Although Kiir's allies have been given limited access to resources, they have often been punished (turning them into enemies) for becoming too greedy or too popular. On the other hand, denying enemies access to resources has made them unpopular, and shaming them or painting them in a bad light has deterred others from joining them, reducing their credibility in the eyes of their ex-supporters but leaving them insecure enough that they still have to rely on Kiir.

While chatting with a senior government official in Juba in April 2013, the author noted how presidential escort vehicles that shut down the roads could have serious negative impacts on the running of the city. Responding coldly, the author's interlocutor told him that 'the function of any state is to invest in its president'.[1] This type of sentiment, which places leaders above everyone else, is common and is a product of violently coercive tactics. Indeed, in South Sudan, the fear of political, economic and social sanctions transformed the masses into a fearful people with a frighteningly high tolerance for the injustices that were committed by the political elites.

While the president pressured lawmakers to create a constitution that gave him absolute control in all branches of the government, the single determining factor that made the use of political fear extremely effective was his control over all the sources of money and jobs within the country. While denial of access to these resources was used to punish Kiir's opponents, access to these resources was granted to those who helped him to spread fear both in the national security and the national army.

A rule by decree

Throughout his governance, President Kiir has ruled by decree – a style of governance that has allowed him to quickly create unchallenged laws (even when those laws violate the Constitution) and fire any government official, from the vice president to members of the state assemblies, cabinet ministers, deputy cabinet ministers, undersecretaries and state governors. For the ruler, one short-term benefit to this style of rule is that it allows him to achieve efficiency by avoiding delays that are usually associated with judicial review processes. A long-term disadvantage to this system is that his successor can undo any of his previous or ongoing decrees by declaring all of his decrees null. The only safeguard against this possibility is to rely on parliamentary scrutiny and judicial reviews. The decrees serve as weapons that instil a great deal of fear in the public. A rule by decree plays a decisive political purpose for the president as a coercive tool for controlling the behaviours of his employees, allowing him to punish disloyalty and reward loyalty. When one watches the national television, an anticipation for a decree that fires existing government officials or hires new ones is a serious cause of anxiety amongst the capital's citizens. Ruling by decree is equivalent to using fear as an instrument of governance. It is also inefficient in that it promotes corruption. Once a person has been appointed by decree into a decision-making position, the president hardly shows any appreciation at the end of his contract, which is usually terminated harshly and without prior notice. Words of thanks are not expected. Some government officials learn that they have been fired while at an international airport or when they are watching South Sudan Broadcasting Cooperation Television (SSBC TV) late at night. The aim is to ensure that those who are fired do not return to their offices, where they may be able to steal documents or cash. Ironically, this promotes the undesired outcome. Some offices keep easily accessible and bulk supplies of US cash in safes for emergencies. This turned out to be necessary after the banks in South Sudan ran out of US currency and consequently rationed the amount of US money that one could withdraw from an account at one time. The fear of being fired at any moment and without warning motivates government officials to grab whatever they can on their way out rather than focusing on initiating long-term developmental projects. Hence, this process introduces a fear of job loss that encourages corruption.

Unleashing hunger to make examples of dissenters

In association with the use of food as a weapon of fear, a coercive strategy called *loony chok* – 'to unleash hunger' – was deployed by the ruling elites against internal dissenters or those suspected of harbouring dangerous dissenting views. The *loony chok* strategy was effective because the system was centrally controlled so that those who did not express loyalty were denied jobs, even in the private sector.

The author once learned of a man, an economist educated at one of the top universities in Europe, who lost his ambassadorial job. Subsequently, rumours were circulated about him so that no one would offer him employment. There were those who the rumours turned into his enemies and others who were afraid of being punished for helping him. A generous hotel owner allowed him to stay at his hotel and paid his expenses for the foreseeable future. Another young man befriended him and covered his food and transportation costs. While he was subjected to live on the handouts from a few generous friends, rumours continued to circulate that he was being monitored. It was alleged that people broke into his room and returned with news of how much he was suffering based on how he was unable to bathe or afford a sufficient amount of clothing. The author enquired about him with two officials, one a deputy minister and another a top administrator in a powerful government ministry. Both gave bizarre reasons for being unable to help, but it could be sensed that the two leaders feared becoming victims themselves. Another businessman offered him a job as a consultant, and after finalizing everything, the contract was terminated hours before the man reported to the office for work. The businessman was threatened and forced to terminate the contract. The system (both the private sector and the public sector) is centrally controlled, and once you are singled out as a target, it can literally starve you to death. When the man first lost his job, he sensed that he was being isolated, and he tried to see President Kiir. Since he was no longer an ambassador, it was difficult for him to set up a meeting. He learned that the president was heading to Israel, so he made his own arrangements to see him there. When he arrived, everyone was surprised, and instead of allowing him to explain his reasons for being there, they circulated a demolishing rumour that he had come to harm the president. This rumour nearly sealed his fate. His own uncles, powerful politicians who were close to President Kiir, would not even help him. He was a victim of his own success (a truly brilliant and articulate economist). In South Sudan, you are doomed the moment that you are accused (falsely or not) of looking down on society's power brokers.

This young man was being used to set an example to those who would dare criticize the most powerful political elites. Like the rule by decree, this forced starvation of dissenters is inefficient because it can push people towards rebellion. For the man in this story, the outbreak of conflict in 2013 made it impossible for him to stay in Juba, and he eventually left the city and joined one of the opposition groups. He eventually ended up finding a job in the Gulf.

To starve dissenters, the powerful elites must first deny them of their supporters. When political rivals are deprived of jobs or public resources, they lose their supporters. As an example, when one group of former political detainees returned to Juba following an agreement with the government, they were accommodated in a hotel under government expenses. While they had access to food, they did not have access to cash. One of them described to the author how vulnerable visitors from their villages would come to visit them and leave empty-handed, which these political detainees found to be uncomfortable or even humiliating. One day, a government official who was sympathetic sneaked some cash into the hotel and gave it to one of them to share amongst the rest. This was their happiest day in Juba. The next day, they were able to give a little something to their dependents and the elders from their communities who visited them.[2] While some of the former political detainees had been doing well financially, having accumulated their wealth during their time in the government like everyone else, their accounts had been frozen when they were detained and lost significant value by the time they could withdraw from them again. Their other assets, such as their homes, were either commandeered or left empty, as prospective homeowners and tenants were afraid to rent or own a home that belonged to a person with affiliations to an opposition group.

Humiliating ex-rivals

Not only are people who are suspected of holding dissenting views hit with various types of coercive repercussions, including forced starvation, but some coercive measures also specifically aim to punish ex-rivals. One of these measures includes humiliation, which involves showing people what might become of an individual if they end up on the wrong side of the political divide. The message is clear: you can never be forgiven, so it is best to avoid taking the rival political faction's side.

President Kiir has been playing a dangerous game of luring his political opponents back to Juba, taking to the pulpit at the SPLM House and insulting his enemies, who are essentially little more than his political prisoners on parole. Consider the case of Hon. Pagan Amum who was lured to come on his own to Juba before signing the Peace Agreement of August 2015.[3] He was assured that he would operate as a general secretary of the SPLM to speed up the reconciliation of the SPLM as per a deal that had been negotiated in Tanzania.

Amum arrived in Juba and went to his hotel, but it took him several weeks to realize that he may have walked into a trap at the enemy's headquarters, unarmed and with no guards. Amum used the Peace Negotiation of 2015 to escape to Addis Ababa. President Kiir permitted Amum to go, hoping that he would stick to the government's side. When Amum rejoined his colleagues in Addis Ababa, the president and his close allies renewed their investigation into Amum's corrupt practices. Again, the way in which Amum was treated in Juba and immediately after he returned to Addis Ababa was intended to scare people from following his and the paths of others who had joined opposition groups.

Another victim of the tactic of humiliation was Deng Alor, the former foreign minister and a native of Abyei who was detained along with Amum and some of their other colleagues at the start of the conflict. At the Council of Ministers' meeting and then again at church, Kiir told Alor, whom he had just reconciled with, that if God had asked him to choose, he would have told God to take Alor and not his younger brother, Amb. Kuol Alor, who had died that week.[4] Alor had complained of weekly bouts of disrespectful treatment during official meetings at the Council of Ministers. When Alor was the minister of foreign affairs, he claimed that the ambassador in Ethiopia was asked not to provide services to him.[5] The outspoken Minister of Information, Michael Makuei Lueth, gave the following rationale behind the humiliating treatment of Deng Alor: 'We want him to resign from his position, but he does not want to do so.'[6]

This humiliation was not limited to Pagan Amum and Deng Alor; it was also extended to the entire group of the SPLM's former political detainees, who comprised eleven top SPLM officials whom President Kiir had arrested after the civil war broke out on 15 December 2013. President Kiir has said on record that he regretted not having the former political detainees killed, who were instead released and sent to Kenya where they received a warm welcome. This angered the president: 'When I watched television after I released them on the same day, I saw them being received on the red carpet by that country and they started talking politics after leaving Juba, so that's why I regretted for saving their lives.'[7] In a meeting held at the SPLM House with former detainees (FDs) in attendance, President Kiir said, 'The Former Political Detainees went to Western capitals to backbite us and stop all the money [from coming] to us, so it is you who have really destroyed South Sudan.'[8]

The former chief of general staff, Paul Malong Awan, was forced out of his position and subsequently put under house arrest in Juba after falling out with President Kiir. Eight students reportedly died and others were injured after a fire burnt down a dormitory at Moi Girls' School in Nairobi at 2.00 am on 1 September 2017.[9] One of Gen. Malong's daughters, Alakiir Malong, was confirmed dead. Kenyan doctors needed Gen. Malong to supply his DNA in order to identify the body of his deceased daughter. During this emotional time, Malong requested to go to Kenya so that he could be with his family, but in an interview with a Dinka-language radio station based in Australia, Malong said that the president had denied his request to leave.[10]

Later on, the body of Malong's daughter was taken from Kenya to Juba and then subsequently transferred to Aweil, Malong's hometown. When Malong requested to join his family for the burial of his daughter, President Kiir once again denied him. Gen. Malong used this treatment as grounds for forming a rebel movement. Malong has not been able to confront the government militarily because no neighboring country has given him a base.[11] After learning that there were publicly available recordings of alleged attempts by Malong to direct his supporters to mobilize for armed opposition, the government cracked down on his suspected supporters, isolated him and confined him to Nairobi.

While political rivals are often the victims of humiliation, when they cannot be reached, which is often the case for exiles, their associates and loved ones become easy secondary targets. The case of Angeth Acol de Dut, the former undersecretary of the Ministry of Labour who is married to Dr Majak D'Agoot (a member of the SPLM's former detainees), illustrates this point. Mrs de Dut shared a short clip on her Facebook wall with the following caption:

> On this day two years ago, I took this short clip as I left Juba, running away to safety. I couldn't talk about the fear I was feeling as I boarded that flight until now. And to this day, I ask, why do others feel they have a right to deny others the right to live freely in South Sudan?[12]

In South Sudan, one has the potential to become an enemy of the state and of the people if they happen to come from what the government has classified as a rival group.

Divide and conquer as a coercive tool of managing groups

When the first government of Southern Sudan was formed in October 2005, competing political elites clashed. Gen. Simon Kun Puoch was informed by President Kiir's circle that he would be decreed in as a national minister within a few hours and that he would join the government of national unity in Khartoum. So, Gen. Simon Kun Puoch prepared to throw a party to celebrate such a big news. However, he had to cancel the party preparation after receiving the official list of the entire government that didn't have his name on it. Brimming with rage, he allegedly arranged an urgent meeting with President Kiir, intending to lecture Kiir on the importance of keeping a promise. Gen. Kun Puoch was hostile to Dr Riek Machar after learning from President Kiir that the decision to remove his name from the list of ministers going to Khartoum was to be blamed on Dr Machar. The president promised him that he would look for ways to address his grievances, and Puoch eventually became a powerful governor of the Upper Nile state and an ally of the president during the conflict because of his fallout with Dr Machar in 2005. Dr Machar didn't like the idea of forming a government without a member from the numerous Lou Nuer whose youth had always stood with him whenever a contest between

Dr Machar and his Dinka rivals (first Dr John Garang and later President Salva Kiir) had turned violent. Dr Machar convinced the president to remove Gen. Kun Puoch, his long-time ally, and inserted Gen. John Luk, a Lou Nuer son, to go to Khartoum to join the government of national unity formed in October 2005. Dr Machar had never denied such an event, which could mean that he did it. Ironically, Dr Machar was holding two positions: the position of vice president as well as the position of the minister of housing, and his wife, Angelina Teny, was also a minister of oil in the Government of National Unity in Khartoum. This hypocrisy on Dr Machar's part only made his then ally Gen. Simon Kun Puoch more bitter. This bitterness was undoubtedly convenient for President Salva Kiir, who exploited it extensively against Dr Machar.[13]

Introduced and operationalized by colonial extractive governments throughout what was then Southern Sudan, the tactic of pitting in-group rivals and their communities against each other remains a dominant characteristic in South Sudanese politics to this day. In order to prevent the governed masses from uniting and demanding accountability and service delivery, Juba divides groups into subgroups and plays adjacent groups against one another. One subgroup is made to perceive itself as pro-government because its influential members are offered a few benefits. Another subgroup is perceived to be anti-government, and some of its members are punished to set examples for the price of their alleged disloyalty. When a central authority intervenes and chooses a side between two communities/groups, this increases the sense of an asymmetrical relationship, which exacerbates the security dilemma between the groups.

Equatoria: Fear arising from military marginalization

Many Equatorian communities (viewed here as though it were an homogenous group, but it is a region comprised of many social groups, but are grouped here just to keep the analysis simpler) view the government as a vehicle for the Dinka to acquire absolute power by using the security apparatus to spread propaganda, to liquidate its opponents/critics, to confiscate land from those less empowered/connected and to amass state resources for personal gain.[14] The government's political legitimacy has been irreversibly compromised. In the past, the technological capability of ethnic rivals to accumulate power was balanced. In a conversation on a South Sudanese policy forum on the relations among groups, Sam Laki, agricultural economics professor at Central State University, noted that 'both Equatorians and the Dinkas were never in control of the police and military, so the amount of pain they inflicted on each other was marginal, and pales in comparison to the pain that they are inflicting on each other now'.[15]

Western Equatoria represents a case where grievances related to marginalization in the military have led to conflicts. Local grievances have been brewing in Western Equatoria long before the 15 December 2013 conflict. They are centred around impunity for incursions by armed Dinka pastoralists who were clashing with the host communities, land-grabbing by Dinka political-military elites, and marginalization in the armed sector. The above-mentioned social-political-economic tension between the communities and the government (rightly viewed as the Dinka government) led to the use of a local armed group (the Arrow Boys, initially formed to protect the communities against Uganda rebels committing atrocities in the area at the time) to protect their communities. The Arrow Boys group eventually gave rise to further groups that became interested in the national politics after the December 2013 conflict. Two important actors associated with the armed groups in the area were Gen. Welebe and Gen. Alfred Fatuyo. Machar's group seemed a much better alternative although not widely accepted in the area since the locals blamed him for the initial presence of the Lord's Resistance Army leader Joseph Konyi in the area. Two of the only three armed groups in the area pledged allegiance to the SPLM-IO. Machar promoted Wesley Welebe and Alfred Fatuyo to the ranks of two stars after the August 2015 peace deal. When Machar and Kiir clashed in 2016, it was Machar's support in Western Equatoria that actually helped him to reach the Congo safely. Unable to win the locals, 'government forces repeatedly deploy counter-insurgency tactics that collectively punish civilian communities to depopulate areas with rebel activity, demoralise the community, and discourage community support for rebellion'.[16]

One way of disadvantaging one group over the other is to empower political leaders from one group while disempowering the ones from the rivalling group. This has been the case in Western Equatoria, where political elites have been divided between government supporters and those in opposition.[17] A similar scenario has played out in Upper Nile State.

The Shilluk versus Padang Dinka: Conflicts over land

The politics of fear related to the uneven distribution of administrative public resources at state levels and access to power and resources at the national level in Juba has triggered sociopolitical identity crises at various levels. Grievances attached to marginalization based on a social identity are now common everywhere. In some places, they have led to outright violence. After taking over the ruling of the then Southern Sudan, the elites began to incorporate the process of distributing powers within each of South Sudan's ten states into their political calculations. Control of the bureaucratic and administrative offices attached to the territory and the resources that can be accessed through control of these administrations[18] became a core of many horizontal grievances. The conflict between the Shilluk and the Padang Dinka in the Upper Nile state, which the Padang Dinka sees as apolitical while the Shilluk sees it as a political conflict, is a conflict over land. Although the conflict over land predates the SPLM-led government, the government in Juba exacerbated the security dilemma between the two communities by appearing to have chosen a side, at least in the perspective of the Shilluk. Creation of counties based on tribal lines increased boundary disputes fitting the following counties against each other: Fashoda County and the newly created Akoka County; Malakal and Bailet over Malakal town; Panyikang County and Bailet County over Anagdiar payam. The Shilluk felt marginalized[19] while the Padang Dinka contested such claims. The rebellions of the Shilluk's Robert Gwang, Johnson Olony and Ayok Ogat between 2010 and 2013 were conflicts over land.[20] During the early months of the South Sudanese Civil War, Juba contracted Johnson Olony, the leader of the the Shilluk Agwelek forces, to rout the SPLA-IO forces from the east bank of the White Nile around Malakal. When that mission was accomplished, the government won in Malakal, and Gen. Olony and his forces acquired weapons. The Shilluk–Padang Dinka rivalry again became the primary antagonism, and Juba decided to side with the Padang Dinka[21] while Olony switched over to the SPLM-IO and sided with Dr Riek Machar. The Padang Dinka-Shilluk rivalry was exacerbated by the proliferation of states in 2015. When the government reverted the country back to ten states, the Padang Dinka protested. The SPLM-IO leadership chose Johnson Olony as the governor of Upper Nile state, and President Kiir has refused to confirm Olony, likely a decision informed by fear of antagonizing the Padang Dinka.

Consequently, the Upper Nile state remained without a governor from February until December 2020.

Arrests

In South Sudan, like the old SPLM/A days of the civil war, criticisms directed at powerful political elites are legislated and severely punished. Indiscriminate state-led violence/arrests against unarmed citizens are intended to magnify the state's coercive capacity and to frighten other critics into hiding and silence. Of course, because no one wants a relative to be the next victim, families and clans press their sons and daughters to mind their own business and to remain silent while the acts of state-sponsored terrorism are carried out against unarmed citizens. This silencing of the people through coercive means has the potential to multiply the number of victims while increasing the illegitimacy of the central authority.[22] After politically motivated arrests, it is common for coercive agents to search for charges that they can file against the arrested victims.

In South Sudan, the reasons people are arrested are typically quite different from the charges that they receive in court. Some people, along with their colleagues, have been dragged to court only to learn that there was not a single specific charge filed against them. For example, Dr Majak D'Agoot was hardly questioned during the Trial of G4. The discrepancy lies in the fact that prosecutors and the arresting officials have to blend their charges with manufactured stories to ensure that their sentencings carry a death sentence or life in prison. Consequently, any outcome in the court of law is either the condemnation of an innocent person or an embarrassed government with prosecutors who are incapable of proving its cases.

According to the anti-reform National Security Act (2014), young people who are labelled as enemies of the state are often the enemies of individual leaders. As an example, Kerubino Wol Agok was arrested without charges for allegedly initiating a riot inside the Blue House Prison, an incident wherein some prisoners disarmed the guards to protest for being denied access to courts. Government officials resorted to retaliatory measures against Agok in the form of a financial sanction against his security guard company, KASS, ordering that its bank accounts at a commercial bank be closed under a directive that was issued from the Central Bank (exposing the Central Bank's independence from security and politically related machinations). This measure fit into the government's use of fear in order to scare people into what might happen to them if their words or actions made them enemies of the state (to avoid losing access to his money within minutes, no wealthy person would take this risk). In addition, other prisoners who considered protesting would learn their lesson. While it was a crime for those prisoners to disarm the guards at the Blue House, it was also criminal for the state to close their bank accounts in retaliation. By doing so, the state of South Sudan criminalized its mode of retaliation. After being pardoned by the president, Wol Agok was eventually forced to declare a rebellion, and a week later, he was killed by the government forces in Lakes State. The graphic images of his dead body were shared widely on social media to send a message to potential youth rebels.

Peter Biar Ajak, a vocal activist who was labelled by the government as an enemy of the state and locked up together with Wol Agok for months in violation of his rights to court process, was neither covered by the president's amnesty to all those who have taken up arms against the state nor by a decree ordering for the release of all the political prisoners and prisoners of war. Once Peter was released, he wisely chose safety by keeping silent. He eventually fled to the United States where it became safe for him to resume political activism. Free men are scared to death by their political leaders, as these individuals hold the right to deny job access to anyone who does not sing their praises.

In September 2018, Majak Aderek, a former SPLA soldier living in Melbourne, travelled to South Sudan to attend his dad's funeral. Upon arriving in Kenya, he decided to travel via the Loki–Kapoeta–Juba–Bor road. His bus stopped in Kapoeta for the night. He took a motorbike to a nearby hotel, where he would spend the evening. On his way to the hotel, someone approached him and asked where he was coming from. Before he finished giving his answer, three other fellows came, and the gang of four began to beat him and hit him with the butt of a rifle. They also insulted him, accusing him of being a member of the South Sudan Young Leaders Forum (a youth organization whose leader, Peter Biar Ajak, had been arrested and accused of various crimes against the state by security agents). Aderek had no idea of what they were accusing him. The armed men took him to their office (a security office), where, luckily, he met an old comrade, a certain major, who convinced the security officers to release him. The major advised the Melbournian to return to where he came from, warning him that it was too dangerous for him to continue on his journey. The man returned to Kenya with no further debate. Coming from abroad to South Sudan is risky, and if you have written anything critical of the government, then the risk is even higher. In sharing these stories, the victims of these crimes are spreading fear, which further helps in keeping voices silent (the true aim of arrests and state-sponsored terrorism).[23]

The National Security Services became a vital tool of silencing dissent through arrests with capabilities of reaching into neighbouring countries to get people. The case of Dong Samuel Luak and Aggrey Idri, who were abducted from Kenya in January 2017, detained at the Blue House Prison and allegedly killed there is illustrative among other examples.[24]

Unknown gunmen

When the sound of a gunshot is heard in Juba but the gunman remains unknown, some citizens argue over which type of gun was used and whether or not it killed anyone based on the sound alone. These quarrels echo the fears of the people who live in South Sudan today. The way in which the community spreads word about a shooting that has resulted in death heightens the fear of those who have heard the news. The function of an unknown gunman's targeted killings is not to quell one critic of the government but to make an example of him – to send a message to everyone else that they should be careful on Facebook and on Twitter, or they might be next. The journalist/ writer or the critic who falls victim is not usually the target; the target is a collection of many voices – the bystanders – who become silent after seeing the consequences of speaking out with their own eyes.

A few small communities that are seen as insufficiently loyal are singled out and used as examples of the consequences of disloyalty. Again, these victimized communities are not the targets; the targets are the many communities that will take corrective measures and pledge their support to avoid being targeted.

South Sudan has continued to bleed since the early morning of 15 December 2013. The unknown gunmen continue to eliminate the best minds and hearts of the educated young people.

Whenever a report comes out exposing the wrongdoings of the powerful elite in South Sudan, those in power dismiss it by claiming that external organizations should not be the watchdogs of internal affairs, knowing full well that the local think tanks that could keep the ruling elite in check are not permitted to investigate their abuses without submitting themselves to grave risk.[25] These external reports are dismissed on the grounds of various contradictions that speculate about the truth, summarize what everyone already knows and provide completely false accounts in response. While some of these claims may have some truth to them, they also illustrate a worrying pattern: that the most vulnerable members in Africa defend its most powerful members.

The strategy for deploying unknown gunmen in Juba is to kill courageous writers so that the rest will run into hiding at the mere sound of the gunfire. This exercise can easily get out of hand, leading the government's levels of repression to easily become too widespread and thereby increasing resentment on a massive scale. The unknown gunmen use coercive violence in a way that is designed to maximize fear (e.g. the choice of the people targeted and the manner in which some of them are killed). Nearly every writer who has been killed or tortured by an unknown assailant has been blamed by the fearful masses for having a 'loud mouth'. The fear that these acts unleash enables this dangerous group of masked men to magnify its coercive capacity. Unknown gunmen in Juba almost exclusively target writers who are critical of the government (they also seem to warn their victims in a number of cases, specifically asking them to stop writing critical opinion pieces against the government). The unknown-gunmen problem has remained unsolved in South Sudan since the brutal murder of Isaiah Abraham in 2012. None of the unknown gunmen have been found.

Interference of security in businesses and surveillance

While it is generally expensive to venture into business in South Sudan, it is more expensive to stay in it. Many businessmen in Juba have said that because the provision of security is largely privatized, the one thing that is absolutely necessary for one to succeed as a business person in Juba is protection. Nevertheless, in order to be protected, one must have the resources to pay for the men who carry the biggest guns in town so that they will come to their rescue whenever their business faces threats from other powerful armed groups. It is nearly impossible for small businesses in South Sudan to attract investors from South Sudanese communities abroad due to their lack of trust and anti-business logic.

In classrooms, national security agents have reportedly registered as students so that they can monitor teachers. The scary environment in which high school teachers operate, coupled with poor salaries of no more than $10 a month, have forced many to give up teaching and to seek opportunity elsewhere.[26]

During the civil war, the business environment grew increasingly hostile. Surprisingly, this hostility stemmed in part from the very authorities who should have protected local businesses. Businesses with the highest potential amidst the conflict were hijacked by armed agents, making it extremely difficult to survive in those sectors. Take, for example, the fishing industry. Those who had gone into the fishing business in 2016, buying fish in Jonglei, the Eastern Lakes and the Terekeke States, had to transport them to Juba by boat and bribe armed agents to get fuel. These businessmen (many of them under 30) were required to pay further bribes to move the fuel to the port, where other agents were likely waiting for more bribes. Failure to pay these illegal bribes led several armed agents to violently rob a number of these businessmen of their products. These same agents also collected illegal taxes on every boat that passed between different routes connecting Bor, Mingkaman, Mongalla and Juba. Once the boats reached Juba with fish, various government agents would descend upon the fishermen, demanding charges that were allegedly on behalf of the National Security, Wildlife, Police and Criminal Investigation and Fishery departments and the State, County and Payam authorities. All of these hurdles hurt the fishing business in South Sudan. Today, Uganda continues to be the main supplier of fish to Juba.

Civil society space

In its first encounter with civil society organization, the South Sudanese government, whose institutions are led by people with little experience in anything but the use of guns, resorted to intimidation tactics to fight off what they mistakenly view as a foreign entity meddling in its internal affairs. As in the classic security dilemma scenario, the government overplayed its hand in its attempt to keep the civil society organizations under control and ended up making its institutions look bad. However, the more the government deployed coercive tactics in the civil society space, the more its image became tainted in the eyes of the public.

The government recognized the power of civil society organizations early on in the conflict and decided to infiltrate them using two channels.[27] First, the government spied on the organizations by infiltrating their memberships with spies. Second, the government recruited people into the civil society organizations to empower the 'right' people, as the civil society organizations are viewed as channels for access to Western money, and to better understand how these organizations provide aid by embracing ideals that appeal to Western countries. These infiltrations created an environment of distrust within the civil society organizations with members increasingly growing suspicious of one another. Although it became clear to many civil society organizations that conducting meetings in Juba was too risky, even meetings that were held in Kenya or Uganda were not considered secure enough to allow members to speak freely. During meetings held in Kampala and Nairobi, several members voiced their concerns about what had taken place in Juba.

The government effectively inhibited the activities of the civil society organizations. Once victimized, the civil society members increased their fears by transmitting those fears amongst themselves. The family members of those involved in civic duties, such as activists and journalists, also functioned as channels for the transmission of fear.

Members of the entire South Sudanese society, out of fear for their own lives or blind support for the ruling elites, have resorted to blaming the victims for their outspokenness while expressing no outrage for the crimes that had been committed against them. Isaiah Diing Abraham Chan Awuol, a former major within the SPLA, had received numerous direct threats for his commentaries and several indirect threats through friends. On 5 December 2012, a group of unidentified gunmen appeared on his doorstep in Gudele estate in Juba, called him outside and shot him dead in front of his house. The killers were not apprehended.[28] Some officials, who were close to Isaiah Abraham and who had expressed outrage publicly, blamed the loss of their government jobs on their reactions. Fearing for their own careers or lives, some members of South Sudanese civil society blamed Awuol for not caving to the threats and warnings that had been sent to him through his friends and loved ones. This became the pattern: state agents committed egregious crimes against a citizen, the crime was overlooked and the blame was pinned on the victim for having a 'big mouth'. Agents from the National Security Services ordered *The Citizen* newspaper to stop printing due to articles it published urging President Salva Kiir to sign a peace deal with the rebels.[29] Nhial Bol Aken, an editor for *The Citizen*, quit journalism in protest after his paper was shutdown. In an interview with SBS Dinka Radio, he cited threats to his safety that were communicated to him through close friends. Certain victims of the unknown gunmen, such as the neurosurgeon Dr Ding Col Dau, were even blamed for returning to their country while the country was at war. Appointments of former critics into government positions are viewed as attempts to silence them.

In addition to physical elimination and arrests, the threats and acts of sexual violence have also been used as weapons of fear. Female activists have reported threats of sexual violence that have been sent to their social media handlers, threatening them to tone down their critical views.

Fear within the civil society community reached its peak in 2015 through 2017 and then decreased by 2018 and 2019. This decline was due to civil society organizations' success in circumventing blockages to the freedom of expression. The organizations discovered a way to air their grievances without attracting the government's attention. The Anataban Campaign used street theatre, graffiti, murals, sculpture and poetry to foster public discussion about the issues of social justice and governance. Other similar campaigns have taken the form of tea parties where citizens gather for tea and discussed issues of concern.

5

Fear of domination triggered by corruption

Scholarly works analysing corruption in South Sudan have sought to show that the political-economic history of South Sudan reads like a tale of massive and protracted robbery.[1] There is also a growing literature from policy perspectives on corruption, which is mostly all about unearthing instances of corruption by following dirty money related to war criminals who compete for control over state assets and the country's abundant natural resources.[2] In the prevailing analyses, two major political events that explain corruption's culture are rarely discussed extensively in connection with the phenomenon. The first event is the 1991 split within the SPLM/A. The second event is the referendum exercise of 2011. The SPLM/A used corruption to survive after the split in 1991 and guard independence against spoilers after 2005. In his Jungle Chronicles book, Commander Atem Yaak, the former director of the Radio SPLA, who had served as the speech-writer of Dr John Garang, and former deputy minister of information in South Sudan, has documented a few incidents in which the SPLM/A seemed to have had strict guidelines on how to handle money before 1991. After 1991, the then chairman of the SPLM/A, Dr John Garang, had to relax strict adherence to anti-corruption measures and allowed his commanders some free hands in their zones of control to motivate them to carry on fighting after the blow of the 1991 split, which had weakened and discouraged many fighters. Atem Yaak Atem had noted, 'SPLA officials stole booty in the form of vehicles and cash after capturing government garrisons and accumulated illegal wealth.'[3] At Rumbek Meeting, in 2004, the then deputy chairman of the SPLM/A, Salva Kiir, raised the issue of corruption: 'Corruption, as a result of the lack of structures, has created a lack of accountability which has reached a proportion that will be difficult to eradicate.'[4] He continued, 'I would also like to say something about rampant corruption in the

Movement. At the moment, some members of the Movement have formed private companies, bought houses, and have huge bank accounts in foreign countries. I wonder what kind of system are we going to establish in South Sudan considering ourselves indulged in this respect.'[5] Commander Michael Makuei Lueth added, 'I am saying that the leadership is not committed to fighting corruption.'[6] Commander Wani Igga echoed similarly, citing how the chairman in a meeting informed the leadership that Commander Deng Alor, the then office manager of the chairman, brought some money from Nigeria, but how that money was spent had never been explained again.[7] External financial supports were some of the sources of lootable resources for the SPLM/A commanders. Some commanders amassed cattle in black markets, and others were taking advantage of humanitarian food. Dr John Garang might have had an idea on how to undo the dangerous system he had allowed to develop, but he, unfortunately, died in 2005. President Salva Kiir took over, and having condemned corruption in 2004 in Rumbek, people expected him to do something to reverse the entrenched corruption. A governor approached Kiir in 2010 to report alarming cases of corruption. Kiir told him, 'These supposedly corrupt people are too powerful. If I touch them now, we will not see independence.'[8] De Waal argued that although widespread corruption in Sudan was economically inefficient, it enabled the ruling elites to consolidate domestic control and minimize internal strife. This gambit made it extremely expensive and challenging for the Sudanese government to sabotage Kiir's political independence goal.[9] Thus, the fear of inadvertently spoiling the South Sudanese's opportunity to exercise their freedom to choose to secede made President Kiir allow his government to engage freely in corruption practices. After independence, it was too late to curb corruption.

Linking fear of domination to corruption

When its benefits are perceived to be collective, corruption, of which bribery is one of its several manifestations, can be seen by the marginalized as a tool that the ruling group uses to exert dominance.[10] By comparison, the ruling group views any discourse about corruption to be propaganda that is used by the 'disgruntled' groups to express their grievances.[11] From either viewpoint, corruption enters into conflict dynamics as one of the tools for stoking fear and manufacturing group-based grievances, which can, in turn, trigger actions that exacerbate the security dilemma between competing groups.

The Chinese government provides food aid to South Sudan in the form of bags of rice. While Western governments have provided this aid to South Sudan, as well. The difference between those donors and the Chinese government is that China leaves the distribution of food in the hands of the South Sudanese government. Consider the following story. A woman seeking food for her hungry children waits in a line for several hours but returns home empty-handed. She cannot hide her disappointment and begins toloudly complain, 'These Dinka people love to govern, and they also love to eat by themselves. They have taken all the money and hidden it in their homes, which is why there is no money in the banks. Now they have also taken the food from the Chinese that was intended for suffering people, and they are hiding it in their houses.'

A group of Dinka men jump to their feet to defend their tribe, which has its fair share of people who are poor and suffering due to the humanitarian disaster. Before things can escalate further, one Dinka man tells them that, given the state of things, and because a handful of Dinka elites are ruining it for everyone, there is no reason to get defensive. These types of conversations are the only way to escape the current state of mistrust and denial.

In places like South Sudan, corruption functions as a manufacturer of grievances amongst the elite groups. For instance, when a powerful decision maker/regulator overtly allocates lucrative rents or government positions to the members of his group, he is creating a fear of domination where his group is perceived by outsiders to be benefitting at the expense of others. For instance, in Western Bahr el Ghazal:

> The Fertit opposition was born out of a fear of marginalization and the long-held perception that members of the Dinka tribe are attempting to seize control of former Western Bahr el Ghazal (WBEG) state. This fear has intensified more recently by the reorganization of South Sudan into 28 states in 2015, which has tilted the demographic balance of parts of the former WBEG in favour of the Dinka, making the indigenous Fertit a minority in their ancestral lands.[12]

The reaction of the disgruntled groups, in turn, creates a fear of victimization, wherein the group that benefits begins to feel victimized. As an obvious implication, the security dilemma is not only exacerbated by racing to arms but also by competition over access to resources. Even if the benefitted group is not gaining significantly, the fear of victimization leaves the decision maker/regulator vulnerable, and his group now has to protect him through political, and if necessary, military means.

Constructed grievances are viewed as political tactics to dominate others or discourses that frame opponents in a negative light. In this context, the politics of fear can broadly be considered to be the manufacturers of group-based grievances. Corruption is involved, as well.

In South Sudan, the lack of opportunities for non-state actors who were not allied to the ruler, the collective benefits of corruption available to those controlling or associated with state power and the absence of legal recourse incited a vicious, bloody battle over state power.

The unequal distribution of resources was exemplified by the ownership of companies operating in the gold and oil sectors. Because the owners of these types of organizations were awarded contracts during each of South Sudan's sizeable corruption scandals, this became an economic problem of how to achieve 'fair division' amongst competing groups. In South Sudan, corruption has perpetuated the inequities of wealth, status and power and has helped to create a form of fear that has divided South Sudanese society into the beneficiaries and the marginalized. The fear arising from grievances that are manufactured by corruption can be aroused by dramatic acts of violence where political leaders use public resources to arm one group so that they may have an advantage over another. Indeed, this occurred when the White Army battled the Murle – the Padang Dinka fought the Chollo. Another way to arouse this type of fear is through large corrupt schemes that are not decried on moral grounds but because each event primarily benefits one group at the expense of another.

If you visit cities where the South Sudanese live, you cannot miss the prevalence of conspicuous consumption: consumption for the sole purpose of displaying wealth and/or social status. This frivolous consumption places a lot of stress on a person's financial limits, and if one happens to be a public servant with access to public resources in an environment with weak regulatory measures, it can encourage a form of competitive corruption between political elites, which can be signalled and transmitted in a number of ways. In 2008, when the elites and their associates learned about government contracts for companies to import dura (grain), so that it could be used to store and fight a predicted future hunger, they rushed to register thousands of companies within weeks. The news spread quickly to the villages, and people rushed to Juba. Some of the top elites' relatives who had just arrived in the villages to Juba became millionaires overnight. In a case of classic elite corruption in Africa, companies took nearly $2 billion for the contracts but never delivered a single grain of dura, giving the scheme its infamous name: the dura saga.

Existing literature contends that the structure of government institutions and the nature of their political processes determine the level of corruption in a given polity.[13] In particular, weak governments that do not control their agencies are said to experience very high levels of corruption.[14] The absence of deterrence lowers the risk of getting caught. Conversely, bureaucratic corruption leads to structural-institutional distortions by limiting the fiscal capacity of the government to efficiently raise sufficient taxes. This affects the government's fiscal decisions[15] and weakens it as a whole. A combination of rents and unaccountable public servants is viewed as one of the main causes of corruption.[16] Jain[17] summarized the causes of corruption into three factors by arguing that the existence of corruption requires discretionary power related to regulations, economic rents linked to power and sufficiently low punishment. However, the distribution of a country's population, rather than its physical expanse or natural endowment of resources, is relatively more significant to its impact on corruption.[18]

Corruption is part of the fabric of social and political relationships.[19] This means that what qualifies as a corrupt practice depends on the social-political-economic regulatory environment. If these change, then so do the practices that are defined as corrupt. Nevertheless, literature that examines South Sudan is more focused on economic analysis than the country's actors and the social factors they contribute.

Corruption can both encourage cross-ethnic solidarity and mobilization that defies divisions spurred by conflict and trigger or deepen conflict and social division.[20] For instance, Olonyi fought against the SPLM-IO in support of the government.[21] Although Kiir and Olonyi were suspicious of each other, corrupt opportunities enabled this alliance to briefly work.[22] A similar relationship developed between Juba and various private armies with local agendas that were directly opposed to the government's national agenda, and yet they sided with it anyway.[23]

Complaints about corruption can provide people with an avenue to express their grievances and protest against their exclusion from power, resources and the benefits of corruption.[24] Corruption and the risk of large-scale ethnic violence are likely to be causally linked, due to the tendency of networks of corruption to form along ethnic lines and benefit certain ethnic groups over others.[25] Societies consider inequalities originating in corruption and rent-seeking to be more unfair than inequalities that originate from productive efforts and market competition.[26] South Sudan's Auditor General, Stephen Wondu, argued that 'ethnicity became the defining factor in the allocation of public offices'.[27] Ann Laudati contended that 'any investigations into conflict must explore how identity has been mobilised for social and political purposes, as well as strategies to access material (natural resource) gains'.[28]

Starting on a wrong footing

From its first days of peace in 2005 and 2006, corruption marred Southern Sudan. In 2008, the Parliament accused Arthur Akuien Chol, the minister of finance at that time, of theft after he purchased vehicles for the government from Cardinal Company in 2006, and the transaction for the purchases was recorded to be double the price of their actual worth.[29] In his defence, Arthur Akuien said on a Dinka language radio based in Australia that 'I was controlling money, but they needed me out'.[30]

Similarly, while the Juba–Nimule road, a 192 km highway that connects Juba to the Ugandan border, was built by contractors under United States Agency for International Development (USAID) at a cost of $225 million, the construction of all the roads within Juba (which, if one were to stretch them out in a line, would be 75 km in length) cost the government $1.7 billion.

One of the most publicized corruption scandals in South Sudan was the 'dura saga'. Dura is a South Sudanese name for sorghum. The scandal centred on government payments of nearly $1 billion for domestic contractors to supply food to state governments ahead of a projected food crisis in 2008. While some companies received advance payments and did not deliver afterwards, others claimed to have delivered the supplies but did not receive any payment. The remarkable element in this scandal was in the number of contracts. Dozens of companies[31] were investigated for having not delivered the contracts while another eighty-one companies protested against the government for failing to pay them for the services they had allegedly delivered. Payments were released on the orders of the implementing agencies even before the work had commenced. Against a budget of $500 million intended for dura purchases in 2008, contracts amounting to $1.6 billion were reportedly awarded to unregistered companies or those incapable of delivering the ordered quantities.[32] Prior to the dura saga, the rent-seeking market was a largely closed market in the sense that it was difficult for beginners to enter it. This difficulty of entering into the market explains why some start-ups who had won big contest prizes were required to offer generous bribes to build trust with those who set the rent. The dura saga was the first attempt to curb the overconcentration in rent flow by dividing up the contracts and sharing them among a larger number of companies and individuals who did not meet the basic requirements for the services that needed rendering. This marked the beginning of what became an atmosphere of competitive corruption, wherein rent allocators competed in collecting rents with the aim of expanding their political support bases. The dura saga triggered a large-scale imitation process, with both regulators and contract seekers competing against each other.

Corruption has led South Sudan directly down a path of profound financial crisis. Debt-free at the time of its independence, by 31 March 2019, the country's total outstanding debt was 177.615 billion South Sudanese Pounds (SSP), of which domestic debt is 33 billion SSP and foreign debt is $933 million – most of which is owed to commercial lenders, such as oil companies, at high interest rates.[33]

The Government of South Sudan's (GoSS's) net income from oil revenues during the first six months of independence was on average $556,300,000 per month. On 22 January 2012, South Sudan began a shutdown of its oil production as a retaliatory measure after Sudan began diverting approximately 120,000 barrels of South Sudanese oil per day, apparently in response to the lack of progress in negotiations on a transit fee for oil from South Sudan that travelled through Sudan. By March 2019, the total oil production stood at

170,000 barrels per day, with the government profit share being 42 per cent. The benchmark price for the main type of oil South Sudan is producing known as the Dar Blend is $55 per barrel. While this is a small improvement in oil revenues accruing to the government's coffers, there is little hope among the masses of much change in the way the government has been operating.

The GoSS and the independent Government of the Republic of South Sudan received approximately $20 billion in oil revenue from 2005 to 2014.[34] Very little of this was spent on development. The comparatively vast amount of money and the political-economic domination that came with it led the ruling elites to behave recklessly. The complete shutdown of national oil production in 2012, an act without precedent anywhere in the world, left South Sudan with critical financial vulnerabilities. While borrowing was the only available option for financing essential government activities, some rent allocators used the opportunity to acquire foreign loans without the approval of the relevant authorities and diverted those loans into their personal accounts. A few months after the oil shutdown, Juba borrowed roughly $1.5 billion[35] from commercial banks, the Bank of South Sudan and a pair of oil-trading companies[36] to offset a foreign currency shortage. No details were published on how the loans were used, and the public only learned of the loans when the government said that the salaries of its civil servants would be delayed to allow for the repayment of loans.[37] Some officials at the Ministry of Finance did not even know that the government had borrowed any money.[38] The government's spending agencies owed local contractors no less than 2.6 billion SSP[39] by July 2015. Between 2013 and 2015, China's National Petroleum Corp., Malaysia's Petronas and ONGC Videsh Ltd of India extended oil-collateralized loans to the government. These debts were to be repaid to the companies in the form of deductions from government oil sales. South Sudanese officials met in June 2014 with these companies to propose an emergency loan of $200 million.[40] The companies were reluctant to extend the loan because South Sudan could not pay back the $1.6 billion it had already borrowed.[41] Though minor, non-oil revenues from customs dues and taxes were mismanaged, low-level officials were permitted to collect rent in these areas without the attention of their superiors, but with the financial difficulties following the oil shutdown, rent allocators who could no longer allocate rents from the oil revenues were forced to look into other sectors that they had initially ignored for being too unprofitable.

At one point, Paulino Wanawilla, the minister of justice, admitted, 'I have pieces of evidence of people in this Ministry of Justice who are legal counsellors and take bribes.'[42] Bribery through the gift of contracts was a major and well-known source of illicit enrichment.

Two of the main features of South Sudanese corruption include violence and massive capital flight. The latter has led to underinvestment in the country and the sale of South Sudan's natural assets, such as land at a bargain price, to foreign investors.

Since the autonomous government of Southern Sudan came into existence in 2006, foreign actors have swarmed to Juba to take advantage of the environment's weak institutions and rapidly expanding economic opportunities. It took seven years for the foreign actors to penetrate the system that was in place at the time of independence. One dominant group of foreign actors included Lebanese traders, some of whom came from Nigeria and others who had travelled from war-ravaged African countries. The Lebanese traders quickly gained an understanding of how South Sudan's patronage system worked, aiming to exploit the weaknesses of local political actors by directly approaching them or their families. In spotting their marks, the traders would look for the following traits: (1) a tendency to display new-found wealth in the form of expensive cars, staying in luxurious hotels without paying the bills, owning expensive houses or modern gadgets and taking luxury vacations and (2) a tendency to believe in rumour mongering and the personal insecurities of local actors. To penetrate the system, the traders offered local actors expensive gifts in the form of houses in Juba, modern gadgets, cash, free homes in Dubai and other international destinations, free hotel accommodations in Juba, free airfare, free hotel accommodations abroad, help with visa processing and the facilitation of moving stolen assets to safe havens. They successfully breached the system through the SPLA, the national security, the police and the presidency.

Different markets of corruption

Construction

In Juba, the absence of clear land policies has led to violence and forceful land acquisitions. Most of the foreign traders in the construction industry there are Chinese, Lebanese, Somalian, Ethiopian, Ugandan and Eritrean, and each group has taken advantage of the legal loopholes of South Sudan and cut illegal land lease deals with individual local actors. The leases are usually for ten to thirty years, and the purported owner is paid $1,500 to $2,500 per month, with the promise that the owner will take over the structures after the end of the leasing period. The problem is that the buildings that are erected have a lifespan of no more than twenty-five years. Indeed, issues arise when (1) the purported owner turns out to be a land grabber, as this leads to conflict amongst the various claimants; (2) the owner realizes that he has been cheated and demands to renegotiate the contract, thereby creating a conflict that pits him against the company leasing his plot; and (3) the foreign actors fight each other over certain strategic locations by trying to encourage the local owners to backtrack on a previously agreed upon sublease contract with the promise of offering a financially improved contract. This motivates violence, which is often transferred to local actors who fight incessantly on behalf of the foreign parties. In addition to dealing directly with individuals, some foreign actors collaborate with local actors, such as government employees, their relatives or the agents of powerful government officials so that they can use government projects to steal from various markets.

Nilepet and the general tendering process of oil blocks

There are many channels for accessing corrupt gains in the oil industry. Formal and recognized channels include (1) various oil accounts set up by local actors in collaboration with oil firms and (2) oil-collateralized loans. In addition, there are informal channels that impact the government's overall share of oil revenues, which include:

1. A monopoly over air services in and out of Paloch – the oil hub of South Sudan.
2. Inflated expenditure costs that are made by taking advantage of the poor accounting of the government's financial sectors and exploiting the tendency for some government employees to lead luxurious lifestyles and stay in expensive hotels.

Nilepet is one of the least transparent organizations in South Sudan. In fact, the entire Ministry of Petroleum does not share data on the oil it markets and sells. It used to publish some data on its website, but this practice stopped several months ago.[43] When the Minister of Petroleum, Ezekiel Lol Gatkuoth, was asked about this on a local TV programme in Juba, he reasoned that the website was down.[44] The marketing committee, which consists of members from both the ministry and Nilepet, recommends the companies to whom they should sell oil, but some people believe that the minister sidesteps the committee's decisions and awards cargoes to companies that are either linked to him or to some other powerful political leaders. Some believe that this practice remains the same when it comes to the tendering process of oil blocks. There is no transparency in the tendering process whatsoever; once someone pays, the block is allocated to them.[45] Oil block acquisition is the mandate of the Ministry of Petroleum, which controls the contracting process for oil companies that are planning to bid and invest in South Sudan.[46] The Petroleum Act of 2012 detailed that blocks must be tendered openly and that companies are subject to certain criteria in order to qualify to hold blocks. Single-sourcing is not allowed by the law. The awarding of block B3 to Oranto was illegal.[47] Nearly everyone I have interviewed believes that the blocks are awarded to companies that are willing to pay bribes. The minister appears to have sidestepped the Petroleum Commission and Authority, which is supposed to serve as an upstream regulator for monitoring acreage winners and other powerful actors who have opted to obtain single-source oil blocks (as was the case with block B3, which was awarded to the Nigerian Oranto) in lieu of companies that have not been properly vetted. The minister of petroleum and other powerful actors are being flown in private jets across the region to negotiate and make offers to companies that are only willing to acquire oil blocks if they may resell them to others.[48] There is a law on oil leases, but it is not being followed.[49] An employee of Nilepet who claims that his involvement in anything to do with the awarding of contracts to companies or individuals is very limited said that a significant number of deals are done behind closed doors and with considerable secrecy.[50]

Although Holdcorp Investment SL claims on its website that it is about to sign a contract on block E2, this agreement has yet to materialize. There is also currently a debate within the presidency on whether blocks E2 and A4 should be awarded to ROG. Both ROG and Holdcorp Investment SL want block E2, which they may end up sharing once it has been awarded to them.

The presidency seems to be divided on the issue. There are people who are willing to award the blocks, and there are those who are blocking the process, fearing that the two companies in question may not be genuinely competent. The following email was written by one of the president's top advisors, who is also a minister of foreign affairs (it was addressed to a '1v', likely referring to the first vice president):

> Anyway for me I didn't mince my words. I told the President straight away that if he insists on awarding the 2 Blocks to ROG none of those Projects will ever materialize. I told him ROG was just going to be like Total and Oranto. Even he was shocked that I could talk to the President like that. They fear the President but for me I call a spade a spade when talking to him because I cannot help him by telling him lies.[51]

The previous email clearly shows that the law is not being followed (and is suffering from executive interferences), as it is the presidency and a few powerful actors who seem to be deciding who the oil blocks will be awarded to rather than the Petroleum Commission and Authority, a responsibility which is stipulated by the law (the Petroleum Act of 2012). Prior to his firing, Ezekiel Lol Gatkuoth was believed to be in the process of signing numerous dubious deals.[52] This inefficiency may include single-sourcing a block to an incompetent company, and immediate gains in the form of bribes may play a dominant role in the decision-making process.

Defence contracts

This material relies in part on the author's earlier investigations for a local newspaper.[53] The basic prerequisites to win a contract to supply goods to the army include possessing a legal registration licence under the South Sudan Companies Act and a minimum bank account balance of 50,000 SSP. After contestants are invited to apply to a contest for a government contract, they are asked to make their best offers. Fully aware of the extraneous resources they will expend to deliver the contract, they incorporate various calculations into their offers. The difficulty in this stage comes from the fact that each contestant is unaware of the offers his competitors are making. The regulator will make his judgement on who he thinks will offer him the best kickbacks based on the individual's or company's previous dealings with him or his fellow regulators. The contestant for an army contract has four groups they will need to deal with: the target department, which needs to be supplied with food, fuel or uniforms; the procurement section, which advertises the needs of the target department and forms a committee that includes a member from that department who will help in the decision about the contract; the army's financial department, which processes the payment and hands it over to the Ministry of Finance; and the Ministry of Finance, which awards money to the winning party once the contract has been executed.

Factors that inhibit the capacity for the local contract winner to deliver include the lack of start-up money, which oftentimes is not objectively assessed prior to awarding the contract; the need to bribe various departments; and the fear of not getting paid within a reasonable interval of time.

A common manoeuvre around the lack of start-up money has been to find someone else with the cash to fund the delivery of the contract. Well aware of the contract winner's lack of funding, potential financiers charge exorbitant interest rates; for instance, most financiers charge a 30 per cent return on the loan. After securing their funds, the contract winner may proceed with their delivery of the contract. Nevertheless, they say have to wait for funding, as there is usually a delay at the Ministry of Finance for processing payments for contract delivery. People often expedite this delay by bribing brokers who are associated with the Ministry of Finance. However, because these bribes, on top of all the payments they have made to secure the contract, typically make the process of delivering goods to government sectors non-profitable, no rational agent who expects to gain from the agreement would continue playing by these rules. Regulators with the power to shorten the payment period on a contract benefit equally to those regulators who design the contests.

The costs of bribery can be so high that to maximize the value of their rent, some contract winners deliver small amounts, deliver nothing at all or escape the agreement by bribing the target department. As an example, a contractor who was supposed to deliver fuel or food to a battalion can alternatively contact the battalion commander to negotiate new terms for the delivery. The contractor can ask the battalion commander to agree to sign a paper that says, 'Goods have been delivered,' who, in turn, can ask for a certain percentage of the contract value to be given to him. Then, the contract winner will go to the border and bribe people there to write a document that says, 'Goods have passed here in Nimule.'[54] After manoeuvring across the border, the contractor will then bribe the Ministry of Finance to speed up the process of getting their payment tabled on the priority list.

A contractor may lose half of a contract valued at two million SSP to bribery, and as such, may not be too interested in delivering the goods or services. They may occasionally deliver a small amount of the goods or services to keep their collaborators out of trouble, like if the case arises where a rent allocator bothers to check up on the absence of the completed delivery. Indeed, something along these lines occurred when, despite the huge budget that had been allocated for the procurement of vehicles for the Ministry of Defence, President Kiir was shocked to learn that 'there are no even vehicles to transport soldiers on missions'.[55] Either vehicles had not been delivered in the quantities requested or the quality of what was priced differed from the quality of what was delivered, and in a country with extremely poor road infrastructure, used cars rarely last for a year.

Since very little is delivered in order to complete the transaction, the contractor does not create jobs and usually lacks an office of their own. A wealthy businessman who made his fortune by collaborating with rent allocators could not answer when he was asked why, when his company boasted close to $80 million in revenue, his only employees were himself and his brother.

Most companies and individuals who engage in the market are primarily interested in securing access to future rents, and they factor this into the current 10 per cent kickback benchmark they offer to rent allocators. For instance, two businessmen in South Sudan won a contest prize worth $1,000,000 in profit a few years ago. Instead of giving 10 per cent to the rent setter as it is customary, one of them suggested that they give the rent allocator $700,000 to secure more contracts in the future.[56] The following table illustrates the corrupt practices that are embodied during the procurement of defence contracts.

The cost of transporting a 50 kg sack of rice, sugar or maize flour from the local market in Juba to the SPLA's headquarters is just 12 SSP plus 4 SSP for loading and unloading – that's only five to ten per cent of the charged differential. What is the reason for overpayment? 'Did they agree with the people paying, to overpay them so that they share the excess?' asked the

Defence food supply contract prices versus retail prices

Item	Quantity	Price Defence pays to a supplier (SSP)	Retail Prices Dec. 2013 (SSP)	Excess Payment (SSP)
Maize	50 kg	284	135	149
Sugar	50 kg	479	220	259
Rice	50 kg	500	188	312
Oil	20 L	228	112	116
Beans	50 kg	360	175	185
Lentils	25 kg	583	132	448
Fuel	1 L	9	6	3

Source: Author's survey.
Note: This data was collected under the author's directive in August 2013 as a part of the directorate of the Military Pension Fund's attempt to evaluate the process of awarding contracts at the Ministry of Defence.

former minister of justice, John Luk, during a probe into the dura saga when a similar pattern of excess payment was witnessed,[57] which clearly pointed to collusive corruption. The official explanation for why excessive payment occurs is to compensate for the typical delay in paying contractors. The secrecy and limited competition in the defence sector can lead to a relatively high level of informal contracts and rent-seeking activities, providing fertile ground for the growth of corrupt practices.[58]

Money exchange market

The rent-seeking that goes into the money exchange market is more complex than the dealings and negotiations involved in defence contracts. The author's interviews with local owners of foreign exchange bureaus and traders who trade in currencies in the parallel market result in some interesting tales. The plane that flies between Egypt and Juba has the largest record of cancelled flights in the entire country. To get US dollars at the commercial exchange rate, which offers better rates than the black market, one must produce documentation that shows their need for dollars. One requirement is a document proving a person's need to travel to a foreign country, such as medical reasons. The applicant needs a visa to the country to which he is travelling and a ticket. The rent-seeker calculates his payoff: the maximum amount allowed minus the amount of effort that is required. His effort includes the ticket cancellation fees and visa fees. Now, the difficult part is the cancellation process. According to the design process, he can only be paid by the security personnel once he has checked in at the airport. Having completed check-in and having exchanged his currency into dollars, he calls Egypt Air to report an emergency that requires him to immediately cancel his flight. As this is allowed in most cases, the rent-seeker gets to return home with his US currency. This process does not go well for every rent-seeker. As an example, one inexperienced rent-seeker who failed to manoeuvre his way out of the airport found himself in Egypt, having to pay for the hotel there and losing all of his money on the ticket.

The Ministry of Finance generates US dollars from oil and non-oil revenues and sells them to the Central Bank at a fixed rate of 2.96 SSP per US dollar (between 2013 and 2015), from which the Central Bank sells to commercial banks at rate of 3.16 SSP per US dollar. Over the course of 2012 and up until April 2014, the parallel market exchange rate fluctuated from 4.0 SSP to 5.8 SSP per US dollar. By August 2015, the rate of exchange had climbed to 17.2 SSP per US dollar and later to 50 SSP per US dollar by July 2016, following the devaluation of the currency in December 2015, when the official exchange rate became 18 SSP against the US dollar. Those with access to the official exchange rate window extracted significant rents from the system,[59] as the gap between the official exchange rate and the parallel market rate remained considerably wide. The oligopolistic cartels in the parallel market are composed of powerful South Sudanese individuals in the security and financial sectors and are often members of the business community with strong ties to influential rent allocators.

Letters of credit, hotel expenses, travelling expenses, crisis management committee

After the oil shutdown in 2012, the system of letters of credit (LCs) was introduced when South Sudan secured a $100 million line of credit from Qatar National Bank (QNB).[60] In the LCs system, the Central Bank of South Sudan (CBoSS) makes block allocations to any concerned loaning agency. The total amount of LCs is in the form of a credit line from QNB to CBoSS, which repays the credit line to the lender (QNB) every three months. The total amount of LCs awarded between April 2014 and April 2015 amounted to $590 million.[61] The system's prime objective was to mitigate the climbing prices of commodities in the local market. However, the traders who were awarded allocations ended up receiving the money without delivering the services, and the authorities did little in the absence of enforceable restrictions on the LCs.

A considerable number of government officials live in hotels that charge $300 per night, and these personal bills usually accumulate over the years. They are also often inflated by the hotel managers who pass them on as public loans. Citizens in Juba believe that the foreign businessmen who manage these hotels siphon public funds into the private accounts of government officials. One writer observed that 'the amount spent to house a minister in one of those hotels for one year would have paid for the construction of a house'.[62] Similarly, oil firms accommodate a considerable number of high-level local staff in expensive hotels, pay for those expenses upfront and then pass those charges surreptitiously to the government to be paid as part of operational expenditures.

In April 2014, a minister travelled to Kigali, Rwanda, with one other person; their traveling expenses for the trip that lasted for two days were billed against the ministry's budget at $28,000.[63] The former head of United Nations Mission in South Sudan (UNMISS) was rumoured to have paid $30,000 per month on rent in Juba, and her landlord was Arthur Akuien, the former minister of finance who was fired and arrested on alleged corruption. Since these non-profit organizations (NPOs) pay for whatever price is asked, politicians race to build expensive houses. People use urban land leases as the basis for getting bank loans to build houses and then use most of the funds for other purposes, contributing to the high cost of urban land and a real estate boom that has persisted even during the crisis.

The civil war did not stamp out corruption but only changed its nature as the government faced bankruptcy and a new scramble to collect rents ensued. Following the December 2013 crisis, a committee called the Crisis Management Committee (CMC) took over paying the army's salaries. In comparison to a soldier's 599 SSP monthly salary, the CMC's lowest paid employee made 500 SSP per day. The government delegation to the Addis Ababa peace talks made between $700 and $2,000 per day.[64] After reports of alarming corruption, the president dissolved the CMC ninety days after its formation.

Anti-corruption measures as weapons of fear

President Kiir's speech during the independence celebration in 2011 promised to fight corruption: 'As President I pledge to you to do all I can to remove this cancer of official corruption.' A year later, in the wake of the exposure of a grand scandal in which billions of dollars were reportedly stolen by the elites, President Kiir delivered a letter to seventy-five officials that read, 'Most of these funds have been taken out of the country and deposited into foreign accounts. Some have purchased properties, often paid in cash.'[65] Still, no action was taken, and the president's promise to expose fifty corrupt senior army officers went unfulfilled. In April 2013, South Sudan's police authorities vowed to arrest suspects involved in the theft of money that went missing from the president's office.[66] Some of those accused and suspended returned to their jobs a month later without any public notice. It became clear that Kiir could not fight corruption without alienating allies whose irresponsible spending had led the nascent nation to economic collapse. Indeed, the political crisis of 2013 was closely related to Kiir's attempts to control and centralize rent-seeking.

In 2012, President Kiir wrote, 'We fought for freedom, justice and equality. Many of our friends died to achieve these objectives. Yet, once we got to power, we forgot what we fought for and began to enrich ourselves at the expense of our people.'[67] In 2017, President Kiir said, 'I decided that the infrastructure or whatever that we want to be done by foreign companies has to be done in exchange for crude oil because our people don't want to see money. If they see money, their hands start shaking.'[68] He added, 'I did not get people who can work, I got people who know how to eat.'[69]

However, anti-corruption measures serve political purposes more than they are used as tools to reform the system. It has been noted that when Deng Alor heard that his name was among the seventy-five officials to whom President Kiir had written, asking them to return $4 billion allegedly stolen due their direct or indirect involvement, the minister reportedly said he would gladly accept the letter and its consequences if the president had written and mailed one of the letters to himself. President Kiir certainly did not like this. Within a few weeks, Alor became one of the first victims of Kiir's anti-corruption measures. In June 2013, Minister of Cabinet Affairs Deng Alor and Minister of Finance Kosti Manibe were accused of transferring over $7 million to a company known as Daffy Investment Ltd without authorization from the president or the cabinet for the alleged purchase of anti-fire safes on behalf of the government. President Kiir suspended them both and lifted their immunities so that they could be investigated for the suspected theft.[70] The investigation did not go far, as the duo were further accused of planning a coup and thrown in jail together with eight other leaders. A committee headed by the minister of cabinet affairs was formed on 27 May 2014 to scrutinize reports on non-oil revenues. The committee received detailed reports from twenty-one agencies about their collections from April 2013 to April 2014, wherein the Civil Aviation Agency listed a grand total collection of 6,590,700 SSP from which 0 per cent had been remitted to the Ministry of Finance.[71] This kind of corruption was only uncovered because of the financial difficulties induced by the current war and the decline in oil prices, as rent allocators who could no longer allocate rents from the oil revenues were forced to look into other sectors that were initially ignored for being too unprofitable.

In the army sector, rent-seeking appears to be a free-for-all market. The top leaders are aware of the corrupt practices, but there is little they can do about it. During one occasion, a top military general had a case brought before him from generals complaining that their allowances were not on par with their colleagues. When one of them was asked how much he was getting in allowances, he said, 'Only SSP 17,000.' It was clear that the money that was provided to senior officers for fuel and the services of their units was treated as their personal allowance, a clear case of corruption for which no one would dare punish them.

While President Kiir is aware of the corruption in his country, he does not willingly encourage it; his allies simply exploit his weaknesses and threaten to defect if he lays his hands on them. In South Sudan, rampant and uncontrolled rent-seeking stripped the country of its resources and made it impossible for the president to govern. The December 2013 conflict was preceded by an increasingly competitive and uncontrolled scramble for rents.

Lual Deng, the managing director of the Ebony Centre, blamed institutional weaknesses for the rampant corruption: 'Wall Street investors would carry the "animal spirit" to the maximum if there were no strong regulations and regulators in place. So, our "lone-eaters" are operating in an environment of "animal spirit" and would take decades to eradicate if South Sudan doesn't build resilient institutions for effective governance soonest.'[72] L. B. Lokosang, a former director who served in the government for three years, observed that 'corruption and impunity have been tolerated even at the highest echelons of the administration'.[73] President Kiir's relationship with some of his aides appeared to have been maintained at the expense of his own credibility. The president's office has been buffeted with recurring embezzlements by his closest aides who have access to the rent allocating nexus, including the window for the official exchange rate. Some aides who were relieved in 2013 on charges of alleged theft in the office of the president returned, only to be relieved again in 2015 after the president's signature was forged by a security officer and used to siphon money into private bank accounts from the country's Central Bank. These allies continued to take advantage of the lacunae in financial management systems to capture rents. Someone in the top hierarchy of the government, who had checked with the Ministry of Industry, Trade and Investment to review the list of individual ministers who had applied directly or indirectly LCs, discovered that there were only two ministers who did not apply to benefit from the LCs.

The pattern of the anti-corruption measures in South Sudan suggest that individuals who have been targeted are those who have fallen out with the president. In November 2014, Kiir threatened punitive action against finance ministry officials after his office was deluged with reports that there were people in the ministry who extorted bribes from companies and individuals before awarding government contracts.[74] In a sting operation, the office of the president asked someone to approach two junior officers with a promise to pay them money to expedite the process to pay funds allocated for the construction of houses for the Presidential Guard Force. This person paid them 50,000 SSP, and each junior officer took half of the payment.[75]

The June 2016 verdict against the sixteen people who had been accused of grand embezzlement in the office of the president has exposed a serious vulnerability in South Sudan's anti-corruption measures: direct or indirect interference with the judicial process from the top leadership. For instance, over the course of the trial, the president publicly expressed disappointment with some of the ringleaders among the accused, his former close aides, for putting his reputation on the line, forging his signature to cash checks from the Central Bank and stealing at a time of great financial difficulty. The end result was a blanket judgement that failed to differentiate the level of culpability amongst the accused.

Conclusion

Following the Comprehensive Peace Agreement (CPA) of 2005, international aid agencies began to shoulder a range of governmental responsibilities, including funding most of the health sector and providing technical advice to line ministries, that would normally have been addressed by the GoSS[76] itself. This aid hid the extent of corruption that continued to spread like an unchecked and hidden disease at the time.

By early 2006, about a year after the CPA was signed, the GoSS had received about $750 million.[77] A subsequent auditing of the GoSS accounts between 2005 and 2006 revealed that over $1 billion had 'disappeared' in that period alone.[78] How could anyone steal more than what was available? While the misappropriated amount may have been uncertain, thus uncertainty was compounded by the fact that the GoSS was not transparent about its share of oil revenues. Indeed, it usually received more in oil revenues from the national government in Khartoum than it was officially declaring – a discrepancy that led some to blame Khartoum for defrauding the south and ignoring the invisible hand of the southern elite. Serious allegations charged some ruling elites for conniving with oil companies and officials from Khartoum to sell and divert part of the oil revenues to their own private accounts during the transitional period (2005–2011).[79]

One of the faces of corruption is nepotism, which manifests itself more frequently at the heights of leadership.[80] Name any South Sudanese politician, and you will realize that a good number of those who are quick to defend him against critics are associated with him either through a direct or an indirect patronage or hail from the same ethnicity/region/clan. It is also common to find an office staffed by the relatives of the most senior official. The 'employment of relatives, which has entrenched tribal loyalty and concentration of resources in Juba, has driven people to Juba but only to find themselves camping in politicians' compounds'.[81] These dependents exert external pressure on the politician to steal for them. Due to a combination of temptation and internal and external pressures, and regardless of budget, government officials award themselves generous allowances that are well above their official salaries.

Due to poor regulatory structures, corruption became decentralized and lacked any effective controlling oversight, resulting in the proliferation of different types of corruption as individuals exploited various kinds of opportunities. The implications here are that South Sudan's political structure is systemically corrupt, and few conventional analyses of corruption and how best to tackle it apply, as these studies assume that those at the top of the system only preside over corrupt practices because they are unaware of their subordinates' activities.[82] At the peak of some of Southern Sudan's largest scandals, rent-seekers demanded rapid payment, a tendency that led to overspending of the country's allocated budgets.[83] This had catastrophic consequences on the national reserve. When too many hands are left to freely and repeatedly reach into the public pot, its resources are emptied, threatening to deprive the influential actors of their authority and control.

South Sudan was not only susceptible to the inheritance of Sudan's defective system from Sudan, from which she broke away in July 2011, but she risked mimicking the faulty economic and political structures of neighbouring countries like Kenya and Uganda as well as the corruption of the guerrilla commanders during the civil war.

While manufactured grievances are more likely to lead to wars that pit social-political groups against each other than are objective grievances, it is objective grievances that serve as the foundation for manufactured grievances. The perceived lack of opportunity for outer groups, the apparent collective benefit of corruption that is available to those who control or are associated with state power and the absence of legal recourse that encourages bloody infighting over state power eventually become mimetic at both the individual and institutional levels, plunging a country into a state of economic, fiscal, security, political and humanitarian chaos in which the symptoms are all too apparent. The dissemination process of corruption began in response to signals from influential regulators and quickly became mimetic, with decision makers, contract seekers, land and mineral concessionaires and institutions being influenced by most of their interacting colleagues' behaviours. The resulting destructive competition among elites and their associates triggered a tragedy of the commons, leading to deleterious consequences and the collapse of the system.

Social media as a transmitting channel of fear

In an interview with DW journalist in 2017, President Salva Kiir claimed that the South Sudanese refugees in neighbouring countries were chased away by social media in a conspiracy against his government.[1] Whether viewed as proactive or reactive, the role of social media can no longer be ignored in the South Sudanese society.[2] Political leaders are worried about it. Social critics such as artists are increasingly mentioning social media in their songs, which affects the communities they live in and their individual lives, both negatively and positively. The multilevel conflicts seen on the ground have been exported to Facebook, and they can be gleaned from the newsfeeds of users in the South Sudanese social media network. On a newsfeed, data shared may address a conflict among the three groups, Dinka, Nuer and non-Nuer and non-Dinka (comprising more than sixty groups, each with varying interests), or may deal with a much lower-level conflict, pitting clans or different ethnic groups against one another at a local state level. The data usually reflect one of the three inciting violence, spoiling coordination or seeking coordination and argumentation.

Facebook and Twitter are effective tools for marketing fear. The PeaceTech Lab has noted in one of its publications on online hate speech that 'most online hate speech has originated among the Diaspora; it has been both an instigator and an echo chamber of the conflict back home'.[3] Instead of serving as a source of support and of positive and constructive contribution, the South Sudanese virtual community has become a lightning rod for online behaviours that are shaped and driven by a small number of influential broadcasters of social disorder. The power of social media has negatively impacted the progression of the conflict in South Sudan. This chapter addresses the propagation of fear/hate through social media and also analyses how South Sudanese political elites and their associates use social media to disseminate mostly false narratives, generating fear and hatred and manipulating community grievances by exploiting cultural biases to market fear and hatred.

Marketing fear online

As we will see, social media has played a vital role in the marketing of fear amongst the South Sudanese. While the country is largely illiterate, those who use social media are exclusively literate. One may challenge this emphasis on the role of social media due to the lack of technological infrastructure in South Sudan, but the social media users have bought Thuraya phones and given them to youth leaders who are engaged in community defence. The same users also contribute money for buying guns and ammunitions that are made readily available by some armed sector conflict entrepreneurs. Conflicts between groups within the Dinka have been blamed on the diaspora. So, the youth at home do not have to have Facebook accounts or Twitter accounts. All they need is a phone to communicate with others. Typical issues that are sure to trigger waves of emotional reaction include those related to social identity.

Not only do people vote against their long-term best interests, they also support items on social media that go against those interests. Take live videos, for instance. If you were to examine the trend of 'likes' and 'positive comments' that negative content receives or the 'negative comments' that positive content receives, you would soon find that even the most fair-minded user supports views and sentiments that are harmful to them in the long run. For example, if you 'loved' a negative comment that targeted an out-group, the counter-negative reaction by the opposing in-group may affect you. The good news is that emotional appeals succeed in the absence of good work, especially when there is a crisis. When communities are made to be busy – working on concrete developmental projects – then any negative content they encounter will be less likely to appeal to them.

On social media, individuals condition their behaviours on the behaviours of influential users who are visible in their social media networks. The more people who conform to an unacceptable act, the more that act becomes normalized. As an example, live videos where insults are hurled at individuals and communities attract greater amounts of traffic now than they did three or four years ago. The philosopher John Stuart Mill once noted that 'the danger which threatens human nature is not the excess, but the deficiency of personal impulses and preferences'.[4] Under this perspective, it has become evident that social media has increased the unconscious normalization of abnormalities. While insulting and painting certain communities in a negative light may be immediately politically optimal for the few influential users who are engaged in this type of act, this dangerous behaviour will bring peace to no one in the long run.

The significant divisions between the South Sudanese people are exacerbated by the fact that the powerful elites and their associates who operate online blame the crimes of their rivals on their communities (e.g. their region, ethnicity or clan) and communalize their individual grievances. Under this direction, fear/hate-generating narratives are propagated through live videos (status updates) so that communities are pitted against one another and endless toxic exchanges that are damaging to the social fabric are triggered.

The war of words that takes place online has helped to entrench hatred and to fuel hostility. Indeed, social media has played a vital role in how the masses have been persuaded to support mass violence. The virtual South Sudanese community comprises troublemakers, activists and generally passive, disgruntled, neutral or satisfied individuals – data that can all be gleaned from the information on their newsfeeds.

Hate speech is propagated by influential users who have a considerable number of followers. These followers enable these users to spread more negative content and encourage them to continue their activity. The users exert their influence by leveraging the power of their positions in the government or in opposition camps, by their associations with the top powerful elites who incentivize them, through silent praise, by spreading certain content through their level of education or by the esteemed positions they hold in non-governmental institutions. There are countless users online who hate a certain political actor, ethnic group or clan because they are copying from those they trust to know better. In sum, online hostilities are essentially group-based grievances that are engineered through the antagonization of others.

An individual user who encounters negative content on her newsfeed may choose to share, like or comment approvingly on the negative content if she trusts the judgement of the person who shared it or to win the favour of the poster or group who supports the idea. Consequently, some people will like a post because it has been liked by another person they hold in high esteem. Indeed, likes, shares and positive comments are rarely about a post's content but rather about the characteristics of those who posted it. A majority of social media actions trace trajectories that have clan, ethnic, regional or political leanings.

Words of mass destruction

It is not the mere existence of old wounds but the deliberate reopening of those wounds that seriously impacts group relationships. The speech of President Kiir that opened and closed with insults directed against his rivals seated in the audience at Nyakuron Cultural Centre a day or so before the conflict broke out was applauded by some lawmakers in the audience with war songs and beating of drums. This speech was circulated on social media, and it angered a number of Nuer people.

In an earlier speech before members of the parliament in which Kiir announced the decision to go to war over Heglig in 2012, all the lawmakers supported the decision with the beating of drums and loud singing of war songs in the parliament. All memories of the civil war were brought back. South Sudanese used social media to start circulating the picture of Gen. James Gaduel Nyakuach, who led the war and caused mass support for the war to hike, giving Kiir and the lawmakers the impression that they were doing the right thing. After regaining sanity, the parliamentarians realized the country had lost over 90 per cent of revenue instantly due to the shutting down of oil due to war. The Government of South Sudan (GoSS) marketed the fear of an external threat to get the masses to support their policies, even policies that are self-destructive. These examples also show that literacy levels are not bullet proof to the gunshot of political trickery.

The fact that institutions equipped with a great deal of resources can be duped may be scary, but what is scarier still is that it is often impossible to convince those who have been duped to reconsider their positions once they have successfully bought into a harmful scheme.

In South Sudan, the political elites are trapped in a loop of avenging past grievances, ensuring that those who have been temporarily deprived of power do not attempt to regain it to take revenge. This war is mostly fought through negative smearing of rivals in the mass media. While an insult or a sign of disrespect (which is called a 'dhääl' in the Dinka language) can manufacture grievances and destroy social fabrics, it is not easy to devise a scheme to legislate insults so that the victims seek some form of redress from their aggressors, especially when the medium of delivery is a social media source. The aggressive party almost always responds violently. Provided they are aware of this cultural tendency, an aggressor who is in a better position may agitate his victims into action by hurling insults at them.

Conflict entrepreneurs have exploited cultural sensitivity to insults to spur their troops into action. Youth from a group that has been called cowards on live videos may attack their rivals to prove that they aren't cowards. Some groups of Dinka youth in Jonglei have composed songs to assert this as the reason for attacking Pibor areas in July 2020.

In an unpublished work by Professor Akolda Ma'an Tier, he observed that a number of political elites played a role in the revenge killings at Lakes State. A similar conclusion was drawn by Gen. Kuol Malith, who served in the area during the civil war. The political elites protected relatives who had committed crimes by recruiting them into the armed sectors, and they sometimes used them as bodyguards. This action increased the grievances amongst the victims' families, who waited for the perfect opportunity to take revenge. When these cycles of violence had reached their boiling point and sown fear of greater conflict, the government in Juba sent the same political elites who started these hostilities to keep the peace. This circumstance is not unique to Lakes State; it has been witnessed in other settings throughout South Sudan, as well. In other areas, the conflict has remained dormant or has been diverted to social media.

At the start of the conflict in 2013, Michael Makuei Lueth, who was the spokesperson of the South Sudanese government and the minister of information during South Sudan's civil war, was alleged to have branded the two counties of Twic East and Duk within Jonglei State as 'rebel communities'. Whether the allegation was real or imagined, the government paid dearly in the negative publicity it received on various internet platforms from members of Twic East. The news of such an insult had emerged on top of an already angry and divided group of communities.

War via live videos and songs among the Dinka of former Bor District

A social group may be formed when two or more families/clans with common or distinct origins merge. The benefits to this merger usually include the improved protection of the people and private and public properties of the social group from hostile outer groups. For some group members, the question of where one comes from is more important than the question of where one is; for others, it is the other way around. Whenever a number of social groups are brought under a common administrative authority, the question of what this collection of groups ought to be called becomes an issue. If you pick a name from one of the groups for a common identity, then this may lead to future conflict due to the importance people attach to their social identities, which are tied to their distinct origins, kinships and histories. Appealing to these social identities is also typically more successful during times of potential threat and conflict. The issue of social identity emerged in recent years among the Nyarweng, Bor, Twic and Hol Dinka groups in Jonglei State.

During a certain period in the history of South Sudan, the four groups mentioned above were collectively known as the Bor Dinka, from being in Bor District, and not many objected to this identification although it was known that Bor belonged to the two of its subsections of Athooc and Gok. The war has introduced identity crisis. This Jonglei case is one in which the divide and conquer did not succeed in creating a conflict. This perhaps may have a lesson. A brief history on the experiences that these communities have shared, how these experiences contributed to their identity and how they have been threatened by the ongoing war and its politics is necessary.

The flood

Between 1961 and 1964, heavy rains in East Africa had increased the water levels of Lakes Victoria and Albert by three metres. Egypt responded to the

Equatorial Lakes' rising levels by increasing their outflow through the Owen Falls Dam, which triggered floods.[5] Vital pastures became inaccessible, thousands of cattle were killed and people died. Threatened by the floodwaters, many young men and women from Nyarweng, Hol, Twic and Bor fled north in droves with other affected Nilotic people living near the Nile. In spite of the usual psychological obstacles that those who had been uprooted from their homes faced, such as discrimination, humiliating insults and exploitation, the displaced youth took advantage of the educational, business and technological prospects that were available to them. When stability returned to South Sudan in 1972, opportunity favoured them, and a good number of the Nyarweng, Hol, Twic and Bor managed to find jobs in the autonomous government of Southern Sudan formed following an agreement in 1972 that ended the Anya-Nya led civil war in Sudan. This enabled them to send their children and relatives to school. While other factors, such as the nepotism of the ruling elites, cannot be dismissed entirely (as some do credit the achievements of these communities to Hon. Abel Alier, a Bor Dinka, and Dr John Garang, a Twic Dinka), the positive impacts of the 1962 flood played a dominant role in creating a space for these communities in the national arena.

When the second civil war erupted in 1983, education (knowledge) and experience (skills) were favourably rewarded, and those who had attended grade school or higher dominated the officer ranks. The handing out of ranks was based on merits as officers were ranked according to their performances in the exams given; those who had university degrees or were outstanding high school graduates did much better than their colleagues with only a rudimentary elementary school education. This led to a domination of intelligent units and officers by the Bor, Twic, Nyarweng and Hol. Of course, others may still credit this domination to nepotism (perhaps an institutionalized one). But this would also lead to the domination of the SPLA at the top by the Bor, Twic, Nyarweng and Hol by 2005 when the war ended. Gradual corrective measures were taken to fire hundreds of officers to create some balance.

The SPLM split of 1991

In 1991, the split within the SPLA resulted in a massacre that came to be known as the Bor massacre and led to massive displacement of the Nyarweng,

Hol, Twic and Bor communities among other communities in the Upper Nile region. Once again, the Nyarweng, Hol, Twic and Bor dominated the camps of displaced persons in Eastern Equatoria and one of the most critical refugee camps in East Africa (Kakuma). The high school scholarship opportunities and the resettlement programmes to resettle refugees in Australia, Canada and the United States were dominated by the Nyarweng, Hol, Twic and Bor. The resettled refugees provided further educational opportunities for their relatives back in Africa (it is currently very unusual to come across a Nyarweng, a Hol, a Twic or a Bor Dinka diaspora who is not paying for a relative's education in Uganda or Kenya). Some of the young people who were educated in neighbouring countries found jobs with non-governmental origanizations (NGO), with the governments or in the private sector, and their families and relatives were able to receive quality educations outside of South Sudan. The private sector in Juba is dominated by members of Nyarweng, Hol, Twic and Bor Dinka. A businessman, Makur, from Eastern Lakes State told me an interesting anecdote a while back in Juba. After being told that Makur, a skinny man who looked like he was in his 20s and who happened to be passing by at the time, was the owner of the building, one young man exclaimed, 'The Bahr al Ghazal people have properly eaten this country to an extent that even this young man owns such a gigantic building.' Makur responded by narrating to the young men that 'every businessman who owns a shop in his building was from Jonglei'. He concluded, 'In fact, we the Bahr Al Ghazal are holding the cow's horns while it is you the Jonglei people who are milking it.'[6]

The 2013 conflict brought suffering and opportunity to the Kakuma refugee camp, which now, like other refugee camps in Uganda, is full once again. Only violent displacement has shaped the destiny of the Nyarweng, Hol, Twic and Bor Dinka, which has enabled these communities to develop distinctively within their ethnic group of the Dinka (rather than the typical collectivist culture, a different value system is being adopted: the slow trend of individualist culture). Their zeal for entrepreneurialism, education and personal discipline is beneficial and can be traced to their extreme exposure to the outside world. Constant displacements have exposed the Nyarweng, Hol, Twic and Bor to new ideas, allowing them to enhance their technological capacity and bring an unmatched sophistication to the way that they approach conflict. If one looks at the various communities and sub-communities in South Sudan, the difference between their achievements and outlooks on life has a lot to do with the level and frequency of their displacements. The shared experiences of constant displacement have allowed the Dinka communities in Jonglei State to forge a social-political identity that has made them a stronger political threat. The best way to deal with a threat like this one is to divide and conquer it. As such, the uneven division of state and national power became the tools that the government indirectly used to undermine any future threats to leadership from these communities.

Ministerial appointments

In South Sudan, ministerial and government appointments are viewed as rewards to the communities where the appointees come from. Under this logic, it makes sense that most people who work for the ministers come from the same areas as the ministers, leading to the likelihood for some form of sanctioned nepotism to arise. Consequently, when an elite has been appointed into a government position in South Sudan, his support base (which is usually made up of his clan or the biocultural network to which his/ her family belongs) celebrates in extravagant style so that certain members within their base will benefit. In other words, access to power and wealth and the way that it is distributed throughout Juba often involves communities. As a result, grievances and fear that is generated amongst the competing elites within each state transfers between those of their respective communities. The politics of dividing the national cake carries with it the serious potential for communal conflicts. The war and its politics have strained the social fabrics of these groups, and the deterioration of relationships between the subsections of each group have already been realized. The failure of the ruling elites to effectively manage diversity throughout South Sudan has triggered further failures in maintaining cohesion within each group. The system of governance in Juba, which divides communities into supporters and enemies, exacerbates the effects of perceived domination and social-political-economic exclusion, which are at the roots of bitterness amongst social-political groups. While these horizontal grievances and group fears are triggered by the choices made by the government in Juba, they can be found in nearly every state.

The bitter conflicts within homogenous groups also show that tribalism is not as important as it is portrayed in the extant literature on the conflict dynamics in South Sudan.

Between October 2005 and July 2013, a number of the sons and daughters from Jonglei State's four Dinka communities of Nyarweng, Hol, Twic and Bor served as ministers or deputy ministers in Khartoum or Juba.

Twic had Dr Majak D'Agoot serving as deputy minister of defence (2011–13), Dr Lual Achuek Lual Deng serving as deputy minister of finance (2005–10) and minister of petroleum (2010–11), Hon. Atem Yaak serving as deputy minister of information (2011–13) and Hon. Rebecca Nyandeng serving as minister of roads and later as an advisor. In addition, Hol had Hon. Rhoda David Alak serving as deputy minister of electricity and dams (2011–13), Nyarweng had Philip Thon Leek serving as minister of transport and roads and Bor had Hon. Kuol Manyang and Hon. Michael Makuei serving as ministers. Between July 2013 and 3 September 2018, while Twic, Nyarweng and Hol had no one from their communities serving as ministers or deputy ministers, three individuals from Bor started as cabinet ministers in July 2013. These individuals included Hon. Kuol Manyang Juuk, Hon. Michael Makuei and Hon. Abdalla Deng Nhial. Nhial only served for two months and was removed by President Kiir as a punishment for slapping an MP, Machok Majong Jong, from Kiir's home turf.[7]

The debates that took place between July 2013 and 15 December 2013 were already turning grievances against the government into grievances against each other among the former Bor District communities.

The Nyarweng and Hol did not participate much in these discussions. Rather, the ongoing discourse became a two-person game that pit the Twic and Bor against each other. The Bor accused the Twic of jealousy, and the Twic accused the Bor of having manipulated the outcome of ministry appointments in their favour. The two communities readied themselves for conflict, but the confrontation was unique in that both sides chose to wage their war with words using social media.

The online war between the two groups (which has recently also been fought with songs) did not necessarily harm Kiir's political needs. For one, it was a welcome distraction that directed attention away from his government.

Amidst the December 2013 conflict, Twic members claimed that Hon. Michael Makuei Lueth had branded their lands as rebel territories. At this time, while Dr Majak D'Agoot was among those who were detained in Juba, Hon. Rebecca Nyandeng gave public interviews to international media outlets where she openly opposed the government. Whether the stigmatization of rebellion had any trace of truth in it or not is history, but this triggered toxic exchanges on Facebook where everybody became the targets of insults and counter insults.

Being called an enemy of the government when the country was at war conjured a number of fears. This triggered a strong defensive reaction from Twic members, particularly among those who were diaspora. Sadly, the reactions of some Twic social media users violated ethical boundaries and the boundaries of mutual respect, as they targeted members of other communities (from Bor and other areas in Bahr Al Ghazal) who were often innocent. This did not help in the process of reconciliation and the mending of the social fabric that had already been strained by the conflict. Unfortunately, instead of being sympathetic and seeking to understand the grievances that were rooted in the dangerous branding, the defensive reactions of some Twic young people were now used as proof to justify why the community was deserving of their negative label. In connection with the early complaint of Twic members about the distribution of power at the national level, the inflation of states from ten to twenty-eight and then thirty-two also created a protest among Twic citizens within the state of Jonglei, as Bor had multiplied into eight counties while Twic had only multiplied into three, which were later increased to five after bitter protests online.

Hol and Nyarweng were the first communities who negatively reacted to the injustices of the twenty-eight states associated with the distribution of counties and members of parliament in the state of Jonglei, which exacerbated the perception of internal domination within the state of Jonglei by the Bor Dinka. The four communities of Hol, Nyarweng, Twic and Bor have formed a community umbrella organization in various places including in diaspora, which is known as the Greater Bor community. To protest what they saw as uneven sharing of power in the state of Jonglei, the Hol and Nyarweng held meetings in Juba and Bor and terminated their participation in the Greater Bor community in Juba, Kenya and the United States and in all other places where this union existed. They pulled their two state members of parliament (Hon. Abiel Chan Anyang and Hon. Athiak Ruei Padier) out of Jonglei State parliament for eight months. When this started, Hol and Nyarweng primarily faulted Hon. Aguer Panyang, from Twic, who stubbornly defied the community opposition to his government and ended up appointing two sons of Hol and Nyarweng as part of his cabinet against the wishes of the community. Governor Aguer eventually added more counties to both Duk and Twic, solving part of the problem, and Duk eventually allowed the two MPs to rejoin the state assembly.[8]

The war of songs rapidly turned the conflict to be between the Twic and Bor. In the absence of a meaningful dialogue, the two groups took their grievances to social media.

War taken to social media

Political tensions within Jonglei managed not to explode into conflict for three reasons. The communities in Jonglei differ in politics, but they pray at the same church, which makes their political differences less violent as there are no rooms for the breakdown of communication channels.[9] The second reason can be attributed to Dr John Garang's historical design. When the SPLA started in 1983, it attracted many warlords who predominantly came from the Dinka and Nuer social groups. Warlords emerged within what is now Jonglei like many communities that had participated in the First Sudanese Civil War (1962–72). Dr Garang literally clipped the wings of the warlords from his home turf areas and instead favoured younger, more educated officers (insisting on basing ranks on performances in an exam given at the training camp, for instance). The high-ranking Anya-Nya officers from Nyarweng, Hol, Twic and Bor realized this early on and began to step out of the way. This significantly downgraded the importance of military ranks amongst the Nyarweng, Hol, Twic and Bor. The generals within the Nyarweng, Hol, Twic and Bor, though still important as political elites, were not necessarily viewed as community leaders unlike in other communities.

Third, while the Nyarweng, Hol, Twic and Bor politicians and their associates engaged in divisive politics to outdo one another, their generals in the SPLA all chose to remain united. They saw no gain in heightening the existing tensions. They were able to think this way because nearly all of them had the equivalent of a high school education, if not a bachelor's degree.

With the Nyarweng, Hol, Twic and Bor generals denying the politicians of a battleground in Jonglei State, the politicians and their associates took to social media, where their weapons became live videos and status updates. Jonglei State has given South Sudan a new form of war – a war that came complete with spectators who could interact by liking or sharing their posts.

War of Songs

Rev. Archibald Shaw has noted that a Dinka song is generally in vogue for a limited time only and that any new circumstance produces a fresh series of appropriate songs.[10] The songs are violating some cultural norms. One community elder has expressed concern about the nature of the dissing songs, noting that 'Dinka usually make themselves known to those they compose songs against in order to give the other party a chance to reply in kind'.[11] There is usually a closure to the fight with songs: 'When people realize that they have already exhausted their ideas, they are taken to court for investigation, punishment and warn not to sing again against each other.'[12] Traditionally, 'elders that are not directly related to the rivals are not normally blemished',[13] which is another rule being violated. For instance, insulting songs that depicted Dr Majak D'Agoot as a traitor and Hon. Rebecca Nyandeng as a killer hit social media in 2014. The songs ended up getting out of control with prominent leaders from Bor, such as Hon. Abel Alier, Gen. Kuol Manyang, Governor Maker Thiong Mal and Hon. Michael Makuei Lueth, including some who are deceased hit with dissing songs from 2018 until 2020.

Timeline of songs between Twic and Bor (2013–20).

2013: In 2010, a wrestling team from Bor won 11–0 against Twic's wrestling team. In 2013, John Ayuen from a Bor's subsection of Abii (Nyara) composed a song referencing this defeat: 'Duɔ̈kkë wunda yötic cë wun ë Twic' – 'Don't treat our team like a Twic's team.' This song would have been a normal practice had it been composed in 2010, but by 2013, there was already tension between the two groups, and every word uttered became sensitive.

2014: Akim Maluk from the Bor's section of Palek, who happens to live in Australia, branded Dr Majak D'Agoot and Hon. Rebecca Nyandeng in a song as the destroyers of Bor.

2016: Joh Ayuen (referenced above) composed another song with a line: 'Kuan anyagat aabukku ke yök ëbën wuɔ Makuei Lueth ku Kuɔl e Manyang, ee rebool e ka yokku ke maan gup' – 'We (I, Kuol Manyang and Michael Makuei) will dig out all the rebels; we hate the rebels.' Given that the Twic claimed that they had been stigmatized as rebels, they interpreted such an implicit reference as an attack on them.

2018: Manyang Achut Mamer from the Bor's section of Atet composed a song labelling Dr Majak D'Agoot as a traitor. Unfortunately, albeit its sensitivity, the song has been memorialized as a part of the Atet youths' official recordings on YouTube as it is sung as the number two song in that album.

In 2018, Twic's singers picked up composition of songs.

2018: Kur Matiop Kur (known as K–2) from the Twic's section of Pakeer composed a song entitled 'Awalwala'. K–2's song pushed things to the next level by declaring that the Jonglei identity originated in Twic and by praising a certain wrestler, Maghot, from Twic in terms that were demeaning to the Bor.

2018: Mabior Majok Ajang from the Twic's section of Pakeer composed a song entitled 'Pinynom ku Ciir e liep' in which he urged Dr Majak D'Agoot not to worry because 'aaye diäär keek lät ke yïin' – 'it is only women who are hurling insults at you'. It is inflammatory to be referred to as a 'woman', as that is culturally associated with being a coward or someone unworthy of being responded to. To add to the inflammation, the Twic swarmed Bor Town in 2019 to cross the river to wrestle with the Aliab team in Eastern Lakes, and while they were preparing to cross the Nile to Mingkaman, they danced and sang this song.

2018: Ayiik Garang-weet from the Twic' section of Ajuong composed another song in which he taunted: 'Menh Ajuong aye rem dhiau maoo e ka guac Gongic' – 'Ajuong's son makes people cry as Gongic is about to be wrestled down.' Gongic is the top wrestler of Bor while Maghot, who is referred to as 'Ajuong's son', is the Twic's top wrestler. Maghot and Gongic drew, but the song has remained as 'Menh Ajuong aye rem dhiau maoo e ka guac Gongic'. While the Twic's team wrestled with the Aliab's team in 2019, this song was played on loudspeakers before an audience numbering more than fifty thousand. Gongic and his teammate certainly did not like this, and when the Twic's team returned to Bor Town, Gongic defeated the Twic's number two in wrestling Deng Dau – Moradong. Deng hit the ground very hard, and he was sick afterwards. The conversations following the defeat of Deng retriggered toxic exchanges on Facebook. The singing had gotten out of hand, with Twic releasing more dissing songs that spared nobody. In 2019 and 2020 singers were increasingly composing vitriolic songs and hiding their voices and accents, circulating their songs via Messenger.

At a national wrestling tournament in Juba, Bor Facebook users increased criticism of the Twic wrestler, Maghot Khot, who was leading the whole team of Jonglei, in the hopes that the wrestling coach would drop him from the top position. To his credit, the coach (also from Bor) stood his ground, but eventually, things were beyond his control. The wrestling team disintegrated along Twic versus Bor contours, with both sides challenging each other into a confrontation. Authorities intervened and stopped the groups before they could begin to fight, which seemed likely given the tension of the circumstances.

Users resorted to composing more insulting songs, with composers from the Twic (and maybe a few of the Bor) leaving no one unscathed, even going as far as to ridicule the dead or elderly statesmen. These songs, in addition to live videos where the posters hurled insults at their leaders, continued to increase. They are discussed endlessly on social media via live videos.

Parallel to these trends was the issue of identity. The toxic politics since 2013 had sharpened identity discourses. The community leaders of the Bor, Twic and Duk (Hol and Nyarweng) in Canada, Australia and the United States held exceedingly disparate views on the relevance of Greater Bor to the umbrella of identity. In the United States, the Bor's leader there claimed that he would not accept any umbrella of identity that excluded the Bor (while this is what the author heard, it is possible that he may have been misquoted). By comparison, the Twic's leaders in both Canada and the United States wanted to use Jonglei as the umbrella of identity and do away with Greater Bor, and the Duk's leaders in Canada and the United States leaned towards using Jonglei as their umbrella of identity but were not opposed to a completely new identity as an alternative.

There are certainly elites who saw and still see conflict as a platform for them to outdo their rivals from within Jonglei. These individuals have done their best to exploit growing tensions in the hopes of sparking violent conflict in Jonglei. Both sides of the conflict in Jonglei have fallen victim to these politicians' machinations: while one side was made to see that it was winning following the July 2013 dissolution of the cabinet, the other side was made to see that it was losing. Individual politicians may win or lose, but the entire community does not benefit at all. Indeed, both natural disasters and man-made insecurities are equally threatening to a community's villagers. Both sides should have realized that the politicians held a hidden design to get one side to redirect its grievances against the national government towards the other, and, in turn, to get the other to become defensive. By falling into this trap, the politicians were able to use the conflict to divide and conquer the masses.

In spite of the pressure from the ruling class for the communities to take arms against each other, they have bravely resisted these destructive machinations and refused to fight. The heartless elites have recently found collaborators who have figured their scheme out once and for all: to use social media to provoke and propagate messages of hate. The chain of provocations started with the online circulation of two songs that portrayed two politicians from one side as 'killers' and another politician from that same side as a 'traitor'. They then released a third song in response to the first two that indirectly called out their opposition, portraying them in inglorious terms, charging them with 'hate' and, unfortunately, suggesting that 'it is better to slit their throats so that they believe us'.[14] The circulation of these songs and the reactions they generated took the war of words to another level. A wrestling tournament in Juba presented another opportunity for exploitation. After Jonglei failed to win the championship due to claims of fighting amongst the wrestlers over the line-ups, the fans began to push their favourite wrestlers to challenge one another immediately. Provocative letters were hastily written and circulated on Facebook and were followed by online bullying. The community leaders called off the wrestling tournament, which took the tension away from the field in Juba and left it to fester online.

A number of 'educated' men and women who predominantly live in the United States, Canada and Australia have resorted to using live videos to engage in a war of words (hurling insults at elders because an insult or insulting song directed at an elder or a leader is a sure way to start a conflict). The goal for most of these users is to build up the fear of violent conflict in order to force the central authority in Juba to split up the new Jonglei State into two or three parts.

In some South Sudanese cultures, a talented person, when provoked, may compose a song to criticize or to speak disrespectfully to his opponent. This may trigger a series of disparaging songs that pit two singers against each other. A host of factors can trigger this duel: an insult, competition over a woman, a dispute over who won a wrestling contest, a dispute over ownership of a territory, etc. The insults can also prevent singers from two communities from working together, tarnishing the reputations of noble men and women from rival communities. Usually, authorities intervene, and the singers are fined. They are asked to sing their songs for the records, and after which, those songs are banned (of course, individuals who know the songs may still sing them, but they cannot be performed in public out of fear that they will incite conflict). Those who are not able to retaliate through song may resort to violence when a song is composed against them.

Once the disparaging songs have been sung in court, they are copyrighted as intellectual properties. The offended party is not expected to continue to claim harm from them. The composer or his community can still occasionally sing them but not with the intent to incite violence. What is overruled is the composition of new songs. The ruling simply breaks the cycle. On occasions when this has happened, there has existed an unwritten code that excludes executive leaders (chiefs) and priests (beny ke bith/yath) from this exercise. This is done to leave the window for reconciliation open.[15] On both sides, social media commenters and young people who compose songs and make live videos fail to observe this regulation. Unlike past events, perhaps the reason is that politics are now at stake.

Participation in the ancient art of songcraft has traditionally been confined to talented singers. With the discovery of writing, people with that ability have used the written word to achieve what others could only achieve with songs. Nevertheless, with the introduction of live videos in 2016, those who lack talent in writing or song composition can now produce live broadcasts for them to insult and disparage their rivals. Nothing has changed. The art has remained the same. It is the medium of communicating that art that has become democratic. Indeed, a live video requires no special talent; it requires only participation.

The rise of disparaging songs and bickering over wrestling positions is not voluntary. These are social channels through which the elites pressure young people into conflict with the help of propaganda through social media. The elites and their collaborators use the politics of fear to coerce their potential victims into actively fuelling the flames that will eventually devour them.

Conclusion

The seven-year-old war of words that has pit communities against one another in Jonglei State is a consequence of elite competition to delegitimize internal rivals and to gain, regain or retain access to power. While there can be short-term winners, every one of the political elites in Jonglei will be long-term losers (anyone of them who aspires for a bigger piece of the pie will have a serious challenge uniting Jonglei State as his/her basic support base). This is precisely the reason that people will eventually realize that they have been playing a zero-sum game. The conflict has reached a critical level – the communities are gradually taking ownership of the problem, and it is unlikely to be solved easily. The only reason this conflict has yet to devolve into a deadly and violent confrontation is that unlike the educated men and women in the diaspora, the men and women of the SPLA in Jonglei have remained united and rejected the politicians' schemes. The war of words has ended in a painful draw, yet nobody is willing to realize that insulting someone from this or that side will produce similar results.

Outside of the affected communities who may view the conflict as part of the larger divide and conquer scheme, the conflict is not necessarily bad for the top national leaders.

Elites spread stories online to discredit their rivals and their support bases and to gain and retain control and power in the state apparatus. The result is the increased suspicion and victimization of South Sudan's different groups. Their rivals' crimes (imagined or real) are then blamed on their communities. These hate-generating narratives pit communities against one another and trigger toxic exchanges that perpetuate deep enmity and damage the social fabric of South Sudanese society. These social media narratives are successful in amplifying social hostility not because the stories are true, but because (1) they are repeated and re-disseminated by individuals using the 'like' and 'share' buttons; (2) there are few interactions to counterbalance misperceptions among different ethnic groups both within and outside of South Sudan where South Sudanese settle in communities defined along tribal lines; and (3) the harmful social media narratives contain built-in appeals to dormant ethnic resentment and hatred underpinned by past episodes of ethnic conflict. It is not the mere existence of old wounds, but, rather, the deliberate reopening of those wounds that seriously impacts group relations. To varying degrees, every society has a foundational sentiment, which, upon being stirred, can strain the social fabric of a society. Furthermore, social media has furnished researchers with a virtual environment of conflict where battles are waged online amongst a virtual population that shares similar attributes with their offline counterparts. At times, the online war of words can become as intense as the war taking place on the ground. Instead of serving as a source of support or providing positive and constructive contributions, the virtual South Sudanese community has fomented certain online behaviours that are shaped and driven by a small number of influential disseminators of social disorder.

Most individuals who use social media condition their behaviour according to the behaviour of their friends. Individuals are more likely to go live on Facebook when their virtual friends and family do. In their live videos, their disgruntlement, neutrality or satisfaction with how the government is performing will be influenced by the virtual actions of their trusted online friends. Some users regard going live on Facebook as an activity only taken by lowly regarded individuals with the sole aim of attacking personalities and communities. Unfortunately, this stigmatization overlooks those who use the tool to constructively benefit their communities and to advance the collective agenda of governance. Because the live video button allows more users to express themselves in their local languages and to reach out to just about anybody who understands those languages, it is complementary to writing platforms, which are restrictive. Like the political environment, whether or not a social media platform becomes toxic depends on the character of the actors who broadcast their opinions. If someone uses live videos to share their constructive and progressive objectives, then their audience will be attracted away from negativity. Through social media, the mass participation in the social-political affairs of South Sudan will eventually produce a country in which no one will feel unsafe for expressing her/his opinion. Social media has legitimized criticisms of South Sudanese leaders.

The role of the external actors in South Sudan's conflict

During the First Sudanese Civil War (1955–72), the Anya-Nya cultivated relations with Israel, providing military and medical supplies as well as managing the propaganda of the rebels, Kenya and Ethiopia, where the rebels had their bases.[1] Through the targeted messaging designed by the SPLM/A's leader Dr John Garang, the SPLM/A expanded the relations during the Second Sudanese Civil War (1983–2005) to include many other African countries, which provided political, financial and military assistance. In East Africa, the SPLM/A enjoys strong ties with the governments of Eritrea, Ethiopia, Kenya, Tanzania and Uganda – with Ethiopia (together with Libya) having provided significant political and military support to the SPLM/A during the earlier days and Eritrea having provided major military assistance in the 1990s, especially to the SPLM/A and its allies in eastern Sudan.[2] In November 1993, the US House of Representatives recognized the right of the people of South Sudan to self-determination, and the SPLM/A began to have warm relations with the United States, Norway, South Africa and a number of other countries in Europe and Asia.[3] The United States has constantly provided the biggest financial support to South Sudan. The relations between South Sudan and Sudan have remained poor until 2019, when Sudan's President Omar Hassan el Bashir was overthrown.[4] The new actors in Khartoum may offer hope for South Sudan and Sudan to resolve major post-independence issues, including the contentious and occasionally violent dispute over the Abyei area.[5]

China, which entered Sudan in 1995, eventually improved its relations with South Sudan after the latter's independence in 2011. The SPLM leadership has maintained ties with Egypt over the past two decades, although successive governments in Cairo did not support the South's right to self-determination, but 'towards the end of the war, Egypt accepted the fact that independence was inevitable'.[6] The South Sudanese Civil War (2013–20) has reconfigured South Sudan's relations with other countries.

Published research by the UN Panel of Experts,[7] the Small Arms Survey[8] and Conflict Armament Research[9] have examined the external financing channels used by the two main actors in the conflict, government (the SPLA) and opposition (the SPLA-IO) to mobilize military resources to wage war. The SPLA and the SPLA-IO have each relied on foreign commercial logistics to deliver weapons and personnel into the conflict's major operational zones. Other external actors have defended their political economic interests by giving a diplomatic support to either of the parties or both. The analysis will focus on China, Israel, Uganda and Sudan, as well as the role of the humanitarian intervention in the conflicts, but let's briefly discuss Egypt and Ethiopia.

Egypt and Ethiopia

South Sudan's primary resource, which has not yet been utilized, is the Nile. A hostile government in Juba would be a nightmare for Egypt: roughly '23 billion cubic metres (BCM) of the total flow of the Nile of 84 BCM measured at Aswan crosses southern Sudan into northern Sudan and eventually into Egypt'.[10] This makes it plausible that Egypt would offer support to the government of South Sudan during a crisis to guarantee the political support, or at least neutrality, of Juba in the ongoing politics of the Nile River in the region. However, a close association between Egypt and South Sudan would make Ethiopia suspicious. Ethiopia has a long history of supporting Southern Sudanese rebels during the Sudanese civil wars. While Ethiopia stood with South Sudanese in the past, and Egypt stood against various Southern Sudanese rebels in support of Khartoum on ideological grounds, things changed when Khartoum was no longer fighting against Juba (2013–20). Now, Juba is seen by some observers as leaning towards Egypt (or is it Egypt that is courting South Sudan to ensure that South Sudan backs her diplomatically or at least remains neutral in the struggle over control for the Nile?). Because of Ethiopia's historically friendly gestures towards the South Sudanese people during times of hardship, the South Sudanese public supports Ethiopia. However, Juba has maintained relatively good relations with both Egypt and Ethiopia. Egypt is already moving to increase her investment in South Sudan. A branch of Alexandria University will open in 2021 in Tonj in South Sudan.[11]

If Juba leans too much towards Egypt, Ethiopia will not sit idly. Notwithstanding its own internal contradictions – which Prime Minister Abiy Ahmed, who had initially raised hopes for democracy, has not effectively managed – Ethiopia may punish such a betrayal or perception of ungratefulness by providing both a rear base and minimal external support to any South Sudanese opposition leadership.

On the other hand, disappointing Egypt while supporting Ethiopia would not be wise, either; it would mean going against Sudan at a time when the relations between the two Sudans are becoming cordial.

China

South Sudan relations with China are usually conducted primarily on a personal level in the Office of the President under the China Desk.[12] South Sudan has the potential to answer the main problems facing China, such as vulnerable agricultural foundation, shortage of farmland and water resources.[13] However, presently, China's involvement in South Sudan is motivated by two interests: first, to maintain a monopoly on the oil sector in a country where a combination of unfortunate circumstances keeps other competitors at bay.[14] Although the state-owned China National Petroleum Corporation (CNPC), one of the largest oil companies in the world, controls around 40 per cent of the two main oil consortia in the country, the holding is almost negligible, accounting for 2 per cent to 5 per cent of China's oil consumption.[15] China's interest in the oil sector may be a relational building venture aimed at a secondary interest. They are able to access the key political actors. Where else could such people be found in a country that depends entirely on oil?

Analysing the data that could be found on the web, the secondary interest seems to be the integration of South Sudan into an envisaged new regional market as a dividend of the Belt and Road Initiative, launched in 2014, which is China's signature vison for reshaping its global engagements.[16] Obviously, the South Sudanese Civil War (2013–20) threatened both of these interests, but China chose to stay rather than fleeing, like many other actors who had entertained entering into South Sudan when the country became independent from Sudan in 2011. Although it officially became an independent country in 2011, South Sudan had existed as a distinct political entity (albeit not under a unified political leadership) with various independent domestic actors who challenged the legitimacy of external authorities that invaded it and represented South Sudan in building external relations from the 1960s through 2011. The modern competition over control among external actors is not a new phenomenon in South Sudan.

Due to the historical importance attached to the Nile River, which cuts South Sudan into two, the region first attracted international competition between 1840 and 1862 among explorers competing to discover the source of the Nile and then once again from 1893 to 1898 when the French and the British almost fought at Fashoda in South Sudan on 3 November 1898, due to the French government's intention to use engineering to obstruct the flow of the Nile in order to hurt Egypt (then a British ally).[17] The politics following the Six-Day War of 1967 brought Israel into South Sudan. The politics of the Cold War pushed South Sudan into an alliance with Cuba, Libya, Russia and other socialist camps, excluding China. The end of the Cold War and the start of the War on Terrorism turned South Sudan into a Western ally by 1995 as the United States supplied it with resources channelled to the SPLM/A through Uganda, Eritrea and Ethiopia. At the same time, China became interested in digging for oil, which was discovered by Chevron and abandoned due to the civil war, in collaboration with Sudan.

What can be learned from this history is that South Sudan has made the habit of making friendships during a crisis, and China may be kin at exploiting such an opportunity to establish a strong relationship with South Sudan. As a latecomer, China has to have a strategy to be able to compete with established external actors in the area.

First, China offers alternative models on political and economic issues and copies the West on some aspects of humanitarian intervention (food aid and medicine[18]). Where the West unhesitatingly uses hard power (carrot and sticks), China goes for soft power aimed at winning over the corrupt elites the West wants to crucify. Where the West insists on seeing stability as a prerequisite for development, China takes the reverse direction: development will lead to stability. This is a formidable formulation, and it may gain traction in development policy forums in Africa as there are already voices echoing this emphasis on development.[19] This may appeal to the ruling elite in Juba because the SPLM published a similar model in Nairobi in February 2000 called 'Peace Through Development: Perspectives and Prospects in the Sudan'. China has always placed development as the top priority. The 13th Five-Year Plan – approved in Congress in March 2016 – defines development as innovative, coordinated, green, open and shared, aimed at building a moderately prosperous society.[20]

Second, in order for China's alternative model of development stability to work, China has to take higher risks than rational economic theories would permit by continuing to invest amidst the conflict in South Sudan.[21] Nevertheless, the civil war offered high risks as well as ample opportunities for China to establish a monopoly where war has deterred others.

Third, China focuses on the stability of the zone of interest (oil areas) rather than focusing on the entire region. For example, China transitioned smoothly into working with South Sudan's government after the latter's independence while at the same time maintaining her relationship with Sudan, despite the fact that South Sudan and Sudan remained hostile to each other. China only wanted corporation in the oilfields. Extending the same strategy, China negotiated with both the SPLA and the SPLA-IO to keep the war away from the oil areas in Paloich areas after oilfields of Unity State were shut down due to conflict activities at the start of the conflict. China's security model of becoming a common friend of two enemies by providing financial and other support to both parties, conditioned upon their guaranteeing the security of oil infrastructure, became unsustainable when new actors entered into the conflict or, in the case of the rebels, not attacking it.[22]

Chinese-produced ammunition is by far the most prevalent ammunition used by all sides in the civil war, which were supplied lawfully to South Sudan's government under 2011 and 2013 contracts until June 2014 and retransferred clandestinely to SPLA-IO forces by elements within the Sudanese government in 2014 and 2015.[23] In September 2014, the Chinese Embassy in Juba informed journalists that China would halt arms shipments to South Sudan, including all outstanding deliveries subject to existing contracts.[24] External material support to the SPLA from China dropped away in the early stages of the war.[25]

Israel

Between 1969 and 1971, Israel supported the Southern Sudanese rebel group, which has been at war with the Sudanese government since the early 1960s.[26] The operation was led by the Mossad, which had correctly realized that it was not enough just to win the war, but it also needed to put out a winning narrative. The Mossad identified Joseph Lagu as the right leader among the South Sudanese leaders to work with, and Israel readily supplied military assets through airdropping and began to secretly produce and disseminate propaganda on behalf of the Anya-Nya.[27] The weapons were meant to strengthen the Southern Sudanese rebels to keep the Khartoum engaged away from the politics following the Six-Day War, which had heightened hostilities between Israel and Egypt under President Gamal Abdel Nasser (1956–70). The propaganda campaign was aimed at countering Egypt's campaign. Egypt's policy towards the armed conflict in South Sudan was characterized by 'condemnation of the rebels and their demands, and resorting to military as well as political solutions'.[28] The means by which the military support was to be delivered to the Anya-Nya was designed to tie Ethiopia and Kenya into the campaign so as to create a zone of influence in the region. Israel left the Anya-Nya alone in December 1971, and the Sudanese government began to negotiate with the Anya-Nya a month later, which led to the Addis Ababa Peace Agreement in 1972, lasting until the SPLM-led Second Sudanese Civil War started in 1983. There is not enough evidence supporting any role that Israel might have played during the Second Sudanese Civil War.

In the South Sudanese Civil War (2013–20), it was not an Israeli policy to support Salva Kiir as much as it was the interest of several Israeli businessmen to sell arms.[29] When the conflict broke out, both Riek Machar and Salva Kiir sought Israeli assistance, and Israel eventually joined and remained on Kiir's side – both for the simple reason that he still runs the country as far as they are concerned and because most Israeli businessmen involved drew much of their knowledge on South Sudan from government officials.[30]

There is also great lack of coordination between the Ministry of Foreign Affairs and the security sector and arms export regulators, so it is difficult to identify a 'policy'.[31]

Israeli arms supplied to South Sudan received significant media attention after the UN Panel of Experts reported that government-sponsored Mathiang Anyoor militia members were using (lawfully supplied) Israeli Galil ACE rifles.[32] These weapons originated in South Sudanese National Security Service (NSS) stockpiles and were deployed by the militia during the initial fighting in Juba in December 2013. The UN Panel of Experts also reported that the NSS had acquired Micro Galil rifles from Ugandan stockpiles in 2014 after the start of the hostilities. The government of Israel had not authorized Uganda to retransfer the weapons. External material support of firearms to the SPLA from Israel dropped away in the early stages of the war, but according to Israel, some other equipment and intelligence systems may continue to flow.[33]

Uganda

Uganda's role in South Sudan has always reflected the state of its internal problems such as coups and guerrilla warfare. During the time of President Apollo Milton Obote (15 April 1966–25 January 1971), Uganda cooperated with Khartoum against the Southern Sudanese rebel movement called the Anya-Nya.[34] In January 1971, Idi Amin overthrew President Obote and took power in Uganda. Amin had good relations with the Anya-Nya, whom he had visited at their base at Owiny Ki-Bul.[35] Uganda's support for the SPLM/A during the second civil war was motivated by a tit for tat policy against Khartoum because the latter was supporting Ugandan rebels of the Lord's Resistance Army (LRA) led by the notorious Joseph Konyi. In the South Sudanese Civil War (2013–20), unlike the Israelis' role in the conflict dynamics that is largely led by a group of businessmen with some relations to South Sudanese leaders, Uganda's involvement in South Sudan is a personal venture of Uganda's President Yoweri Museveni, a former guerrilla commander, who had ruled Uganda for nearly thirty years at the time he defeated his rival Kizza Besigye for the third time in February 2011. In fact, the relationship between Kiir and Museveni is more or less like a mentor–mentee relationship.

The SBS Dinka Radio interview with Gen. Paul Malong on 20 July 2020 revealed that through the advice of Gen. Paul Malong, President Salva Kiir sent $5 million USD to Museveni to support his re-election campaign. In return,

Museveni, a leading rancher in Uganda, sold some of his cows to Salva Kiir. According to Malong, the transaction was facilitated by Gen. Edward Kalekezi Kayihurua, the then inspector general of police of the Uganda Police Force from 2005 until 5 March 2018. Kiir's office did not pay all the money. Gen. Kayihurua approached Gen. Paul Malong Awan and informed him that he was afraid that President Museveni may accuse him of having stolen his money. Gen. Malong used his own money (about $40,000) to clear the arrears.[36] According to Malong, when the two leaders saw each other, Museveni joked, telling Kiir, 'I heard that you did not like me.' Malong said that Museveni asked Kiir, 'Why did you give your enemy ammunitions, referring to the campaign donation as such?'[37] Museveni had been a familiar face among the SPLM/A leaders due to his friendship with John Garang, which developed at the University of Dar es Salaam in Tanzania, and his backing of the SPLM/A, which was at its highest point in the 1990s when the United States channelled support to the SPLA through Uganda, Eritrea and Ethiopia. For example, the Ugandan People's Defense Forces (UPDF) helped the SPLA to capture the town of Kaya in 1997 a few days before the march on Yei.[38] Ugandan soldiers positioned their machine guns on site at Koboko Mountain to support the SPLA's successful incursion into Yei, a military offensive in the end facilitated primarily by an Ethiopian tank unit.[39] Since the demise of John Garang in a plane crash given him by President Museveni in July 2005, President Kiir had counted on Museveni in case Khartoum would obstruct the referendum exercise scheduled to take place on 9 January 2011.[40]

A careful look at the history of the social group called Bahima from which Museveni came shows that his involvement in South Sudan has an ideological dimension. The Bahinda, a clan within the cattle-keeping Bahima, ruled the Ankole kingdom. This kingdom expanded in population and geographically and had existed for at least 500 years in modern-day Uganda, and it had had at least twenty-three Omugabes (rulers) from antiquity to 1967.[41] How did the minority achieve such a difficult task? Much can be learned from this clan's art of governance. One of their gimmicks was to financially support the most popular candidates from various groups within the kingdom to become the chiefs of their groups.[42] This comes with a risk because a famous chief could overthrow them. But they had figured it all out: they worked with such a powerful chief, guiding his hands to become very corrupt (encouraged to marry many wives and asked to raise taxes) so that by the time he was about to rebel, the people were already calling for his removal, and the Omugabe (king) showed up to support the masses against the chief. The whole scenario was a cycle.[43] Although he has rebuffed attempts by some elites to revive the Ankole Kingdom, Museveni's style of governance seems to be drawn from the Bahinda's dictatorship handbook described in the preceding narrative, and some have drawn parallels with Kiir's governance style. The rise and fall of both Gen. Kayihurua and Gen. Paul Malong[44] illustrate the gimmicks of the Bahinda at play. Gen. Malong was made all powerful by Kiir, and by the time he became too powerful, he had already lost the support of his Aweil support base, which allowed Kiir to fire him without much difficulty.[45]

The involvement of Uganda in South Sudan's conflict was motivated by multiple issues. In the early months of the conflict, and periodically after, there was some direct support from the UPDF on the ground. This was followed by the arms transfers and various business dealings.[46]

In 2017, at a meeting with the SPLM leaders who were detained following the conflict outbreak in Juba in 2013, it became apparent that Museveni had mentioned two dimensions that guided his intervention in South Sudan. First, Museveni had a strong hatred for the SPLA-IO's leader, Dr Riek Machar, which stemmed from the history of the Second Sudanese Civil War in which Machar switched sides after the 1991 split and joined the side of the enemy, President Omar al Bashir.[47]

Museveni had accused Machar of betrayal – particularly because the Ugandan rebels of the LRA were backed by the government of Sudan, and Machar was seen as having a link with them. These factors heightened Museveni's hatred for Machar.[48] People have noted that Museveni does think of himself as a founding member of the SPLM.[49]

Second, Museveni believed that Machar using the Nuer (the White Army militia that fought with the UPDF in Bor) was going to orchestrate a genocide, and that had to be stopped before it escalated. In this sense, Museveni thought that he had acted in the interest of humanity to prevent Machar from reaching Juba[50] when he had indeed engaged in the politics of fear.

Third, Museveni's intervention ensured the security of the asymmetrical cross-border trade that favours Uganda. Ugandan exports to South Sudan increased from $60 million USD in 2005 to $635 million in 2008.[51] The government of South Sudan swiftly paid money for the contracts awarded to Ugandan traders for government services,[52] and the UPDF fighters were paid on time and at a much higher rate than the SPLA soldiers.[53]

According to the African Development Bank's estimates, 'South Sudan currently imports as much as 50 per cent of its needs, including 40 per cent of its cereals from neighbouring countries, particularly Kenya, Uganda and Ethiopia'.[54] According to the permanent secretary of the Ugandan Ministry of Tourism, Trade and Industry, Southern Sudan represented almost 40 per cent of the Ugandan export market.[55]

The Ugandan government has openly provided both arms and troops to assist the SPLA's military efforts since the start of the conflict in December 2013. The asymmetrical relationship between the two nations favours Uganda, and it could become unsustainable in the long run just as a similar relationship between Uganda and Congo did.[56]

Sudan

The opening of the White Nile to navigation between 1839 and 1841 exposed Southern Sudan to large-scale violent activities carried out by ivory and slave traders and later by various external regimes that came to violently impose the idea of a government. From 1839 to 2019 (180 years), the people of South Sudan had constantly known wars. Unfortunately, the political history of South Sudan reads like a mere account of Eastern and Western excursions into the southern hemisphere. A Turko-Egyptian regime ruled what is now South Sudan from 1821 to 1885. During that time, while government soldiers and armed traders hunted for slaves and animal products, administrators exacted exorbitant taxes upon the population. From 1898 to 1956, an Anglo-Egyptian regime ruled over the region. Their main interest was to control the Nile River, and their journey there led to other ventures, such as the work of social anthropologists, who gave the world its current view of the various groups inhabiting South Sudan.[57] The process put in place by the British government, such as the system of chiefship, helped to broker new regulatory orders, rights and resources that ultimately led to the creation of the state itself.[58] The relations between Southern Sudan and the British weren't always helpful. For example, the South Sudanese historian Lazarus Leek Mawut argued that 'the South suffered not so much from neglect by British officials as from their over-protectiveness'.[59] One instance of such overprotectiveness was the isolation of Southern Sudan from the rest of Sudan when the region was declared a closed area to foreigners except by permission of the governor general.[60] The economic and political exclusion of peripheral areas, which has its roots in this overprotectiveness, would eventually cause South Sudan to break away from Sudan over hundred years later. The United States would repeat the British's mistake by being too overprotective of South Sudan by giving them financial assistance in excess and ensuring that the sanctions on Sudan did not affect them. The ruling elite in Juba became reckless with their oil resources.

From 1956 to 2005, South Sudan was managed from Khartoum in theory but not in practice. The sole interest of the various governments in Khartoum was to control the region's resources and to culturally dominate its people. Rebels from Southern Sudan waged two civil wars between 1962 and 1972 and between 1983 and 2005 for self-determination and to change Khartoum's system of governance, respectively. The peace accord of 2005 allowed North and South Sudan to exist as one country while dividing the country's governance under two different systems during the interim period of 2005 to 2011. After the south separated and became an independent country in 2011, the north and south were gradually separated back into two countries that were governed under a single system as the security sectors in both countries influenced each other in their dealings with the civil populations, but the two countries remained hostile as one government supported the rebels in the other country and vice versa.

From 2005 to 2013, a brief period ensued in which an experiment in self-rule had soured in the hands of South Sudanese political leaders who fought amongst each other for dominance, plunging their country into a civil war into which Sudan was drawn in support of the rebels against the government in Juba.

During the South Sudanese Civil War, external material support to the government of South Sudan has been crucial for its survival, but in the classical security dilemma, this has triggered support for the SPLM/A-IO. Sudan has provided the supply of weapons, training and rear bases for the SPLM/A-IO both in Upper Nile and Jonglei, which has increased tensions between

Sudan and Uganda.[61] The SPLM/A-IO used 2014-manufactured Sudanese ammunition prior to the September-December 2014 airdrops in Jonglei, suggesting more than one case of supply from Khartoum to the SPLA-IO.[62] The UN experts found evidence that Sudan delivered weapons three times between March and June 2019.[63]

While all of the external actors in South Sudan's conflict are viewed from their military support or lack of it, those external actors providing food deserve some attention too because food has been weaponized.

After the demise of Omar el Bashir's government, relations between Juba and Khartoum have become friendly. The formation of the government of national unity in Juba in February this year has also made President Kiir to rely less on Uganda's military support. Additionally, South Sudan has brokered a peace deal between the new Sudanese government and a number of rebel groups. An ideology of 'One people, Two countries' could garner support in both Khartoum and Juba. This could be Juba's key to dealing with Uganda and other neighbours with hegemonic proclivities.

While Khartoum has successfully delinked Sudan from some old allies and reconnected with the West and Israel, the worsening economic crisis and failure to reach an agreement with the Sudan Liberation Movement (SLM) and Sudan People's Liberation Movement–North (SPLM-N) present a challenge.[64] Improving the relations between Juba and Khartoum may provide some hope of reducing this threat because the SPLM-N is historically linked to the ruling SPLM in Juba.

Humanitarian intervention

In South Sudan, there is very little room for internal agitation towards reform, which can be attested to the 'frequent sacking of officials who hold differing views with Kiir on issues relating to governance, which are generally not known to the wider public as they are considered either in-house affairs or administrative matters handled privately'.[65] Kiir has asserted that 'he will no longer tolerate those criticising the same system in which they serve while pretending to be cleaned when interacting with the members of the general public or members of the diplomatic communities'.[66] With an increasing intolerance for internal criticism, disgruntled members gravitate towards opposition platforms to agitate (sometimes using violent means) for reform.[67] The elites are trapped in cycles of persisting violence, and the international community continues to provide humanitarian assistance matching the increasing needs of the victims.

The challenge facing development actors in South Sudan is how to increase accountability and sustainability in humanitarian intervention while at the same time not risking abandoning people in times of significant need, such as during violent conflicts. The development partners shouldered primary responsibilities of the government of Southern Sudan from 2005 to 2011 and continued to do so after independence as South Sudan's education, food provision, healthcare and even road infrastructure fell under the control of humanitarian agencies. External groups fail because their humanitarian efforts are susceptible to manipulation and are therefore easily manipulated by both regime and insurgency leaders to advance their own interests, including sustaining war. In some sense, food suppliers may be viewed at the same level as the weapons suppliers. Although humanitarian intervention may be well meaning and intended to alleviate suffering, its susceptibility to manipulation by the warring parties often produces unexpected results.

Humanitarian agencies reporting on a crisis to raise awareness and to encourage donors to provide financial support resort to using a bit of fear to help draw attention. Fear is an excellent tool for promoting their cause, boosting memberships and donations or enhancing political clout.[68]

Both armed opposition groups and the South Sudanese government benefit from how the humanitarian agencies fearfully report about the conflict. Attempts to provide food, medicine and shelter, without the right safeguards and planning, can easily be exploited by the rebels and the government.

The rebels often find ways to capture humanitarian supplies through various ways and use them to provide material support to their forces. Shortly after the war broke out in 2013, the UN accused[69] both the government forces and rebels of stealing humanitarian supplies. Some rebels also recruit new fighters from refugee camps – sometimes by force. Furthermore, warring parties often try to present the humanitarian presence as a gift to their support bases in order to boost their own legitimacy. In 2019, President Salva Kiir branded the distribution of ten thousand bags of rice, which came from Chinese food assistance, as his own gift to the people.[70]

South Sudan's government has also been adept at reporting crises to humanitarian agencies. State officials have sometimes used alarming coverage of the disasters to raise fears that the country is on the brink of collapse, an outcome in which international partners are united in trying to avoid.[71] By drawing on this narrative of desperation – a ploy that's been described[72] as 'playing the fragile state card' – the government can easily manipulate foreign actors and appeal to international financial institutions for funds. In Sarah de Simone's 'Playing the "fragile state" card: The SPLM and state extraversion in South Sudan' (2018), Simone revealed that the SPLM/A political elites promptly incorporated the flow of external resources into its extravagant strategies of state-building by appropriating both material assets and discourse that played the 'fragile state' card, raising fears of governance failure and state collapse.[73]

This tactic was likely deployed to persuade the European Union to start a programme[74] that had paid $40 each to thirty thousand primary school teachers each month since April 2017. While the vulnerable people of South Sudan need and appreciate all the external help they can get in health, education and other basic needs, there is a humanitarian dilemma: how to increase accountability and sustainability during humanitarian response efforts while not risking the abandonment of people who require aid. There is a need to prevent external governments from shouldering the primary responsibilities of the local governments, which tend to be reckless with their own domestic resources as it has been the case in South Sudan.

Warring parties also benefit from the humanitarian presence by turning to straightforward extortion. While fighters have imposed semi-arbitrary charges,[75] such as 'sitting fees' and 'airport fees for relief efforts, in March 2017, the government increased work permits for foreigners a hundred times.[76] A large humanitarian presence can also benefit warring parties in more indirect ways. Although food aid keeps the price of goods down, NGOs workers also inject dollars into the market through their own spending.

South Sudan's peace architecture

There is a gap in South Sudan's peace architecture that focuses on reconciliation and power-sharing agreements among the political elites who are responsible for the war. Mediators who have tried to end South Sudan's deadly civil war have typically attempted to do so by 'buying peace'.[1] As the death toll has risen and the humanitarian situation has deteriorated, international and regional diplomats have tried to get warring parties to stop fighting by offering them a share of the national pie. For example, a regional body of the Intergovernmental Authority on Development (IGAD) mediated a peace deal that set out to establish a power-sharing compromise between President Salva Kiir and the rebel leader Riek Machar in August 2015.[2] As part of the agreement, the latter agreed to cease hostilities and fill the role of vice president. Machar had previously held this position. He remained in office until July 2013, when internal tensions in the government escalated into civil war. After twenty months of fighting and the signing of the Peace Agreement of 2015, Machar returned to his old office in April 2016.

Things quickly fell apart, and by July 2016, the fighting had resumed. Since then, more rebel groups have joined the opposition, and the conflict has evolved and spread. According to UN estimates, tens of thousands of people have been killed, around two million have been displaced, and seven million have needed humanitarian assistance. As the level of destruction continues to rise, mass corruption and the economic and political crises worsen.[3] The warring parties once again renegotiated an old peaceful settlement in 2018, which brought them back to the same government by 22 February 2020. The parties have been working on negotiating who gets what in the unity government.

Buying peace can be an appealing strategy, for it offers a short-term solution.[4] Nonetheless, there are several reasons why power-sharing agreements fail. For one, they ignore the root cause of the conflict, which can only be addressed by the IGAD finding durable solutions to the concerns of ordinary people, who are often marginalized in peace agreements. Take the South Sudan Democratic Movement, one of a dozen groups of rebels in the country, for example. Many of the armed men in it were from the Shilluk subgroup in one of South Sudan's ten states called Upper Nile and were led by John Olony. He was pushed into rebellion due to his Shilluk community's grievances related to the uneven sharing of administrative power in the Upper Nile state. Olony agreed to end hostilities with the government in 2013. He fought alongside the government forces in Malakal against the Sudan People's Liberation Movement-In Opposition (SPLM-IO), and, in return, he was given weapons and military positions in the government. That relationship ended when the original grievances remained unaddressed, and Olony returned to war against the government.

Stopping war through the power-sharing formula also means that notions of justice and accountability are often dismissed or they are included in the peace agreement, but with no commitment to implement them. The Revitalized Peace Agreement of September 2018 has four substantive chapters that directly relate to accountability and justice: Chapter II (Permanent ceasefire and transitional security arrangements), Chapter V (Transitional justice, accountability, reconciliation, and healing), Chapter III (Humanitarian assistance and reconstruction) and Chapter IV (Resource, economics and financial management). Although the agreement is beautiful on paper, there is no political will to implement such ideas. For example, when Kiir and Machar agreed to become ruling partners again in April 2016, the brutal violence that had impacted countless people over the previous two years was largely swept under the rug. In the interest of a quick peace agreement, the victims' wounds were left unhealed. Instead, they reopened in the form of revenge attacks when the conflict restarted a few months later.[5]

Buying peace alters the incentives of potential rebels, which may increase their demands and use violence as a bargaining tool. For example, David Yau Yau has played the system with great skill.[6] He rebelled in 2010 after losing elections to an MP from his area. After his first agreement with the government, David Yau was integrated into the SPLA as a major general, which was a gigantic leap for someone who never had a rank. He rebelled again in 2012. In May 2014, a peace agreement between the government and the Cobra

Faction led by David Yau Yau (classified as a terrorist in one database held at a university in the United States after a series of massacres blamed on his militia in several villages, including the killing of eighty-one civilians in Maar and Paliau) promised the 'reintegration' of the Cobra Faction forces into the national army (the SPLA then and now the SSPDF). To date, that reintegration has not taken place, but David Yau Yau himself has been reintegrated into the national army as a lieutenant general. He has since become a deputy defence minister and then a governor of a state. Citing a UN security analyst, the former Canadian ambassador estimated the strength of the Cobra Faction forces around fifteen thousand to twenty thousand. The status of a mobilized and armed force that is answerable to an individual associated would no longer be an armed youth, but rather a private army. Usually, private armies are created in a similar manner. A group of armed youth who have decided to defend their communities are usually captured by an elite who can use them to help him to ascend to power, and he will either lose control of them or they will remain as his private army. This is a legacy of peacemaking process. David Yau Yau took advantage of the dire situation of the government in 2014 and made his wish list. The government had to give him nearly everything he had asked: an autonomous mini-state within Jonglei that is only answerable to Juba directly, some militias to be promoted as generals and the incorporation of his militias into the national army. The Greater Pibor Administrative Area was created not to end conflict among the warring communities in Jonglei; it was a political strategy to drain the swamp of fish so that the main armed opposition of Dr Riek Machar could not capture that area. Of course, for political reasons, those who negotiated the deal with David Yau Yau had to say that it was meant for the peace in Jonglei. Still, such propaganda leads to a contradiction: Jonglei communities were denied participation during the negotiation process.

The power-sharing peace agreement has laid out a formula for distributing cabinet ministries among five groups: SPLM-IG (twenty cabinet positions), SPLM-IO (nine cabinet positions), SSOA (three cabinet positions), SPLM-FDs (two cabinet positions) and OPP (one cabinet position).

Unfortunately, the two parties that had used violence, namely, the SPLM-IG and the SPLM-IO, took a combined reward package that amounts to 98 per cent in terms of dollars, an estimate obtained by looking at the national budget allocated to each of the ministries. This is rewarding violence.

Ultimately, buying peace by offering rewards to warring elites benefits only those at the top, and it encourages dissatisfied actors to defect and make demands for what they believe they are due.[7] As an example, the SPLM-IO splintering in July 2016 was motivated by a feeling among leaders, such as Taban Deng and Ezekiel Lol, that they should have been offered more and could get better returns by switching sides – a move that contributed to the resumption of conflict. In another example, when the SPLM-IO chose their nine cabinet members, Gen. James Koang Chuol, a co-chair for the Joint Defense Board – a body tasked to help reintegrate the armed opposition forces into the national army as stipulated in the agreement – defected to the SPLM-IG in protest.[8] The governed masses play a minimal role in South Sudan's peace processes.

Looking to the future, the new changes in Khartoum after Al Bashir's demise have come with opportunities and risks for South Sudan. If Juba does not carefully balance its relations with Uganda and Sudan on one hand and Egypt and Ethiopia on the other, any of the disadvantaged countries could encourage a regime change in Juba. Good relations between Sudan and South Sudan is the only key to ending violent conflict in both countries. The leaders in Juba and Khartoum should pursue an ideology of 'One people, two countries'. This will assure the South Sudanese public that their independence will be protected while assuring the people in Sudan that they can benefit from the resources in South Sudan provided that South Sudan is stable. It is in the best interest of South Sudan to remain neutral on the internal issues in Ethiopia and to push for regional intervention to de-escalate conflict in Ethiopia, because if the civil war grows in Ethiopia it will spill over to South Sudan through the restive Upper Nile and Jonglei states. A successful peace architecture should also address external shocks.

Conclusion

In South Sudan, the mothers of some free thinkers pray for their sons to stay away from discussions about politics. Their relatives and best friends also reach out to discourage them from doing so. The fears these loved ones have are not without merit. Scores have died for expressing their political opinions in South Sudan. The pervasive fear that results causes many locals to blame the victims for their big mouths. A certain order has been achieved in ensuring that the masses largely remain silent. Nevertheless, systems in which the powerful elites use coercive means to minimize self-expression and force critical voices into silence or embrace collective thought are doomed to collapse, and the societies in which they operate will only move backwards.

The recurring theme in this book is the argument that the use of the politics of fear has been a successful strategy in controlling South Sudan's population and the country's conflict dynamics.

The elites' politicization of ethnic identity and the promotion of danger, insecurity, resentment and hatred has been successfully used to dominate rivals and to control populations, suggesting that manufactured group-based grievances are more potent in determining the outbreak of an ethnic conflict than contextual factors. Political fear is an instrument that the elite rule or insurgent advance use, and it is created and sustained by political leaders or activists who stand to gain from it (by achieving a specific political goal or to support their moral and political beliefs).[1] One mode of fear arises when leaders or militants define what ought to be the public's chief object of fear. It is not created out of nothing; it is based on some real threat or the memory of a threat. It is the leaders who identify a threat to the population who interpret the nature and origins of that threat and propose a method to remedy it. This idea usually presumes that the leaders and people to which they are appealing share a common identity (ethnic, regional or religious are the common identities in the Sudans) and that both groups are equally threatened by virtue of that identity. The object of fear is the prospect of an undesirable event or outcome emanating from specific objects. The other kind of fear arises from how social, political and economic hierarchies determine access to resources and power (as covered in Chapter 1), which is a fear of domination that may be triggered by corruption. Its specific function is internal intimidation and to use sanctions or the threat of sanctions to ensure that one group retains or augments its power at the expense of another. This type of fear enables one group to rule another.

It is not only powerless social actors who experience fear. Elites may fear that their privileged positions are threatened when the system they dominate undergoes a relative shift in its relationship to power. This is the fear that is common among some radical Dinka elites who tell others that if a non-Dinka takes over, then the Dinka people will not be safe.[2]

Group-based grievances are manufactured in South Sudan through a patronage system of rewarding compliant supporters at the expense of others and by the dissemination of negative messages through mass media by the influential elites.

Studies have predominantly focused on contextual factors as the dominant explanatory variables of the South Sudanese conflict. The greed versus grievance paradigm approaches the conflict from the material conditions of rebels, giving little consideration to other relevant agents, such as the ruling elite, who may manufacture grievances and exploit group identities to achieve certain aims. The current text argues that it is not the mere existence of a previous affliction that triggers ethnic conflict but the deliberate reminder by the powerful elites that the affliction existed. The neopatrimonialism paradigm highlights a limited number of contextual factors, such as historical legacies and historical grievances, that typically overlook the communal grievances or internal shocks that are constructed by the powerful elite. It instead focuses on the risk management skills of the powerful elite and pays negligible consideration to the effects of their manipulative tactics.

This book stresses that the elites' role in constructing fractionalization is significant, thereby increasing the risk of armed conflict. It uses the security dilemma framework and empirical data to show how the politics of fear reactivated the once-dormant conflicts in South Sudan in 2013 and have continued to intensify ongoing confrontation. To manage fear amongst themselves and to maintain their hopes of ensuring the political survival or demise of their rivals, the elites resorted to manipulating group identities and using fear, hatred, resentment and rage (or what Tang called 'psychological regulators').[3] The elites adopted coercive strategies to silence or radicalize in-group moderate elites and to deal with opposing out-group elites through bribery and the exploitation of internal grievances. Those who feared for their lives shifted from moderate to extremist. The loss of political influence among the moderate elites confirms what Snyder and Ballentine asserted: that during successful ethnic mobilization, the more fearful and hateful voices prevail in the marketplace of ideas.[4]

South Sudanese political elites and their associates have spread largely false narratives using social media, effectively generating fear and hatred, and these narratives have continued to aggravate South Sudan's conflict dynamics. Elites spread these narratives to discredit their rivals and their support bases and to gain or retain power and control over the state apparatus. The spread of this content amplifies the suspicion and victimization of South Sudan's different groups, triggering toxic exchanges that damage the social fabric of its society.

Manufactured group-based grievances are sometimes considered a product of the politics of fear. Thus, the politics of fear is a key process, the build-up to ethnic wars. Only by more deeply explicating ethnic mobilization can ethnic war be better understood and the potentially brutal fallout be countered. Those who are well informed – it is hoped – are less hateful and fearful of others than those who are ill-informed. They view the survival of their groups not in isolation but as if they are bound to the survival, security and prosperity of other groups.

The politics of fear can also be in many other international and political contexts and be observed in political elites who resort to manipulating economic and security concerns to legitimize their own existence, as well. When elites disagree on a fair formula for sharing power and access to resources, they resort to using political fear to outdo each other and to manipulate the masses into supporting their policies. Nevertheless, when used by multiple elites with conflicting interests, the politics of fear can generate a collective outcome that is vastly different from what any party might have expected. While one party may escalate threatening gestures, hoping that the attacked party will cooperate to avoid conflict, the other may feel that its security hinges on launching a counter-attack. This generates a security dilemma, exacerbating what may have been a dormant conflict and potentially triggering chaos.

Notes

Preface

1   John Young, 'Isolation and endurance: Riek Machar and the SPLM-IO in 2016–17' (Geneva: Small Arms Survey, 2017), available at http://www.smallarmssurveysudan.org/fileadmin/docs/working-papers/HSBA-SPLM-IO-Update-Oct-2017.pdf (accessed: 28 November 2019).
2   Author's phone exchange with an analyst who spoke with the official, 30 July 2020.
3   SBS Dinka Radio, Ajak Deng Chiengkou's interview with Paul Malong Awan, 29 July 2020, available at https://www.sbs.com.au/language/dinka/audio/paul-malong-president-salva-kiir-does-not-know-how-to-resolve-problems.
4   https://www.theeastafrican.co.ke/news/ea/South-Sudan-unity-government/4552908-5436306-12d2vt1z/index.html.
5   John Young, *South Sudan's Civil War: Violence, Insurgency and Failed Peacemaking* (London: Zed Books, 2019), Chapter 1.
6   Fixing South Sudan Show, *South Sudan Imatong State Gov Tobiolo Oromo on SPLA-Civil Relations*, 4 March 2018 (Online), available at https://www.youtube.com/watch?v=nNGsyYPRqe0 (accessed: 23 November 2019).
7   Z. R. Al Hussein, 'South Sudan: Dangerous rise in ethnic hate speech must be reined in', *United Nations Human Rights Office of the High Commissioner*, 25 October 2016 (online), available at http://www.ohchr.org/EN/NewsEvents/Pages/DisplayNews.aspx?NewsID=20757 (accessed: 14 June 2017).

1 The role of historical legacy in South Sudan's conflict dynamics

1   Alex de Waal, 'When kleptocracy becomes insolvent: Brute causes of the civil war in South Sudan', *African Affairs*, vol. 113, no. 452 (July 2014), pp. 347–69, https://doi.org/10.1093/afraf/adu028.
2   Douglas H. Johnson, *The Root Causes of Sudan's Civil Wars: Old Wars and New Wars (Expanded 3rd Edition)* (Melton: Boydell & Brewer, 2016), pp. 10–13, www.jstor.org/stable/10.7722/j.ctt1h64pck (accessed: 29 July 2020).
3   Lilian Sanderson, 'Educational development in the Southern Sudan: 1900–1948', *Sudan Notes and Records*, vol. 43, 105–17, www.jstor.org/stable/41716825 (accessed: 27 July 2020).

4   Scopas S. Poggo, *The First Sudanese Civil War: Africans, Arabs, and Israelis in the Southern Sudan, 1955–1972* (New York: Palgrave Macmillan, 2009).

5   See Regassa Bayissa, 'The derg-SPLM/A cooperation: An aspect of ethio-Sudan proxy wars', *Ethiopian Journal of the Social Sciences and Humanities*, vol. 5, no. 2 (December 2007), 19–44.

6   The author benefitted from phone conversations he had with two insiders in Juba who chose not to be cited directly, April 2013 and March 2020.

7   Lovise Aalen, 'Ethiopian state support to insurgency in Southern Sudan from 1962 to 1983: Local, regional and global connections', *Journal of Eastern African Studies*, vol. 8, no. 4 (2014), 626–41, DOI: 10.1080/17531055.2014.949403.

8   P. A. Nyaba, *The Politics of Liberation in South Sudan: An Insider's View* (Kampala: Fountain), p. 34.

9   M. A. Dor, V. Jabri, J. Spence and King's College London, 'Conflict resolution as a learning process : The sudanese people's liberation movement/army 1983-2005', dissertation (King's College London, 2017), p. 54.

10 https://www.economist.com/international/1998/03/26/sudans-rebels-change-their-spots.

11 R. Williams and D. Deng, 'The legacy of Kokora in South Sudan', Briefing Paper, Intersections of Truth, Justice and Reconciliation in South Sudan, 2015.

12 Nyaba, *The Politics of Liberation in South Sudan*, p. 52.

13 Author's phone interview with an SPLA commander in April 2019.

14 Author's exchanges with two senior SPLA officers in Juba, 2013.

15 https://www.economist.com/international/1998/03/26/sudans-rebels-change-their-spots.

16 https://www.economist.com/international/1998/03/26/sudans-rebels-change-their-spots.

17 Atem Yaak Atem, *Jungle Chronicles and Other Writings: Recollections of a South Sudanese* (Australia: Africa World Books), pp. 275–6.

18 Nyaba, *The Politics of Liberation in South Sudan*, pp. 49–50.

19 Majak D'Agoôt, 'Reappraising the effectiveness of intelligence methods of a violent non-state sovereignty: A case-study of the SPLA insurgency in the Sudan (1983–2005), Intelligence and National Security (2020), p. 6. DOI: 10.1080/02684527.2020.1866380.

20 M. L. Kuol, 'Administration of justice in (SPLA/M) liberated areas: Court cases in war-torn Southern Sudan', Research paper (1997), pp. 13–14.

21 https://www.sbs.com.au/language/english/audio/majur-nhial-i-was-arrested-seven-times-sentenced-to-death-for-three-of-those-but-i-survived-because-of-dr-john-garang.

22 Author's Facebook exchange with journalist Ngor Arol Garang, 24 July 2020.

23 Author's Facebook exchange with Bishop Moses Deng Bol, who comes from the same village as President Salva Kiir, 24 July 2020.

24 https://www.sudantribune.com/spip.php?article69612.

25 African Rights, *Food and Power in Sudan: A Critique of Humanitarianism*, p. 64 (London: African Rights, 1997).

26 John Prendergast, *Crisis Response: Humanitarian Band-Aids in Sudan and Somalia*, p. 57. (London: Pluto Press, 1997).

27 Atem, *Jungle Chronicles*, p. 321.

28 https://thesentry.org/reports/warcrimesshouldntpay/.

29 The author learned of the correct original version of the song from Mabor Manyang, Juba, 2013.

30 The author heard testimonies of victims through various phone conversations, one WhatsApp exchange and more than twenty commentaries on Facebook, June and July 2020.

31 On 16 June 2014, Rev. Nathaniel Athian Mayen, who lives in Canada, started this conversation about the atrocities committed by the SPLA and, in particular, Commander Jok Reng Magot, which has drawn a huge debate among the victims and the relatives of the said alternate commander; An interview with a chief quoted in M. A. M. Guarak, *Integration and Fragmentation of the Sudan: An African Renaissance* (United Kingdom: AuthorHouse, 2011), p. 214; Chief Dau Tor Akuei, the longest serving chief in Kongor, Twic East, was a victim of Jok Reng's violent recruitment,available at https://paanluelwel.com/2020/03/22/celebrating-the-life-of-sultan-dau-tor-akuei-the-longest-serving-chief-in-twic-east/ (accessed: 25 November 2020).

32 The author heard of this story from Machor Makuek in 1998 in Jonglei village.

33 The author learned of the story from Machor Makuek in 1998 in Jonglei village.

34 'Radio SPLA (Second Sudanese Civil War, 1988)', *YouTube*, uploaded by Jonny (14 February 2014), https://www.youtube.com/watch?v=jwYIAZzLKAU.

35 Nyaba, *The Politics of Liberation in South Sudan*, pp. 55–6.

36 Atem, *Jungle Chronicles*, p. 281.

37 'Wɛŋ Röl' himself told the author the story in 2014 in Juba.

38 https://files.eric.ed.gov/fulltext/ED495403.pdf, p. 57.

39 The author heard the anecdote from the youth leader Kuol Achiek Mach, who came from the same area as the actors mentioned, in Juba in 2014.

40 Gill Lusk 'Democracy and liberation movements: The case of the SPLA', *Middle East Report* (January/February 1992), p. 174.

41 John Young, *South Sudan's Civil War: Violence, Insurgency and Failed Peacemaking*, p. 41 (London: Zed Books, 2019).

42 Atem, *Jungle Chronicles*, p. 334.

43 Ibid., p. 336.

44 Ibid., p. 318.

45 Ibid., p. 337.

46 Ibid., p. 308.

47 Ibid., p. 285.

48 Ibid.

49 The author heard the anecdote at a dinner in Juba in April 2013 with Dr Mansour Khalid.

50 Atem, *Jungle Chronicles*, pp. 326–7.

51 Yehudit Ronen, 'Ethiopia's involvement in the Sudanese Civil War: Was it as significant as Khartoum claimed?', *Northeast African Studies*, vol. 9, no. 1 (2002), pp. 103–26, www.jstor.org/stable/41931302 (accessed: 22 July 2020).

2 Integrating existing approaches

1 Barry Posen, 'The security dilemma and ethnic conflict', *Survival*, vol. 35, no. 1 (1993), pp. 27–47.

2 Barry Posen, 'The security dilemma and ethnic conflict', in M. Brown (ed.), *Ethnic Conflict and International Security*, pp. 10–124 (Cambridge, MA: MIT Press, 1997).

3 Chaim Kaufmann, 'Possible and impossible solutions to ethnic civil wars', *International Security*, vol. 20, no. 4 (1996), pp. 146–7.

4 J. J. Mearsheimer and S. Van Evera, 'When peace means war: The partition that dare not speak its name', *The New Republic* (18 December 1995), p. 18; Chaim Kaufmann, 'Intervention in ethnic and ideological civil wars: Why one can be done and the other can't', *Security Studies*, vol. 6, no. 1 (1996), pp. 62–100.

5 Shiping Tang, 'The security dilemma and ethnic conflict: Toward a dynamic and integrative theory of ethnic conflict', *Review of International Studies*, vol. 37, no. 2 (2011), pp. 511–36.

6 Ibid.

7 Ibid.

8 Ingrid Marie Breidlid and Michael J. Arensen, 'The Nuer White Armies: Comprehending South Sudan's most infamous community defence group', in Victoria Brereton (ed.), *Informal Armies: Community Defence Groups in South Sudan's Civil War*, pp. 29–39 (Saferworld, 2017); Hilde F. Johnson, *South Sudan: The Untold Story from Independence to War*, p. 253 (London: I.B. Tauris, 2016); Mareike Schomerus and Charles Taban, 'Arrow boys, armed groups and the SPLA: Intensifying insecurity in the Western Equatorian states', in Victoria Brereton (ed.), *Informal Armies: Community Defence Groups in South Sudan's Civil War*, pp. 6–16 (Saferworld, 2017); Luka Biong and Deng Kuol, 'Dinka youth in civil war: Between cattle, community and government', in Victoria Brereton (ed.), *Informal Armies: Community Defence Groups in South Sudan's Civil War*, pp. 19–26 (Saferworld, 2017); Øystein H. Rolandsen and I. M. Breidlid, 'What is youth violence in Jonglei?', *PRIO paper* (Oslo: PRIO).

9   Ole Frahm, 'Making borders and identities in South Sudan', *Journal of Contemporary African Studies*, vol. 33, no. 2 (2015), pp. 1–17.

10 Saferworld, *Informal Armies: Community Defence Groups in South Sudan's Civil War*, p. 2, available at https://www.saferworld.org.uk/resources/ publications/1108-informal-armies-community-defence-groups-in-south-sudanas-civil-war (accessed: 24 November 2020).

11 Posen, 'The security dilemma and ethnic conflict'.

12 Paul Collier and Anke Hoeffler, 'On economic causes of civil war', *Oxford Economic Papers*, vol. 50, no. 4 (1998), pp. 563–73.

13 Paul Collier and Anke Hoeffler, 'Greed and grievance in civil war', *Oxford Economic Papers*, vol. 56, no. 4 (2004), pp. 563–95.

14 Paul Collier, Anke Hoeffler and Dominic Rohner, 'Beyond greed and grievance: Feasibility and civil war', *Oxford Economic Papers*, vol. 61, no. 1 (2009), pp. 1–27.

15 Collier and Hoeffler, 'Greed and grievance', p. 563.

16 Aleksi Ylonen, 'Grievances and the roots of insurgencies: Southern Sudan and Darfur', *Peace, Conflict and Development: An Interdisciplinary Journal*, vol. 7 (2005), pp. 99–134.

17 Justin Leach, *War and Politics in Sudan: Cultural Identities and the Challenges of the Peace Process*, pp. 223–4 (London: I.B. Tauris, 2013).

18 David Keen, 'Greed and grievance in civil war', *International Affairs*, vol. 88, no. 4 (2012), pp. 757–77.

19 Christopher Clapham (ed.), *Private Patronage and Public Power: Political Clientelism in the Modern State*, pp. 162–92 (New York: St Martin's Press, 1982).

20 Michael Bratton and Nicholas van de Walle, *Democratic Experiments in Africa: Regime Transitions in Comparative Perspective*, p. 277 (Cambridge: Cambridge University Press, 1997).

21 Paul D. Williams, *War and Conflict in Africa*, p. 55 (Cambridge: Polity, 2016).

22 Ibid.

23 Ibid.

24 Alex de Waal, *The Real Politics of the Horn of Africa: Money, War and the Business of Power*, pp. 91–6 (Cambridge: Polity, 2015).

25 Alex de Waal, 'When kleptocracy becomes insolvent: Brute causes of the civil war in South Sudan', *African Affairs*, vol. 113, no. 452 (2014), pp. 347–69.

26 Daniel Akech Thiong, email exchange with Dr Nicki Kindersley, 20 October 2019; Commentary on the political marketplace by a presenter Markus Hoehne at London School of Ecomomics, 17 October 2019.

27 Clémence Pinaud, 'South Sudan: Civil war, predation and the making of a military aristocracy', *African Affairs*, vol. 113, no. 451 (2014), pp. 192–211.

28 Philippe Le Billon, 'The political ecology of war: Natural resources and armed conflicts', *Political Geography*, vol. 20, no. 5 (2001), pp. 561–84.

29 A. K Jain, 'Corruption: A review', *Journal of Economic Surveys*, vol. 15 (2001), pp. 71–121.

30 Mohamed Suliman, 'Civil war in Sudan: The impact of ecological degradation', *Contributions in Black Studies*, vol. 15, no. 1 (1997), pp. 99–121.

31 William Reno, 'Economies of war and their transformation: Sudan and the variable impact of natural resources on conflict', *Journal of Modern African Studies*, vol. 40, no. 1 (2002), pp. 83–104.

32 Shiping Tang, Yihan Xiong and Hui Li, 'Does oil cause ethnic war? Comparing evidence from process-tracing with quantitative results', *Security Studies*, vol. 26, no. 3 (2017), pp. 359–90. doi: http://dx.doi.org/10.1080/09636412.2017.130 6392.

33 Jok Madut Jok, *Breaking Sudan: The Search for Peace* (London: Oneworld, 2017).

34 Douglas H. Johnson, 'Briefing: The crisis in South Sudan', *African Affairs*, vol. 113, no. 451 (2014), pp. 300–9.

35 Øystein H. Rolandsen, 'Another civil war in South Sudan: The failure of guerrilla government?', *Journal of Eastern African Studies*, vol. 9, no. 1 (2015), pp. 163–74.

36 Øystein H. Rolandsen and M. W. Daly, *A History of South Sudan: From Slavery to Independence* (Cambridge: Cambridge University Press, 2016).

37 Speech of the chairman and commander-in-Chief to the First SPLM/SPLA National Convention, 2 April 1994, available at https://paanluelwel.com/wp-content/uploads/2019/06/1994-chukudum-convention-opening-and-closing-remarks-of-dr-john-garang-de-mabior-1.pdf.

38 Shiping Tang, 'The onset of ethnic war: A general theory', *Sociological Theory*, vol. 33, no. 3 (2015), pp. 256–79.

39 Collier, Hoeffler and Rohner, 'Beyond greed and grievance'.

40 William Reno, 'Patronage politics and the behavior of armed groups', *Civil Wars*, vol. 9, no. 4 (2007), pp. 324–42.

41 François Debrix and Alexander D. Barder, 'Nothing to fear but fear: Governmentality and the biopolitical production of terror', *International Political Sociology*, vol. 3, no. 4 (2009), pp. 398–413.

42 Ole Frahm, *How a State Is Made: Statebuilding and Nationbuilding in South Sudan in the Light of Its African Peers*, p. 281 (Berlin: Humboldt University, 2014), available at http://edoc.hu-berlin.de/dissertationen/frahm-ole-2014-12-16/PDF/frahm.pdf (downloaded: 31 October 2019).

43 Posen, 'The security dilemma and ethnic conflict'.

44 Reno, 'Patronage politics'.

45 Barry O'Neill, 'A measure for crisis instability with an application to space-based antimissile systems', *Journal of Conflict Resolution*, vol. 31, no. 4 (1987), pp. 631–72.

46 David A. Lake and Donald Rothchild, 'Containing fear: The origins and management of ethnic conflict', *International Security*, vol. 21, no. 2 (1996), pp. 41–75.

47 *African Arguments*, 'Choosing to be a Dinka: Selecting ethnicity remains to be an elite privilege' (28 February 2013), available at http://africanarguments. org/2014/02/28/choosing-to-be-a-dinka-selecting-ethnicity-remains-an-elite-privilege/ (accessed: 2 April 2017).

48 Frahm, *How a State Is Made*, p. 282.

49 Steven Wöndu, *From Bush to Bush: Journey to Liberty in South Sudan*, pp. 244–50 (Nairobi, Kenya: Kenway, 2011).

50 Francis M. Deng, *War of Visions: Conflict of Identities in Sudan* (Washington, DC: Brookings Institution, 1995).

51 Frahm, *How a State Is Made*, p. 282.

52 https://theguardian.com/science/head-quarters/2018/mar/27/ how-social-science-can-help-us-understand-moral-tribalism-in-politics.

53 P. Paglia, 'Ethnicity and tribalism: Are these the root causes of the Sudanese civil conflicts? African conflicts and the role of ethnicity: A case study of Sudan', *Africa Economic Analysis*, p. 36, available at https://citeseerx.ist.psu.edu/ viewdoc/download?doi=10.1.1.553.8793&rep=rep1&type=pdf (accessed: 24 November 2020).

54 Ibid.

55 Johnson, 'Briefing: The crisis in South Sudan'.

56 Michael J. Arensen, and Ingrid Marie Breidlid, '"Anyone who can carry a gun can go": The role of the white army in the current conflict in South Sudan', *PRIO Paper* (Oslo: PRIO).

57 Michael J. Arensen and Ingrid Marie Breidlid, 'Demystifying the white army: Nuer armed civilians' involvement in the South Sudanese crisis', *Conflict Trends*, vol. 3 (2014), pp. 32–9.

58 Tang, 'The onset of ethnic war'.

59 Ann Laudati, 'Victims of discourse: Mobilizing narratives of fear and insecurity in post-conflict South Sudan – the case of Jonglei State', *African Geographical Review*, vol. 30, no. 1 (2011), p. 17.

60 Arensen and Breidlid, 'Demystifying the white army'.

61 Alex de Waal, Interviewed for *CFR*, 14 September 2016, available at http://www. cfr.org/south- sudan/understanding-roots-conflict-south-sudan/p38298?cid=nlc-dailybrief-daily_news_brief--link29-20160922&sp_mid=52363867&sp_ rid=c2NvbGxtYW5AY2ZyLm9yZwS2> (accessed: 26 March 2017).

62 Arensen and Breidlid, 'Demystifying the white army'.

63 Syed Mansoob Murshed and Mohammad Zulfan Tadjoeddin, 'Revisiting the greed and grievance explanations for violent internal conflict', *Journal of International Development*, vol. 21, no. 1 (2009), pp. 87–111.

64 Tang, 'The onset of ethnic war'.

3 Internal dynamics of South Sudan's ruling elite

1 Nyith Chol, the SPLM commissar, explained the Nuer's definition of government on Radio SPLA's Nuer Language Programme in 1986.

2 Majak D'Agoôt, 'Taming the dominant gun class in South Sudan', Special Report No. 4: Envisioning A Stable South Sudan (29 May 2018), available at https://africacenter.org/spotlight/taming-the-dominant-gun-class-in-south-sudan/.

3 Daniel Akech Thiong, 'How the politics of fear generated chaos in South Sudan', *African Affairs*, vol. 117, no. 469 (October 2018), pp. 613–35, https://doi.org/10.1093/afraf/ady031.

4 Republic of South Sudan, *Transitional Constitution of the Republic of South Sudan. Article 101/105* (2011), available at https://www.ilo.org/dyn/natlex/docs/MONOGRAPH/90704/116697/F762589088/SSD90704%202011C.pdf (accessed: 19 May 2018).

5 *Sudan Tribune*, 'Kiir threatens to dissolve parliament unless it supports Wani Igga's appointment' (24 August 2013), available at http://www.sudantribune.com/spip.php?article47776 (accessed: 14 June 2017).

6 'Crisis instability is the danger of war due to each side's fear that the other will attack'. See Barry O'Neill, 'A measure for crisis instability with an application to space-based antimissile systems', *Journal of Conflict Resolution*, vol. 31, no. 4 (1987), pp. 631–72; Alex de Waal, 'When kleptocracy becomes insolvent: Brute causes of the civil war in South Sudan', *African Affairs*, vol. 113, no. 452 (2014), pp. 347–69.

7 Salve Kiir, Interview with President Salva Kiir, interview by Jeff Koinange for *KTN News Kenya*, 3 August 2016 (online), available at https://www.youtube.com/watch?v=hOQEyFk-4do (accessed: 17 March 2017).

8 François Debrix and Alexander Barder, 'Nothing to fear but fear: Governmentality and the biopolitical production of terror', *International Political Sociology*, vol. 3, no. 4 (2009), pp. 398–413.

9 Cassandra Vinograd, 'The revenge of Salva Kiir: South Sudan's president has outmaneuvered his opponents politically. Now he has carte blanche to crush them militarily', 2 January 2017, 2.44 am, https://foreignpolicy.com/2017/01/02/the-revenge-of-salva-kiir-south-sudan-genocide-ethnic-cleansing/.

10 John Young, 'Isolation and endurance: Riek Machar and the SPLM-IO in 2016–2017' (Switzerland: Small Arms Survey, 2017), available at http://www.smallarmssurveysudan.org/fileadmin/docs/working-papers/HSBA-SPLM-IO-Update-Oct-2017.pdf (accessed: 28 November 2019).

11 Jacob T. Levy, 'Authoritarianism and Post-Truth Politics', Niskanen Center (30 November 2016), available at https://www.niskanencenter.org/authoritarianism-post-truth-politics/ (accessed: 28 November 2019).

12 Ajak Deng Chiengkou's interview with Telar Deng, 30 December 2014, Nairobi, available at https://www.sbs.com.au/language/english/audio/president-kiir-was-responsible-for-every-decision-but-not-me-first-exclusive-interview-with-telar-deng-ring.

13 Nicholas Coghlan, who was a Canadian ambassador to South Sudan during the conflict, decried this as a big mistake in his 6 November 2019 tweet.

14 https://www.sudantribune.com/spip.php?article46496.

15 *National Conference of SPLA Board – President's Salva Kiir Speech* (15 December 2013), available at https://www.youtube.com/watch?v=5y3bp6Oehis (accessed: 28 November 2019).

16 Ibid.

17 John Young, *South Sudan's Civil War: Violence, Insurgency and Failed Peacemaking*, p. 112 (London: Zed Books, 2019).

18 Young, 'Isolation and endurance'.

19 Peter A. Nyaba, *South Sudan: Elites, Ethnicity, Endless Wars and the Stunted State* (Dar es Salaam, Tanzania: Mkuki na Nyota, 2019).

20 https://radiopublic.com/sbs-dinka-sbs-dinka-Wo3bvr/s1!903cc.

21 Thiong, 'How the politics of fear generated chaos in South Sudan'.

22 Lesley A. Warner, 'The disintegration of the military integration process stability in South Sudan (2006–2013)', *Stability: International Journal of Security & Development*, vol. 5, no. 1 (2016), pp. 1–20, doi: http://dx.doi.org/10.5334/sta.460.

23 Ibid.

24 Author's WhatsApp conversation with two former SPLA commanders, April 2020

25 Lauren Hutton, *Prolonging the Agony of UNMISS: The Implementation Challenges of a New Mandate during a Civil War* (Clingendael: Netherlands Institute of International Relations, 2014), available at http://www.clingendael.nl/sites/default/files/Prolonging%20the%20agony%20of%20 UNMISS%20-%20 Lauren%20Hutton.pdf (accessed: 26 September 2019).

26 Yuki Yoshida, 'Interethnic conflict in Jonglei State, South Sudan: Emerging ethnic hatred between the Lou Nuer and the Murle', *African Journal on Conflict Resolution*, vol. 13, no. 2 (2013), p. 39.

27 Jeremy Astill-Brown, 'South Sudan's Slide into Conflict: Revisiting the Past and Reassessing Partnerships' (2014), p. 8, available at https://www.chathamhouse.org/sites/default/files/field/field_document/20141203SouthSudan ConflictAstillBrown.pdf.

28 Michael Johnston, 'The political consequences of corruption: A reassessment', *Comparative Politics*, vol. 18, no. 4 (1996), pp. 459–77; p. 464.

29 The author was in the audience as he was consulting, at the time, with the Military Pension Fund.

30 *Sudan Tribune*, 'South Sudan's Kiir accuses army of corruption' (20 September 2013), available at http://www.sudantribune.com/spip.php?article48115.

31 O. D. Ajak, interviewed by Ajak Deng Chiengkou for *SBS Dinka Radio* (4 May 2015) available at https://www.sbs.com.au/language/english/audio/general-oyay-president-kiir-was-always-suspicious-of-spla (accessed: 24 November 2020).

32 https://paanluelwel.com/2014/02/09/edward-lino-there-was-no-coup-in-juba/.

33 The question was attributed to Amb. Chol Tong Mayay, and the answer was attributed to Gen. Gier Chuang by the interlocutor who recounted the story to the author in Juba, February 2018.

34 Author's WhatsApp interview with former minister in the national government of Sudan, September 2019.

35 Author's WhatsApp interview with SPLA general, 23 September 2019.

36 Author's WhatsApp interview and phone conversation with former government official, 22 September 2019.

37 Author's WhatsApp interview with SPLA general, September 2019.

38 Ingrid Marie Breidlid and Michael J. Arensen, 'The Nuer White Armies: Comprehending South Sudan's most infamous community defence group', in Victoria Brereton (ed.), *Informal Armies: Community Defence Groups in South Sudan's Civil War*, pp. 29–39 (Saferworld, 2017).

39 Mareike Schomerus and Charles Taban, 'Arrow boys, armed groups and the SPLA: Intensifying insecurity in the Western Equatorian states' in Victoria Brereton (ed.), *Informal Armies: Community Defence Groups in South Sudan's Civil War*, pp. 6–16 (Saferworld, 2017).

40 Small Arms Survey, *The Crisis in South Sudan: A Podcast with HSBA Consultant Joshua Craze* [Podcast]. 19 May 2014.

41 Luka Biong Deng Kuol, 'Dinka youth in civil war: Between cattle, community and government', in Victoria Brereton (ed.), *Informal Armies: Community Defence Groups in South Sudan's Civil War*, pp. 19–26 (Saferworld, 2017).

42 Øystein H. Rolandsen and I. M. Breidlid, 'What is Youth Violence in Jonglei', *PRIO Paper* (Oslo: Prio).

43 *Sudan Tribune*, 'Dinka Bor attack on Murle community leaves dozens dead, says Pibor commissioner' (8 February 2012), available at http://www.sudantribune.com/Dinka-Bor-attack-on-Murle,41548 (accessed: 20 March 2017).

44 L. Baguoot (2017), available at http://www.facebook.com (accessed: 14 March 2017).

45 D. de Manyang (2017), available at http://www.facebook.com (accessed: 14 March 2017).

46 Ole Frahm, 'Making borders and identities in South Sudan', *Journal of Contemporary African Studies*, vol. 33, no. 2 (2015), pp. 1–17.

47 Jok Madut Jok, 'Introduction: The state, security and community defence groups in South Sudan', in Victoria Brereton (ed.), *Informal Armies: Community Defence Groups in South Sudan's Civil War*, pp. 2–4 (Saferworld, 2017).

48 Barry Posen, 'The security dilemma and ethnic conflict', *Survival*, vol. 35 (1993), pp. 27–47.

49 Hilde Johnson *South Sudan: The Untold Story from Independence to War*, pp. 94–5 (London: I.B. Tauris, 2016).

50 Ole Frahm, *How a State Is Made: Statebuilding and Nationbuilding in South Sudan in the Light of Its African Peers*, p. 281 (Berlin: Humboldt University, 2014), available at http://edoc.hu-berlin.de/dissertationen/frahm-ole-2014-12-16/PDF/frahm.pdf (downloaded: 31 October 2019).

51 Ibid.

52 Abraham Awolich and Zacharia Ding Akol, 'The SPLM leadership contest: An opportunity for change or a crisis of governance?' *SUDD Institute policy brief* (2013); John Young, *The Fate of Sudan: Origins and Consequences of a Flawed Peace Process* (London: Zed Books, 2012).

53 T. Deng (2018), available at http://www.facebook.com (accessed: 19 April 2018).

54 Majak D'Agoôt, 'Assessing the utility of risk management theory in the governance of new states: Lessons from South Sudan', *Journal of Risk Research*, vol. 203, no. 1 (2019), pp. 1–17, doi: 10.1080/13669877.2019.1569089.

55 Ibid.

56 Ibid.

57 Radio Tamazuj, *Greater Bahr el-Ghazal Governors Pledge Support to Kiir in Next Election* (2013), available at https://radiotamazuj.org/en/news/article/greater-bahr-el-ghazal-governors-pledge-support-to-kiir-in-next-election (accessed: 18 June 2017).

58 Author's email to Mawut Reech, 20 March 2017.

59 Øystein H. Rolandsen, 'Another civil war in South Sudan: The failure of Guerrilla Government?', *Journal of Eastern African Studies*, vol. 9, no. 1 (2015), p. 171.

60 D'Agoôt, 'Assessing the utility of risk management theory', p. 10.

61 Rolandsen, Another civil war in South Sudan, p. 170.

62 Nicholas Coghlan, *Collapse of a Country: A Diplomat's Memoir of South Sudan*, pp. 117–18 (Montreal: McGill-Queens University Press, 2017).

63 Matthew R. Bailey and Peter D. Balsam, Memory reconsolidation: Time to change your mind, *Current Biology*, vol. 23, no. 6 (2013), pp. 243–5.

64 Edward Abyei Lino, 'Looking at ourselves the way we know not!' (Southsudannation.com), available at http://www.southsudannation.com/looking-at-ourselves-the-way-we-know-not/.

65 Shiping Tang, 'The security dilemma and ethnic conflict: Toward a dynamic and integrative theory of ethnic conflict', *Review of International Studies*, vol. 37, no. 2 (2011), pp. 511–36.

66 Ibid.

67 Radio Tamazuj, *Foreign Minister Says He Was Being 'Humiliated' in Juba* (2018), available at https://radiotamazuj.org/en/news/article/foreign-minister-says-he-was-being-humiliated-in-juba (accessed: 21 May 2018).

68 Eye Radio, *Gov't Reacts to Malong's Move* (2018), available at http://www.eyeradio.org/govt-reacts-malongs- move/ (ccessed: 29 May 2018).

69 Radio Tamazuj, *Foreign Minister Says He Was Being 'Humiliated' in Juba*.

70 Shiping Tang, 'Fear in international politics: Two positions', *International Studies Review*, vol. 10, no. 3 (2008), pp. 451–71.

71 Ibid.

72 Hélène Fatima Idris, *Modern Developments in the Dinka language; Göteborg African Informal Series – No 3*, p. 21 (Göteborg: Department of Oriental and African Languages, 2004).

73 Author's telephone conversation with Dr Majak D'Agoot, 1 October 2016.

74 Johnson, *South Sudan*, pp. 94–5.

75 *Sudan Tribune*, 'S. Sudanese rebels establish military command, create 21 states' (31 December 2014), available at http://www.sudantribune.com/spip.php?article53509 (accessed: 20 March 2017).

76 C. J. Jok (2019), 19 January, available at http://www.facebook.com (accessed: 19 January 2019).

77 Douglas H. Johnson, 'Why Abyei matters: The breaking point of Sudan's comprehensive peace agreement', *African Affairs*, vol. 107, no. 426 (2008), pp. 1–19.

78 Radio Tamazuj, *President Kiir's Legal Advisor Redraws Red Line on Interim Government* (2014), available at https://radiotamazuj.org/en/news/article/president-kiir-s-legal-advisor-redraws-red-line-on-interim-government (accessed: 14 June 2017).

79 Ibid.

80 *Sudan Tribune*, S. Sudan army chief rejects IGAD power-sharing proposal (30 June 2015), available at http://sudantribune.com/spip.php?article55883 (accessed: 14 June 2017).

81 Radio Tamazuj, *Makuei Slams Pagan Amum for Signing IGAD Document* (2015), available at https://radiotamazuj.org/en/news/article/makuei-slams-pagan-amum-for-signing-igad-document (accessed: 14 June 2017).

82 Radio Tamazuj, *South Sudan Broadcast Minister Instructs Gov't Media to Stop War Propaganda* (2015), available at: https://radiotamazuj.org/en/news/article/south-sudan-broadcast-minister-instructs-govt-media-to-stop-war-propaganda (accessed: 14 June 2017).

83 Radio Tamazuj, *Kiir Says He Fears SPLM Will Turn Against Him After Peace* (2015), available at https://radiotamazuj.org/en/news/article/kiir-says-he-fears-splm-will-turn-against-him-after-peace (accessed: 14 June 2017).

84 Radio Tamazuj, *Dinka Council of Elders Says No Short Cut to Presidency* (2017), available at https://radiotamazuj.org/en/news/article/dinka-council-of-elde0rs-says-no-short-cut-to-presidency (accessed: 14 June 2017).

85 Radio Tamazuj, *Dinka Council of Elders Warns War Over Additional UNMISS Troops* (2016), available at https://radiotamazuj.org/en/news/article/dinka-council-of-elders-warns-war-over-additional-unmiss-troops (accessed: 14 June 2017).

86 Ibid.

87 United Nations Panel of Experts on South Sudan, *South Sudan's UN Panel of Experts Report* (2016).

88 Edward Glaeser, 'The political economy of hatred', *Quarterly Journal of Economics*, vol. 120, no. 1 (2005), pp. 45–86.

89 Shiping Tang, 'The onset of ethnic war: A general theory', *Sociological Theory*, vol. 33, no. 3 (2015), pp. 256–79.

90 https://www.zehabesha.com/south-sudan-rebels-seize-pagak-as-government-troops-flee-to-ethiopia/.

91 https://www.nyamile.com/2019/09/22/spla-io-commander-abandons-machar-over-deliberate-attacks-against-gajaak/.

92 *Sudan Tribune, Greater Equatoria demands federal system in South Sudan* (17 April 2011), available at http://www.sudantribune.com/spip.php?iframe&page=imprimable&id_article=38608 (accessed: 14 June 2017).

93 Ibid.

94 Malakal Post, 'Lt. Gen. Thomas Cirillo Swaka's resignation letter', *Malakal Post* (11 February 2017); Radio Tamazuj *Gen. Thomas Cirillo Declares New Rebel Group* (2017), available at https://radiotamazuj.org/en/news/article/gen-thomas-cirillo-declares-new-rebel-group (accessed: 29 May 2018).

95 http://www.smallarmssurveysudan.org/fileadmin/docs/archive/south-sudan/conflict-crisis-2013–15/HSBA-Conflict-in-WES-July-2016.pdf.

96 Small Arms Survey, *David Yau Yau's Rebellion* (2013), available at http://www.smallarmssurveysudan.org/fileadmin/docs/facts-figures/south-sudan/armed-groups/southern-dissident-militias/HSBA-Armed-Groups-Yau-Yau.pdf (accessed: 25 March 2017).

97 Author's Facebook message to Kuir Garang, May 2016.

98 Author's email to Ngor Deng, 19 March 2017; Author's email to Mawut Reech, 20 March 2017.

99 Author's email to John Ghereng Maduk, 19 March 2017.

100 Saferworld, *Informal Armies: Community Defense Groups in South Sudan's Civil War*, available at https://www.saferworld.org.uk/resources/publications/1108-informal-armies-community-defence-groups-in-south-sudanas-civil-war (accessed: 25 November 2020).

101 Author's Facebook message to Dr August Ting, an assistant professor at the university of Juba and a researcher with the Sudd Institute, 13 April 2017.

102 Author's email to Mawut Reech, 20 March 2017.

103 Author's email to Mawut Reech, 20 March 2017; Author's Facebook message to Aduei Riak, 14 March 2017.

104 Author's email to John Ghereng Maduk, 19 March 2017.

105 Cherry Leonardi, '"Liberation" or capture: Youth in between "hakuma", and "home" during civil war and its aftermath in Southern Sudan', *African Affairs*, vol. 106, no. 424 (2007), pp. 391–412.

106 Mark Irving Lichbach, 'Deterrence or escalation? The puzzle of aggregate studies of repression and dissent', *Journal of Conflict Resolution*, vol. 31, no. 2 (1987), pp. 266–97.

107 International Crisis Group, *South Sudan: A civil war by any other name.* (Belgium: International Crisis Group, 2014); John Young, *A fractious rebellion: Inside the SPLM-IO* (Switzerland: Small Arms Survey, 2015).

108 Tang, 'Security dilemma'.

109 Ibid.

110 Michael D. Makowsky and Jared Rubin, 'An agent-based model of centralized institutions, social network technology, and revolution', *PLoS ONE*, vol. 8, no. 11 (2013), available at https://doi.org/10.1371/journal.pone.0080380.

111 Enough Project, *Violent kleptocracies: How they're destroying parts of Africa and how they can be dismantled* (2016), available at: http://enoughproject.org/reports/violent-kleptocracies-how-theyre-destroying-partsafrica-and-how-they-can-be-dismantled (accessed: 16 May 2018).

112 de Waal, 'When kleptocracy becomes insolvent'.

113 D. A. Kuol, Interview by Mading Ngor for *Fixing South Sudan: Ideas for the new nation*, Dolku Media (30 November 2018), available at https://www.youtube.com/watch?v=_U_pcSQWRMk (accessed: 25 November 2020).

114 Author's phone interview with an SPLM-IO official who was a member of parliament before the conflict in 2013, 2019.

115 Author's Facebook exchange with a social media commentator, Mawut Reech, 2018.

116 Author's in person exchanges with someone close to the president, Juba, December 2013.

117 Ibid.

118 D. A. Kuol, interview by Mading Ngor.

4 Governing through fearful means

1 Author's conversation with a government official, who has expressed not to be named, Juba, April 2013.

2 The author learned of this anecdote in 2018 in Kampala from a former political detainee.

3 *African Arguments*, 'Blessed rain and old faces: Pa'gan Amum's return to the SPLM – by James Copnall in Juba' (24 June 2015), available at https://africanarguments.org/2015/06/24/blessed-rain-and-old-faces-pagan-amums-return-to-the-splm-by-james-copnall-in-juba/.

4 Radio Tamazuj, 'Foreign minister says he was being 'humiliated' in Juba' (2018), available at https://radiotamazuj.org/en/news/article/foreign-minister-says-he-was-being-humiliated-in-juba.

5 Ibid.

6 Ibid.

7 Radio Tamazuj, 'Kiir regrets sparing lives of Machar, Pagan's group' (2018), Available at https://radiotamazuj.org/en/news/article/kiir-regrets-sparing-lives-of-machar-pagan-group.

8 https://www.voanews.com/a/south-sudan-kiir-blames-outsiders-for-peace-deal-inaction/4777327.html.

9 *Aljazeera*, 'At least eight students killed in Nairobi school fire' (2 September 2017), available at https://www.aljazeera.com/news/2017/9/2/at-least-eight-students-killed-in-nairobi-school-fire.

10 SBS Dinka Radio, 'Paul Malong: "Doctors need my DNA in order to identify the body of my daughter in Kenya but the presidency refused as per now"' (2017), available at https://www.sbs.com.au/language/english/audio/paul-malong-doctors-need-my-dna-in-order-to-identify-the-body-of-my-daughter-in-kenya-but-the-presidency-refused-as-per-now.

11 Malong Awan, 29 July 2020, https://www.sbs.com.au/language/dinka/audio/ paul-malong-president-salva-kiir-does-not-know-how-to-resolve-problems.

12 A. Acol de Dut (2018), available at http://www.facebook.com (accessed: 25 October 2018).

13 Author's exchanges with a number of former associates of both Dr Machar and Gen. Simon Kun Puoch in Juba in 2013 and on WhatsApp in 2019.

14 https://www.refworld.org/pdfid/57469cf64.pdf; Author's email to Konyen Nakuwa, 10 February 2016.

15 Daniel Akech Thiong, 'How the politics of fear generated chaos in South Sudan', *African Affairs*, vol. 117, no. 469 (October 2018).

16 docs/archive/south-sudan/conflict-crisis-2013–15/HSBA-Conflict-in-WES-July-2016.pdf.

17 http://www.smallarmssurveysudan.org/fileadmin/docs/archive/south-sudan/ conflict-crisis-2013-15/HSBA-Conflict-in-WES-July-2016.pdf (accessed: 25 November 2020).

18 http://www.smallarmssurveysudan.org/fileadmin/docs/reports/HSBA-Report-South-Sudan-Shilluk.pdf, p. 32.

19 Ibid., p. 30.

20 Ibid.

21 Ibid., p. 47.

22 https://www.state.gov/reports/2019-country-reports-on-human-rights-practices/ south-sudan/.

23 The author learned of this story from a friend who had spoken with the victim while he was on his way from Loki to Eldoret in September 2018.

24 https://www.hrw.org/news/2019/04/30/south-sudan-investigate-apparent-2017-killingactivists#; https://www.hrw.org/report/2020/12/14/ what-crime-was-i-paying/abuses-south-sudans-national-security-service.

25 https://eyeradio.org/evidence-of-the-sentry-corruption-expose-is-weak-kiirs-office/; https://www.reuters.com/article/us-southsudan-politics-idUSKCN11N06H.

26 A. Kalei (2018), available at http://www.facebook.com (accessed: 13 September 2018).

27 This section relies on discussions the author had with a number of civil society leaders and activists in 2015, 2016 and 2017 in Nairobi, Juba and skype, WhatsApp and phone.

28 http://www.unesco.org/new/en/communication-and-information/ freedom-of-expression/safety-of-journalists/beyond-the-statistics/ isaiah-diing-abraham-chan-awuol/.

29 https://www.deseret.com/2015/8/5/20485113/south-sudan-shutters-2-newspapers-in-apparent-crackdown.

5 Fear of domination triggered by corruption

1 Alex de Waal, 'When kleptocracy becomes insolvent: Brute causes of the civil war in South Sudan', *African Affairs*, vol. 113, no. 452 (July 2014), pp. 347–69, available at https://doi.org/10.1093/afraf/adu028.

2 https://thesentry.org/reports/warcrimesshouldntpay/; https://www.globalwitness. org/en/campaigns/south-sudan/capture-on-the-nile/.

3 Atem Yaak Atem, *Jungle Chronicles and Other Writings: Recollections of a South Sudanese*, p. 321. (Australia: Africa World Books, 2017).

4 https://sudantribune.com/spip.php?article26320.

5 Ibid.

6 Ibid.

7 Ibid.

8 Author's WhatsApp exchange with former governor of Lakes State, Chol Tong, 25 October 2020.

9 de Waal, 'When kleptocracy becomes insolvent'.

10 Camilla Orjuela, 'Corruption and identity politics in divided societies', *Third World Quarterly*, vol. 35, no. 5 (2014), 753–69, DOI: 10.1080/01436597.2014.921426.

11 Ibid.

12 http://www.smallarmssurveysudan.org/fileadmin/docs/briefing-papers/HSBA-BP-Fertit.pdf.

13 Andrei Shleifer and Robert W. Vishny, 'Corruption', *The Quarterly Journal of Economics*, vol. 108, no. 3 (1993), pp. 599–617; Susan Rose-Ackerman, '*Corruption and Government*' (Cambridge: Cambridge University Press, 1999); Daron Acemoglu, 'Root causes: A historical approach to assessing the role of institutions in economic development', *Finance & Development*, vol. 40 (2003), pp. 27–30.

14 Shleifer and Vishny, 'Corruption'.

15 Ourania Dimakou, 'Bureaucratic corruption and the dynamic interaction between monetary and fiscal policy', *European Journal of Political Economy*, vol. 40 (2015), pp. 57–78.

16 Alejandro Gaviria, 'Assessing the effects of corruption and crime on firm performance: Evidence from Latin America', *Emerging Markets Review*, vol. 3 (2002), pp. 245–68.

17 A. K Jain, 'Corruption: A review', *Journal of Economic Surveys*, vol. 15 (2001), pp. 71–121.

18 Rajeev K. Goel and Michael A. Nelson, 'Causes of corruption: History, geography and government', *Journal of Policy Modeling*, vol. 32 (2010), pp. 433–47.

19 Philippe Le Billon, 'Buying peace or fueling war: The role of corruption in armed conflicts', *Journal of International Development*, vol. 15, no. 4 (2003), pp. 413–26.

20 Orjuela, 'Corruption and identity politics in divided societies'.

21 http://www.smallarmssurveysudan.org/fileadmin/docs/reports/HSBA-Report-South-Sudan-Shilluk.pdf.

22 Ibid.

23 http://www.smallarmssurveysudan.org/fileadmin/docs/facts-figures/south-sudan/armed-groups/southern-dissident-militias/HSBA-Armed-Groups-Yau-Yau.pdf; http://www.smallarmssurveysudan.org/fileadmin/docs/working-papers/HSBA-WP42-Unity-Dec-2016.pdf.

24 Orjuela, 'Corruption and identity politics in divided societies'.

25 Natascha S. Neudorfer and Ulrike G. Theuerkauf, 'Buying war not peace: The influence of corruption on the risk of ethnic war', *Comparative Political Studies*, vol. 47, no. 13 (2014), pp. 1856–86.

26 Alberto Alesinaa and George-Marios Angeletos, 'Corruption, inequality, and fairness', *Journal of Monetary Economics*, vol. 52 (2005), pp. 1227–44.

27 Steven Wöndu, *From Bush to Bush: Journey to Liberty in South Sudan*, pp. 244–50 (Nairobi, Kenya: Kenway, 2011).

28 Ann Laudati, 'Victims of discourse: Mobilizing narratives of fear and insecurity in post-conflict South Sudan – the case of Jonglei State', *African Geographical Review*, vol. 30, no. 1 (2011), p. 17.

29 *Sudan Tribune*, 'SPLA top generals asked by anti-corruption to declare their assets' (27 February 2012), available at http://www.sudantribune.com/spip.php?article41727 (accessed: 22 March 2015).

30 Ajak Deng Chiengkou, Interview with former minister of finance Arthur Akuien Chol (2019), available at https://www.sbs.com.au/language/english/audio/i-was-controlling-money-but-they-needed-me-out-south-sudanese-former-minister-of-finance-speaks (accessed: 28 November 2019).

31 South Sudan News Agency, 'The *dura saga* fat cats' (2013), available at https://paanluelwel.com/2013/01/06/the-dura-saga-fat-cats/ (accessed: 6 April 2015).

32 *Sudan Tribune*, S. Sudan: billions lost in fake contracts, inflated payrolls (17 July 2012), available at http://www.sudantribune.com/spip.php?article43293 (accessed: 7 April 2015).

33 http://www.mofep-grss.org/wp-content/uploads/2019/07/Budget-Speech-draft-FY-19-20-Final.pdf.

34 Yurendra Basnett and James Alic Garang, Exiting the cycle of conflict in South Sudan: Diversifying trade for sustained and inclusive prosperity, Research paper, ODI (2014), available at http://www.odi.org/sites/odi.org.uk/files/odi-assets/publications-opinion-files/9605.pdf.

35 Media sources incorrectly listed the figure borrowed as $5 billion. Charlton Doki, 'Civil servants unpaid as S. Sudan struggles to repay loans' (21 November 2013), available at: http://www.voanews.com/content/south-sudan-civil-service-foreign-loans-salaries/1795044.html (accessed: 7 April 2015).

36 Ministry of Finance, email to the media, 25 November 2013.

37 *Sudan Tribune*, 'S. Sudan silent on $4.5bn loan obtained after oil shutdown' (22 November 2013), available at http://www.sudantribune.com/spip.php?article48903 (accessed: 7 April 2015).

38 Ibid.

39 The official exchange rate is $1 = 2.9 SSP, with the unofficial rate increasing to $1 = 5 SSP in late 2014 and to as high as 1 = 17.2 SSP in August 2015.

40 http://www.wsj.com/articles/south-sudans-debt-rises-as-oil-ebbs-1407280169.

41 Ibid.

42 *Sudan Tribune* 'S. Sudan justice minister acknowledges graft in government' (16 November 2015), available at http://www.sudantribune.com/spip.php?article57062 (accessed: 17 November 2015).

43 https://www.state.gov/e/eb/rls/othr/ics/investmentclimatestatements/index.htm?dlid=281466&year=2018#wrapper.

44 https://www.youtube.com/watch?v=SDfTfPdJoCY.

45 Author's WhatsApp conversation with Indian-Ugandan businessman, 26 November 2018.

46 Author's WhatsApp conversation with Nilepet official, 3 December 2018.

47 Author's WhatsApp conversation with former Ministry of Petroleum official, 4 December 2018.

48 Author's telephone conversation with Indian-Ugandan businessman, 4 December 2018.

49 Author's WhatsApp conversation with economist/consultant to the Ministry of Finance, 3 December 2018.

50 Author's WhatsApp conversation with Nilepet director, 27 November 2018.

51 Author's email to Indian-Ugandan businessman, 3 December 2018.

52 Author's conversation with Nilepet director, 26 November 2018.

53 Daniel Akech Thiong, 'How contracts are inflated in South Sudan' (2014), available at http://www.gurtong.net/ECM/Editorial/tabid/124/ctl/ArticleView/mid/519/articleId/15309/How-Contracts-Are-Inflated-In-South-Sudan.aspx (accessed: 7 April 2015).

54 Nimule is the border post on the road to Uganda.

55 *Sudan Tribune*, '*South Sudan's Kiir accuses army of corruption*' (20 September 2017), available at http://www.sudantribune.com/spip.php?article48115 (accessed: 22 March 2015).

56 One of the two traders told the story to the author in Juba, June 2014.

57 M. D Rwakaringi, 'South Sudan to probe 'dura saga' grain swindle' (2013), available at https://www.voanews.com/africa/south-sudan-probe-dura-saga-grain-swindle (accessed: 24 November 2020).

58 Giorgio D'Agostino, John Paul Dunne and Luca Pieroni, 'Corruption and growth in Africa', *European Journal of Political Economy*, vol. 43 (2016), pp. 71–88.

59 Christopher Adam and Lee Crawfurd, L *Exchange Rate Options for South Sudan* (2012), available at http://users.ox.ac.uk/~cadam/pdfs/Adam_Crawfurd_Exchange%20Rate%20Options%20for%20South%20Sudan_Version2_1_May_2012.pdf (accessed: 25 November 2020).

60 *Sudan Tribune*, 'Qatar to loan South Sudan $100 million: Official' (10 May 2012), available at http://www.sudantribune.com/spip.php?article42555.

61 *Development Policy Forum discussion on the LCs saga* (2015).

62 Bona Malwal, *Sudan and South Sudan: From One to Two*, pp. 198–9 (Oxford: Palgrave Macmillan, 2014).

63 The office manager ran out of ink and had to ask the author to print the document, which is how the author obtained these data in April 2014.

64 Radio Tamazuj, 'South Sudanese chief negotiator paid "allowance"' of $2000 per day' (2014), available at https://radiotamazuj.org/en/news/article/south-sudanese-chief-negotiator-paid-allowance-of-2000-per-day#:~:text=Multiple%20sources%20say%20that%20chief,South%20Sudanese%20cabinet%20and%2-0presidency (accessed: 26 November 2020).

65 H. Holland, 'South Sudan officials have stolen $4 billion: President' (2012), available at https://www.reuters.com/article/us-southsudan-corruption/south-sudan-officials-have-stolen-4-billion-president-idUSBRE8530QI20120604 (accessed: 26 November 2020).

66 *Sudan Tribune*, 'S. Sudan police to arrest officials over cash stolen from presidency' (2 April 2013), available at http://www.sudantribune.com/spip.php?article46054 (accessed: 25 March 2015).

67 Reuters, 'South Sudan officials have stolen $4 bln: president' (2012), available at https://af.reuters.com/article/topNews/idAFJOE85304X20120604?sp=true (accessed: 27 November 2019).

68 Radio Tamazuj, 'Kiir laments corruption: "I got people who know how to eat"' (2018), available at https://radiotamazuj.org/en/news/article/kiir-laments-corruption-i-got-people-who-know-how-to-eat (accessed: 27 November 2019).

69 Ibid.

70 *Sudan Tribune*, 'South Sudan president suspends two ministers for corruption probe' (18 June 2013), available at http://www.sudantribune.com/spip.php?article46997 (accessed: 25 March 2015).

71 Radio Tamazuj, 'South Sudan vice-president acknowledges massive corruption in collection of non-oil revenues' (2014), available at https://radiotamazuj.org/en/

article/south-sudan-vp-acknowledges-massive-corruption-collection-non-oil-revenues (accessed: 28 March 2014).

72 Author's email correspondence with Lual Deng, 8 August 2015.

73 Author's email correspondence with L. B. Lokosang, 8 August 2015.

74 *Sudan Tribune*, 'S. Sudan presidency warns finance officials over bribery' (18 November 2014), available at http://www.sudantribune.com/spip. php?article53080 (accessed: 25 March 2015).

75 Ibid.

76 In this book, 'Southern Sudan' is used to refer to the southern region of united Sudan until 2011 and 'South Sudan' is used to refer to the independent country thereafter.

77 J. Werve (ed.), *The Corruption Notebooks*, pp. 231–2 (Washington, DC: Global Integrity, 2006).

78 *Sudan Tribune*, 'SPLA top generals asked by anti-corruption to declare their assets' (27 February 2012), available at http://www.sudantribune.com/spip. php?article41727 (accessed: 13 April 2015).

79 Author's email to Ngor Garang, 6 August 2015.

80 Author's email to Charles Bakheit, 5 August 2015.

81 Author's email to Garang Atem, 2 August 2015.

82 Johann Graf Lambsdorff, 'Corruption and rent-seeking', *Public Choice*, vol. 113 (2002), p. 1.

83 Radio Tamazuj, 'War economy: South Sudan fiscal report delayed after Q1 overspend' (2015), available at https://radiotamazuj.org/en/article/war-economy-south-sudan-fiscal-report-delayed-after-q1-overspend (accessed: 28 March 2015).

6 Social media as a transmitting channel of fear

1 DW, 'South Sudan President Salva Kiir downplays refugee crisis' (2017), available at https://www.dw.com/en/south-sudan-president-salva-kiir-downplays-refugee-crisis/a-40209980 (accessed: 21 September 2020).

2 ITU News, .How South Sudan is using icts to improve lives' (7 November 2018), available at https://news.itu.int/newest-nation-on-earth-using-icts-south-sudan/ (accessed: 24 September 2020).

3 https://static1.squarespace.com/static/54257189e4b0ac0d5fca1566/t/5c799e9424a6 94995f583879/1551474335039/PeaceTech+Lab+-+South+Sudan+Lexicon+II.pdf.

4 John S. Mill, J. Bentham, and J. Austin, *Utilitarianism; and, On liberty: Including Mill's "Essay on Bentham" and Selections from the Writings of Jeremy Bentham and John Austin*, ed. M. Warnock, p. 135 (Malden, MA: Blackwell, 2003).

5   P. P. Howell, *The Nile: Sharing a Scarce Resource*, p. 124 (Cambridge: Cambridge University Press, 1996); Robert O. Collins, *Civil Wars and Revolution in the Sudan: Essays on the Sudan, Southern Sudan and Darfur 1962–2004*, p. 35 (Hollywood: Tsehai, 2005).

6   Author's conversation with a businessman Makur Chep, Juba, July 2019.

7   *Sudan Tribune*, 'Warrap youth condemn minister's assault on MP' (22 November 2013).

8   I thank Chiengkuach Mabil and other friends from Hol and Nyarweng, who helped in providing data that made up this paragraph.

9   Author's Facebook exchange with Rt. Rev. Moses Deng Bol, Archbishop of the Internal Province of Western Bahr Al Ghazal of the Episcopal Church of South Sudan, 14 January 2020.

10 Archibald Shaw, 'Jieng (Dinka) Songs', *Man*, vol. 17 (1917), pp. 46–50.

11 Solomon Ateng Amos Agok, wrote on his Facebook wall, 25 January 2020.

12 Ibid.

13 Ibid.

14 A line from the 2018: Kur Matiop Kur (known as K–2) from the Twic's section of Pakeer who composed a song entitled 'Awalwala'.

15 Author's WhatsApp conversation with Dr Majak D'Agoot, 2018.

7 The role of the external actors in South Sudan's conflict

1   Scopas S. Poggo, *The First Sudanese Civil War: Africans, Arabs, and Israelis in the Southern Sudan, 1955–1972* (New York: Palgrave Macmillan, February 2009).

2   See the report by Ted Dagne, a specialist in African Affairs and personal friend of Dr John Garang, available at https://fas.org/sgp/crs/row/R41900.pdf.

3   Ibid.

4   BBC, 'Sudan coup: Why Omar al-Bashir was overthrown' (15 April 2019), available at https://www.bbc.com/news/world-africa-47852496.

5   *African Arguments*, 'Abyei: Sudan and South Sudan's new chance to solve old disputes' (21 October 2019), available at https://africanarguments. org/2019/10/21/abyei-sudan-south-sudan-new-chance-old-disputes/.

6   See the Congressional Research Service report by Ted Dagne, a specialist in African affairs and personal friend of Dr John Garang, available at https://fas.org/ sgp/crs/row/R41900.pdf.

7   https://www.undocs.org/S/2020/342; AI (2017); UNSC (2016a, paras 65–87; 2017, paras 109–28; 2018a, paras 69–82).

8   John Young, 'A Fractious Rebellion: Inside the SPLM-IO', Working Paper No. 39 (Small Arms Survey, September 2015), available at http://www.

smallarmssurveysudan.org/fileadmin/docs/working-papers/HSBA-WP39-SPLM-IO.pdf.

9   https://www.conflictarm.com/wp-content/uploads/2015/06/Weapons_and_ammunition_airdropped_to_SPLA-iO_forces_in_South_Sudan.pdf.

10 Salman M. A. Salman, 'The new state of South Sudan and the hydro-politics of the Nile Basin', *Water International*, vol. 36, no. 2 (2011), pp. 154–66, DOI: 10.1080/02508060.2011.557997.

11 https://www.sudanspost.com/egypt-to-open-alexandria-university-branch-in-tonj-by-april-next-year-changson/.

12 Author's exchanges via Messenger with Dr James Okuk, CSPS senior research fellow and political analyst based in Juba, 21 July 2020.

13 https://www.un.org/esa/agenda21/natlinfo/countr/china/2007_fullreport.pdf.

14 https://thediplomat.com/2019/02/how-china-came-to-dominate-south-sudans-oil/.

15 https://qz.com/africa/1111402/south-sudan-china-win-win-diplomacy-struggles/.

16 https://africacenter.org/spotlight/implications-for-africa-china-one-belt-one-road-strategy/.

17 Roger G. Brown, *Fashoda Reconsidered: The Impact of Domestic Politics on French Policy in Africa, 1893–1898* (Baltimore: Johns Hopkins University Press, 1970); Robert O. Collins, *The Southern Sudan. 1883–1893: A struggle for control* (New Haven: Yale University Press, 1962); Robert O. Collins, *King Leopold, England and the Upper Nile, 1889–1909*, p. 50 (New Haven: Yale University Press, 1968).

18 L. Kuo, 'There's at least one place in Africa where China's "win win" diplomacy is failing', Quartz Africa (21 November 2017), available at https://qz.com/africa/1111402/south-sudan-china-win-win-diplomacy-struggles/ (accessed: 26 November 2020).

19 Lesley Connolly, 'The need for a holistic approach to peace and development in the Gambia', *Journal of Peacebuilding & Development*, vol. 13, no. 1 (2018), pp. 96–102, DOI: 10.1080/15423166.2017.1415769.

20 https://sustainabledevelopment.un.org/index.php?page=view&type=30022&nr=81&menu=3170.

21 https://www.hartenergy.com/exclusives/south-sudan-when-oil-becomes-curse-31242; https://en.tempo.co/read/539251/14-chinese-workers-killed-in-south-sudan.

22 https://www.crisisgroup.org/africa/horn-africa/south-sudan/288-china-s-foreign-policy-experiment-south-sudan.

23 https://www.conflictarm.com/wp-content/uploads/2015/06/Weapons_and_ammunition_airdropped_to_SPLA-iO_forces_in_South_Sudan.pdf.

24 https://foreignpolicy.com/2018/11/29/how-eu-and-chinese-arms-diverted-to-south-sudan-fueled-its-civil-war-small-arms-warfare-east-africa-conflict-china-weapons-exports-humanitarian-crisis-juba-peace-deal-salva-kiir/.

25 https://www.conflictarm.com/wp-content/uploads/2015/06/Weapons_and_ammunition_airdropped_to_SPLA-iO_forces_in_South_Sudan.pdf.

26 Scopas S. Poggo, *The First Sudanese Civil War: Africans, Arabs, and Israelis in the Southern Sudan, 1955–1972* (New York: Palgrave Macmillan, February 2009).

27 Yotam Gidron, '"One People, One Struggle": Anya-Nya propaganda and the Israeli Mossad in Southern Sudan, 1969–1971', *Journal of Eastern African Studies*, vol. 12, no. 3 (2018), 428–53, DOI: 10.1080/17531055.2018.1480103.

28 Atem Yaak Atem, *Jungle Chronicles and Other Writings: Recollections of a South Sudanese*, p. 314 (Australia: Africa World Books, 2017).

29 Author's exchanges with Yotam Gidron, researcher with the International Refugee Rights Initiative and a PhD student in African history at Durham University, who has written on Israel in Africa, 20 July 2020.

30 Ibid.

31 Ibid.

32 https://www.conflictarm.com/reports/weapon-supplies-into-south-sudans-civil-war/

33 Ibid.

34 Atem, *Jungle Chronicles,* p. 324.

35 Gidron, 'One People, One Struggle'.

36 SBS Dinka Radio interview with Gen. Malong Awan, 20 July 2020, available at https://www.sbs.com.au/language/english/audio/paul-malong-akol-koor-is-forcing-out-people-he-regarded-an-obstacle-to-his-mission-of-taking-the-presidency-from-kiir (accessed: 26 November 2020).

37 SBS Dinka Radio interview with Gen. Malong Awan, 20 July 2020, available at https://www.sbs.com.au/language/english/audio/paul-malong-akol-koor-is-forcing-out-people-he-regarded-an-obstacle-to-his-mission-of-taking-the-presidency-from-kiir?fbclid=IwAR3uA12LilWuBEszL_50lPFeiDJQI5bkdMAbfLkGf5PLX3Twz9RH9PUNnFk.

38 Mareike Schomerus, '"They forget what they came for": Uganda's army in Sudan', *Journal of Eastern African Studies*, vol. 6, no. 1 (2012), 124–53, p. 128, DOI: 10.1080/17531055.2012.664707.

39 Ibid.

40 ACCORD (n.d.), 'South Sudan – Uganda Relations', available at https://www.accord.org.za/conflict-trends/south-sudan-uganda-relations/ (Accessed: 26 November 2020). .

41 K. Oberg, 'The Kingdom of Ankole in Uganda' in M. Fortes and E. E. Evans-Pritchard (eds), *African Political Systems*, pp. 121–62 (London: Oxford University Press, 1940); Edward L. Steinhart, *Conflict and Collaboration: The*

Kingdoms of Western Uganda, 1890–1907 (Princeton, NJ: Princeton University Press, 1977).

42 Author's conversation with a Ugandan business man in Juba, who shared the insights, which he said he heard from a Ugandan political scientist, Juba, February 2020.

43 Ibid.

44 http://www.smallarmssurveysudan.org/fileadmin/docs/briefing-papers/HSBA-BP-Mathiang-Anyoor.pdf.

45 Author's Facebook exchange with Aken Tong, social commentator from Gen. Malong's home turf, 8 June 2020.

46 Author's exchanges with an analyst based in Washington, DC, who did not give permission to be named; Author's WhatsApp exchange with a Ugandan business owner based in Juba, 17 July 2020.

47 Author's WhatsApp exchange with an SPLM-FDs leader in July 2020.

48 Author's conversation with a member of the SPLM's former detainees who had attended the meetings with Museveni, July 2018.

49 Author's Twitter conversation with an American analyst who did not want to be mentioned, 19 July 2020.

50 Author's conversation with a member of the SPLM's former detainees who had attended the meetings with Museveni, July 2018.

51 https://www.afdb.org/fileadmin/uploads/afdb/Documents/Project-and-Operations/South_Sudan_-_A_Study_on_Competitiveness_and_Cross_Border_Trade_With_Neighbouring_Countries.pdf.

52 https://www.independent.co.ug/south-sudan-billions-excite-uganda-traders/.

53 Author's exchanges with a Ugandan businessman in Juba, 21 July 2020.

54 Mogiya Nduru, 'Turning to Agriculture', *Inter Press Service* (8 April 2016), available at http://www.ipsnews.net/2016/04/need-to-encourage-agriculture/ (accessed: 26 March 2020).

55 Mareike Schomerus and Kristof Titeca 'Deals and dealings: Inconclusive peace and treacherous trade along the South Sudan–Uganda border', *Africa Spectrum*, vol. 47, no. 2–3 (2012), p. 13 (accessed: 21 July 2020, from www.jstor.org/stable/23350449).

56 John F. Clark, 'Explaining Ugandan intervention in Congo: Evidence and interpretations'. *Journal of Modern African Studies*, vol. 39, no. 2 (2001), pp. 261–87, available at: www.jstor.org/stable/3557264 (accessed: 22 July 2020).

57 E. E. Evans-Pritchard, 'The Nuer of the Southern Sudan', in E. E. Evans-Pritchard and M. Fortes (eds) *African Political Systems*, p. 296 (London: Oxford University Press, 1940); Sharon E. Hutchinson, *Nuer Dilemmas: Coping with Money, War, and the State*, pp. 103, 281, 284 (Berkely: University of California Press, 1996).

58 Cherry Leonardi, *Dealing with Government in South Sudan: Histories of Chiefship, Community and State*, p. 3 (Woodbridge, UK: Boydell and Brewer, 2013).

59 Lazarus L. Mawut, 'The Southern Sudan under British rule 1898–1924: The constraints reassessed'. PhD thesis, Durham University, available at http://etheses. dur.ac.uk/971/.

60 Ibid.

61 http://www.smallarmssurveysudan.org/fileadmin/docs/working-papers/HSBA-WP39-SPLM-IO.pdf.

62 https://www.conflictarm.com/wp-content/uploads/2015/06/Weapons_and_ammunition_airdropped_to_SPLA-iO_forces_in_South_Sudan.pdf, p. 5.

63 https://www.hrw.org/news/2020/05/08/un-security-council-should-renew-south-sudan-arms-embargo#.

64 https://www.aljazeera.com/news/2020/10/3/sudans-government-rebels-set-to-sign-landmak-deal.

65 *Sudan Tribune*, 'South Sudan's Kiir fired deputy foreign affairs minister over "repulsive remark": Source' (7 May 2013), available at https://www.sudantribune.com/spip.php?article46496.

66 Ibid.

67 Kiir's nephew, Thiik Thiik Mayardit, in an interview with a Dinka language radio, hosted by the journalist Ajak Deng Chiengkou, has claimed that 'officials working for President Kiir created many enemies for him', available at https://www.mixcloud.com/dinka2/thiik-thiikofficials-working-for-president-kiir-created-many-enemies-for-him-thiik-thiikofficials-wo/ (accessed: 28 November 2019).

68 Daniel Gardner, *The Science of Fear: How the Culture of Fear Manipulates Your Brain*, p. 128 (New York: Plume, 2009).

69 Reuters, 'U.N. says South Sudan army, rebels stealing humanitarian aid' (2014), available at https://www.reuters.com/article/us-southsudan-unrest-un-idUSBREA0E03M20140115.

70 The 211 Magazine, 'President Salva Kiir donates 10,000 bags of rice to Bahr El Ghazal', available at https://www.youtube.com/watch?v=nEkJzbtvLao (accessed 26 November 2020).

71 Daniel van Oudenaren, 'Politicised humanitarian aid is fuelling South Sudan's civil war' (27 February 2017), available at https://www.thenewhumanitarian.org/opinion/2017/02/27/politicised-humanitarian-aid-fuelling-south-sudan-s-civil-war.

72 Sarah de Simone, 'Playing the 'fragile state' card: The SPLM and state extraversion in South Sudan', *The Journal of Modern African Studies*, vol. 56, no. 3 (2018), 395–420. DOI:10.1017/S0022278X18000290.

73 Ibid.

74 Daniel Akech Thiong, 'South Sudan: How warring parties play international donors', African Arguments (20 March 2019), available at https://africanarguments.org/2019/03/20/south-sudan-aid-warring-parties-play-international-donors/ (accessed: 26 November 2020).

75 Christine Monaghan, 'In South Sudan, denial of humanitarian aid is a war tactic' (2018), available at http://www.ipsnews.net/2018/05/south-sudan-denial-humanitarian-aid-war-tactic/.

76 Robbie Gramer, Famine-wracked South Sudan now wants to charge aid workers for help (2017), available at https://foreignpolicy.com/2017/03/09/famine-wracked-south-sudan-now-wants-to-charge-aid-workers-for-help/.

8 South Sudan's peace architecture

1 Felix Haass and Martin Ottmann, 'Profits from peace: The political economy of power-sharing and corruption', *World Development*, vol. 99 (2017), pp. 60–74; Christopher M. Faulkner, 'Buying peace? Civil war peace duration and private military and security companies', *Civil Wars*, vol. 21, no. 1 (2019), 83–103. DOI: 10.1080/13698249.2017.1406037; Daniel Akech Thiong, 'South Sudan: Buying off elites to stop fighting will not work. Here is what might', *African Arguments* (12 March 2018), available at https://africanarguments.org/2018/03/12/south-sudan-buying-off-elites-to-stop-fighting-wont-work-heres-what-might/ (accessed: 26 March 2020).

2 William Davison, 'Failing South Sudan: First as tragedy, then as farce', *African Arguments* (4 October 2016), available at https://africanarguments.org/2016/10/04/failing-south-sudan-first-as-tragedy-then-as-farce/.

3 United Nations Office for the Coordination of Humanitarian Affairs, 'South Sudan', available at https://www.unocha.org/south-sudan (accessed: 26 March 2020).

4 Philippe Le Billon, 'Buying peace or fuelling war: The role of corruption in armed conflicts', *Journal of International Development*, vol. 15 (2003), pp. 413–26; Haass and Ottmann, 'Profits from peace', pp. 60–7.

5 John Young, 'A fractious rebellion: Inside the SPLM-IO' (Small Arms Survey, Human Security Baseline Assessment (HSBA) Working Paper 39, September 2015), available at http://www.smallarmssurveysudan.org/fileadmin/docs/working-papers/HSBA-WP39-SPLM-IO.pdf.

6 Small Arms Survey, 'David Yau Yau's rebellion' (2013), available at http://www.smallarmssurveysudan.org/fileadmin/docs/facts-figures/south-sudan/armed-groups/southern-dissident-militias/HSBA-Armed-Groups-Yau-Yau.pdf.

7 Daniel Akech Thiong, 'South Sudan: How warring parties play international donors', *African Arguments* (20 March 2019), available at https://africanarguments.org/2019/03/20/south-sudan-aid-warring-parties-play-international-donors/.

8 Radio Tamazuj, 'SPLA-IO'S deputy chief of staff defects to Kiir' (17 March 2020), available at https://radiotamazuj.org/en/news/article/spla-io-s-deputy-chief-of-staff-defects-to-kiir (accessed: 26 March 2020).

Conclusion

1 C. Robin, *Fear : The History of a Political Idea* (Oxford: Oxford University Press, 2016).

2 Jongkor Mayol, 'CCSS Host Mr. Morwell Ater Morwell. Juba regime and new national dialogue, what is the intentions' available at https://www.youtube.com/watch?v=Px2sy00loQA (accessed: 26 November 2020).

3 Shiping Tang, 'The onset of ethnic war: A general theory', *Sociological Theory*, vol. 33, no. 3 (2015), pp. 256–79.

4 Jack Snyder and Karen Ballentine, 'Nationalism and the marketplace of ideas', *International Security*, vol. 21, no. 2 (1996), pp. 5–40.

Bibliography

Acemoglu, D. (2003). 'Root causes: A historical approach to assessing the role of institutions in economic development', *Finance & Development*, 40, pp. 27–30.

Adam, C., and Crawfurd, L. (2012). *Exchange Rate Options for South Sudan*, mimeo prepared for DFID-Sudan. Available at http://users.ox.ac.uk/~cadam/pdfs/Adam_Crawfurd_Exchange%20Rate%20Options%20for%20South%20Sudan_Version2_1_May_2012.pdf (accessed: 24 November 2020).

African Arguments (2013). 'Choosing to be a Dinka: Selecting ethnicity remains to be an elite privilege', 28 February. Available at http://africanarguments.org/2014/02/28/choosing-to-be-a-dinka-selecting-ethnicity-remains-an-elite-privilege/ (accessed: 2 April 2017).

Ajak, O. D. (2015). Interviewed by Ajak Deng Chiengkou for *SBS Dinka Radio* (26 April).

Al Hussein, Z. R. (2016). 'South Sudan: Dangerous rise in ethnic hate speech must be reined in', *United Nations Human Rights Office of the High Commissioner*, 25 October [online]. Available at http://www.ohchr.org/EN/NewsEvents/Pages/DisplayNews.aspx?NewsID=20757 (accessed: 14 June 2017).

Alesinaa, A., and Angeletos, G.-M. (2005). 'Corruption, inequality, and fairness', *Journal of Monetary Economics*, 52, pp. 1227–44.

Anderson, R. M., and May, R. M. (1991). *Infectious Diseases of Humans: Dynamics and Control*. Oxford: Oxford University Press.

Awolich, A., and Ding Akol, Z. (2013). 'The SPLM leadership contest: An opportunity for change or a crisis of governance?' *SUDD Institute Policy Brief*.

Baguoot, L. (2017). Available at http://www.facebook.com (accessed: 14 March 2017).

Bailey, N. T. J. (1975). *The Mathematical Theory of Infectious Diseases and Its Applications*. 2nd edn. London: Griffin.

Bamerjee, A. V. (1992). 'A simple model of herd behavior', *Quarterly Journal of Economics*, 107 (3), pp. 797–817.

Basnett, Y., and Garang, J. A. (2014). 'Exiting the cycle of conflict in South Sudan: diversifying trade for sustained and inclusive prosperity', ODI Working Paper. Available at http://www.odi.org/sites/odi.org.uk/fi les/odi-assets/publications-opinion-fi les/9605.pdf.

Becker, S., Egger, P. H., and Seidel, T. (2008). 'Corruption epidemics', *Stirling Economics Discussion Paper, 2008–09*.

Bikhchandani, S., Hirshleifer, D., and Welch, I. (1992). 'A theory of fads, fashion, custom, and cultural change as informational cascades', *Journal of Political Economy*, 100 (5), pp. 992–1026.

Bikhchandani, S., Hirshleifer, D., and Welch, I. (1998). 'Learning from the behavior of others: Conformity, fads, and informational cascades', *Journal of Economic Perspectives*, 12 (3), pp. 151–70.

Billon, P. L. (2001). 'The political ecology of war: Natural resources and armed conflicts', *Political Geography*, 20 (5), pp. 561–84.

Biong, L., and Kuol, D. (2017). 'Dinka youth in civil war: Between cattle, community and government', in Victoria Brereton (ed.). *Informal Armies: Community Defence Groups in South Sudan's Civil War*. Saferworld, pp. 19–26.

Blanchard, Ph., et al. (2005). 'The epidemics of corruption'. Available at arXiv:physics/0505031 [physics.soc-ph].

Bratton, M., and van de Walle, N. (1997). *Democratic Experiments in Africa: Regime Transitions in Comparative Perspective*. Cambridge: Cambridge University Press, p. 277.

Breidlid, A., Said, A. A., Breidlid, A. K., Farren, A., and Wawa, Y. H. (2014). *A Concise History of South Sudan*. Kampala, Uganda: Fountain, pp. 112–13.

Breidlid, I. M., and Arensen, M. J. (2017). 'The Nuer White Armies: Comprehending South Sudan's most infamous community defence group', in Victoria Brereton (ed.). *Informal Armies: Community Defence Groups in South Sudan's Civil War*. Saferworld, pp. 29–39.

Chiengkou, A. (2019). Interview with former minister of finance Arthur Akuien Chol. Available at https://www.sbs.com.au/language/english/audio/i-was-controlling-money-but-they-needed-me-out-south-sudanese-former-minister-of-finance-speaks (accessed: 28 November 2019).

Clapham, C. S. (ed.) (1982). *Private Patronage and Public Power: Political Clientelism in the Modern State*. New York: St. Martin's Press, pp. 162–92.

Clapham, C. S. (2017). *The Horn of Africa: State Formation and Decay*. London: Hurst.

Coghlan, N. (2017). *Collapse of a Country: A Diplomat's Memoir of South Sudan*. Montreal: McGill-Queens University Press, pp. 117–18.

Collier, P., and Hoeffler, A. (1998). 'On economic causes of civil war', *Oxford Economic Papers*, 50 (4), pp. 563–73.

Collier, P., and Hoeffler, A. (2004). 'Greed and grievance in civil war', *Oxford Economic Papers*, 56 (4), pp. 563–95.

Collier, P., Hoeffler, A., and Rohner, D. (2009). 'Beyond greed and grievance: Feasibility and civil war', *Oxford Economic Papers*, 61 (1), pp. 1–27.

Collins, R. O. (2005). *Civil Wars and Revolution in the Sudan: Essays on the Sudan, Southern Sudan and Darfur 1962–2004*. Hollywood: Tsehai.

Corradi, J. E., Fagen, P. W., and Garretón, Manuel A. (1992). *Fear at the Edge: State Terror and Resistance in Latin America*. Berkeley: University of California Press, pp. 3–4.

D'Agoôt, M. (2018). 'Taming the dominant gun class in South Sudan', Special Report No. 4: Envisioning A Stable South Sudan. Available at https://africacenter.org/spotlight/taming-the-dominant-gun-class-in-south-sudan/.

D'Agoôt, M. (2019). 'Assessing the utility of risk management theory in the governance of new states: Lessons from South Sudan', *Journal of Risk Research*, 23 (2), pp. 201–26. doi: 10.1080/13669877.2019.1569089.

D'Agostino, G., Dunne, J. P., and Pieroni, L. (2016). 'Corruption and growth in Africa', *European Journal of Political Economy*, 43, pp. 71–88.

De Manyang, D. (2017). Available at http://www.facebook.com (accessed: 14 March 2017).

De Simone, S. (2018). 'Playing the 'fragile state' card: The SPLM and state extraversion in South Sudan', *Journal of Modern African Studies*, 56 (3), pp. 395–420. doi:10.1017/S0022278X18000290.

De Waal, A. (2014). 'When kleptocracy becomes insolvent: Brute causes of the civil war in South Sudan', *African Affairs*, 113 (452), pp. 347–69.

De Waal, A. (2015). *The Real Politics of the Horn of Africa: Money, War and the Business of Power*. Cambridge: Polity, pp. 91– 6.

Debrix, F., and Barder, A. D. (2009). 'Nothing to fear but fear: Governmentality and the biopolitical production of terror', *International Political Sociology*, 3 (4), pp. 398–413.

Deng, F. M. (1995). *War of Visions: Conflict of Identities in Sudan*. Washington, DC: Brookings Institution.

Deng, T. (2018). Available at http://www.facebook.com (accessed: 19 April 2018).

Development Policy Forum (2015). 'Development Policy Forum discussion on the LCs saga'. Google group discussion.

Dimakou, O. (2015). 'Bureaucratic corruption and the dynamic interaction between monetary and fiscal policy', *European Journal of Political Economy*, 40, pp. 57–78.

Doki, C. (2013). 'Civil servants unpaid as S. Sudan struggles to repay loans'. Available at http://www.voanews.com/content/south-sudan-civil-service-foreign-loans-salaries/1795044.html (accessed: 7 April 2015).

Enough Project (2016). 'Violent kleptocracies: How they're destroying parts of Africa and how they can be dismantled'. Available at https://enoughproject.org/reports/violent-kleptocracies-how-theyre-destroying-parts-africa-and-how-they-can-be-dismantled (accessed: 24 November 2020).

Evans-Pritchard, E. E. (1940). 'The Nuer of the Southern Sudan', in E. E. Evans-Pritchard and M. Fortes (eds). *African political systems*. London: Oxford University Press, p. 296.

Fajgelbaum, P., Goldberg, P., Kennedy, P., and Khandelwal, A. (2019). 'The return to protectionism'. Available at https://voxeu.org/article/return-protectionism.

Fortes, M., Evans-Pritchard, E. E. and International African Institute (1955). *African Political Systems*. London: Oxford University Press.

Frahm, O. (2014). *How a State Is Made: Statebuilding and Nationbuilding in South Sudan in the Light of Its African Peers*. Berlin: Humboldt University, p. 281. Available at http://edoc.hu-berlin.de/dissertationen/frahm-ole-2014-12-16/PDF/frahm.pdf (accessed: 31 October 2019).

Frahm, O. (2015). 'Making borders and identities in South Sudan', *Journal of Contemporary African Studies*, 33 (2), pp. 1–17.

Frank, T. (2005). *What's the Matter with Kansas? How Conservatives Won the Heart of America*. New York: Metropolitan/Owl Book, pp. 76–7.

Gardner, D. (2009). *The Science of Fear: How the Culture of Fear Manipulates Your Brain*. New York: Plume, pp. 128, 142.

Gaviria, A. (2002). 'Assessing the effects of corruption and crime on firm performance: Evidence from Latin America', *Emerging Markets Review*, 3, pp. 245–68.

Glaeser, E. L. (2005). 'The political economy of hatred', *Quarterly Journal of Economics*, 120 (1), pp. 45–86.

Goel, R. K., and Nelson, M. A. (2010). 'Causes of corruption: History, geography and government', *Journal of Policy Modeling*, 32, pp. 433–47.

Gonzales, M. G., and Delgado, R. (2015). *Politics of Fear: How Republicans Use Money, Race and the Media to Win*. 8th edn. Florence: Taylor and Francis.

Gramer, R. (2017). 'Famine-wracked South Sudan now wants to charge aid workers for help'. Available at https://foreignpolicy.com/2017/03/09/famine-wracked-south-sudan-now-wants-to-charge-aid-workers-for-help/.

Granovetter, M. (1978). 'Threshold models of collective behavior', *American Journal of Sociology*, 83 (6), p. 1420.

Hathroubi, S., and Trabelsi, H. (2014). 'Epidemic corruption: A bio-economic homology', *European Scientific Journal*, 10 (10).

Holland, H. (2012). South Sudan officials have stolen $4 billion: president. Available at https://www.reuters.com/article/us-southsudan-corruption/south-sudan-officials-have-stolen-4-billion-president-idUSBRE8530QI20120604 (accessed: 24 November 2020).

Howell, P. P. (1996). *The Nile: Sharing a Scarce Resource*. Cambridge: Cambridge University Press, p. 124.

Hutchinson, S. E. (1996). *Nuer Dilemmas: Coping With Money, War, and the State.* Berkeley: University of California Press.

Hutton, L. (2014). 'Prolonging the agony of UNMISS: The implementation challenges of a new mandate during a civil war'. Available at https://www.clingendael.org/ sites/default/files/pdfs/Prolonging%20the%20agony%20of%20UNMISS%20-%20 Lauren%20Hutton.pdf (accessed: 24 November 2020).

Idris, H. F. (2004). 'Modern Developments in the Dinka language'. Goteborg African Informal Series – No. 3; Dept of Oriental and African languages, p. 21.

International Crisis Group (2014). *South Sudan: A Civil War by Any Other Name.* Belgium: International Crisis Group.

Jaspars, S. (2019). *Food Aid in Sudan: A History of Power, Politics and Profit.* London: Zed Books.

Johnson, D. H. (2008). 'Why Abyei matters: The breaking point of Sudan's comprehensive peace agreement', *African Affairs*, 107 (426), pp. 1–19.

Johnson, D. H. (2014). 'Briefing: The crisis in South Sudan', *African Affairs*, 113 (451), pp. 300–9.

Johnson, H. (2016). *South Sudan: The Untold Story from Independence to War.* London: I.B. Tauris, pp. 94–5.

Johnston, M. (1996). 'The political consequences of corruption: A reassessment', *Comparative Politics*, 18 (4), pp. 459–77.

Jok, C. J. (2019). Available at http://www.facebook.com (accessed: 19 January 2019).

Jok, J. M. (2017). *Breaking Sudan: The Search for Peace.* London: Oneworld.

Kaufmann, C. (1996). 'Possible and impossible solutions to ethnic civil wars', *International Security*, 20 (4), pp. 146–7.

Keen, D. (2012). 'Greed and grievance in civil war', *International Affairs*, 88 (4), pp. 757–77.

Kiir, S. (2016). Interview with President Salva Kiir. Interview by Jeff Koinage for *KTN News Kenya*, 3 August [online]. Available at https://www.youtube.com/ watch?v=hOQEyFk-4do (accessed: 17 March 2017).

Kuol, D. A. (2018). Interview by Mading Ngor for 'Fixing South Sudan: Ideas for the new nation', Dolku Media, 30 November. Available at https://www.youtube.com/ watch?v=_U_pcSQWRMk (accessed: 5 December 2018).

Kuol, L. B. D. (2017). 'Dinka youth in civil war: Between cattle, community and government', in Victoria Brereton (ed.), *Informal Armies: Community Defence Groups in South Sudan's Civil War.* Saferworld, pp. 19–26.

Lake, D. A., and Rothchild, D. (1996). 'Containing fear: The origins and management of ethnic conflict', *International Security*, 21 (2), pp. 41–75.

Lambsdorff, J. G. (2002). 'Corruption and rent-seeking', *Public Choice*, 113, p. 1.

Laudati, A. (2011). 'Victims of discourse: Mobilizing narratives of fear and insecurity in post-conflict South Sudan – the case of Jonglei State', *African Geographical Review*, 30 (1), p. 17.

Le Billon, P. (2003). 'Buying peace or fueling war: The role of corruption in armed conflicts', *Journal of International Development*, 15, pp. 413–26.

Leach, J. (2013). *War and Politics in Sudan: Cultural Identities and the Challenges of the Peace Process*. London: I.B. Tauris, pp. 223–4.

Leonardi, C. (2007). '"Liberation" or capture: Youth in between "hakuma", and "home" during civil war and its aftermath in Southern Sudan', *African Affairs*, 106 (424), pp. 391–412.

Leonardi, C. (2013). *Dealing with Government in South Sudan: Histories of Chiefship, Community and State*. Woodbridge, UK: Boydell and Brewer.

Levy, Jacob T. (2016). 'Authoritarianism and post-truth politics'. Niskanen Center, 30 November. Available at https://www.niskanencenter.org/authoritarianism-post-truth-politics/ (accessed: 28 November 2019).

Lichbach, M. I. (1987). 'Deterrence or escalation? The puzzle of aggregate studies of repression and dissent', *Journal of Conflict Resolution*, 31 (2), pp. 266–97.

Lohmann, S. (1994). 'The dynamics of informational cascades: The monday demonstrations in Leipzig, East Germany, 1989-91', *World Politics*, 47 (1), pp. 42–101.

Makowsky, M. D., and Rubin, J. (2013). 'An agent-based model of centralized institutions, social network technology, and revolution', *PLoS ONE*, 8 (11). Available at https://doi.org/10.1371/journal.pone.0080380.

Malwal, B. (2014). *Sudan and South Sudan: From One to Two*. Oxford: Palgrave Macmillan, pp. 198–9.

Mearsheimer, J. J., and Van Evera, S. (1995). 'When peace means war: The partition that dare not speak its name', *The New Republic* (18 December), p. 18.

Ministry of Finance (2013). Email to the media, 25 November.

Monaghan, C. (2018). 'In South Sudan, denial of humanitarian aid is a war tactic'. Available at http://www.ipsnews.net/2018/05/south-sudan-denial-humanitarian-aid-war-tactic/.

Murshed, S. M., and Tadjoeddin, M. Z. (2009). 'Revisiting the greed and grievance explanations for violent internal conflict', *Journal of International Development*, 21 (1), pp. 87–111.

Neudorfer, N. S., and Theuerkauf, U. G. (2014). 'Buying war not peace: The influence of corruption on the risk of ethnic war', *Comparative Political Studies*, 47 (13), pp. 1856–86.

Ngor, Mading. (2018). 'South Sudan Imatong State Gov Tobiolo Oromo on SPLA-civil relations'. Available at https://www.youtube.com/watch?v=nNGsyYPRqe0 (accessed: 23 November 19).

Nyaba, P. A. (2019). *South Sudan: Elites, Ethnicity, Endless Wars and the Stunted State*. Dar es Salaam, Tanzania: Mkuki na Nyota.

Nyaba, P. A (1997). *The Politics of Liberation in South Sudan: An Insider's View*. Kampala: Fountain.

O'Neill, B. (1987). 'A measure for crisis instability with an application to space-based antimissile systems', *Journal of Conflict Resolution*, 31 (4), pp. 631–72.

Orjuela, C. (2014). 'Corruption and identity politics in divided societies', *Third World Quarterly*, 35 (5), pp. 753–69.

Paanluel (2013). 'The dura aga fat cats'. Available at https://paanluelwel.com/2013/01/06/the-dura-saga-fat-cats/ (accessed: 24 November 2020).

Paglia, P. (n.d.). 'Ethnicity and tribalism: Are these the root causes of the Sudanese civil conflicts? African conflicts and the role of ethnicity: A case study of Sudan', *Africa Economic Analysis*, p. 36. Available at https://citeseerx.ist.psu.edu/viewdoc/download?doi=10.1.1.553.8793&rep=rep1&type=pdf (accessed: 24 November 2020).

Pinaud, C. (2014). 'South Sudan: Civil war, predation and the making of a military aristocracy', *African Affairs*, 113 (451), pp. 192–211.

Poggo, S. S. (2009). *The First Sudanese Civil War: Africans, Arabs, and Israelis in the Southern Sudan, 1955–1972*, New York: Palgrave Macmillan.

Posen, B. (1993). 'The security dilemma and ethnic conflict', *Survival*, 35 (1), pp. 27–47.

Posen, B. (1997). 'The security dilemma and ethnic conflict', in Michael E. Brown (ed.). *Ethnic Conflict and International Security*. Cambridge, MA: MIT Press, pp. 10–124.

Radio Tamazuj (2013). 'Greater Bahr el-Ghazal governors pledge support to Kiir in next election'. Available at https://radiotamazuj.org/en/news/article/greater-bahr-el-ghazal-governors-pledge-support-to-kiir-in-next-election (accessed: 18 June 2017).

Radio Tamazuj (2014). 'President Kiir's legal advisor redraws red line on interim government'. Available at https://radiotamazuj.org/en/news/article/president-kiir-s-legal-advisor-redraws-red-line-on-interim-government (accessed: 14 June 2017).

Radio Tamazuj (2014). 'South Sudan vice-president acknowledges massive corruption in collection of non-oil revenues'. Available at https://radiotamazuj.org/en/news/article/south-sudan-vp- acknowledges-massive-corruption-in-collection-of-non-oil-revenues (accessed: 24 November 2020).

Radio Tamazuj (2014). 'South Sudanese chief negotiator paid 'allowance' of $2000 per day'. Available at https://radiotamazuj.org/en/news/article/south-sudanese-chief-negotiator-paid-allowance-of-2000-per-day (accessed: 24 November 2020).

Radio Tamazuj (2015). 'Kiir says he fears SPLM will turn against him after peace'. Available at https://radiotamazuj.org/en/news/article/kiir-says-he-fears-splm-will-turn-against-him-after-peace (accessed: 14 June 2017).

Radio Tamazuj (2015). 'Makuei slams Pagan Amum for signing IGAD document'. Available at https://radiotamazuj.org/en/news/article/makuei-slams-pagan-amum-for-signing-igad-document (accessed: 14 June 2017).

Radio Tamazuj (2015). 'South Sudan broadcast minister instructs gov't media to stop war propaganda'. Available at https://radiotamazuj.org/en/news/article/south-sudan-broadcast-minister-instructs-govt-media-to-stop-war-propaganda (accessed: 14 June 2017).

Radio Tamazuj (2015). 'War economy: South Sudan fiscal report delayed after Q1 overspend'. Available at https://radiotamazuj.org/en/news/article/war-economy-south-sudan-fiscal-report-delayed-after-q1-overspend (accessed: 24 November 2020).

Radio Tamazuj (2016). 'Dinka council of elders warns war over additional UNMISS troops'. Available at https://radiotamazuj.org/en/news/article/dinka-council-of-elders-warns-war-over-additional-unmiss-troops (accessed: 14 June 2017).

Radio Tamazuj (2017). 'Dinka council of elders says no short cut to presidency'. Available at https://radiotamazuj.org/en/news/article/dinka-council-of-elders-says-no-short-cut-to-presidency (accessed: 14 June 2017).

Radio Tamazuj (2017). 'Gen. Thomas Cirillo declares new rebel group'. Available at https://radiotamazuj.org/en/news/article/gen-thomas-cirillo-declares-new-rebel-group (accessed: 29 May 2018).

Radio Tamazuj (2018). 'Foreign minister says he was being 'humiliated' in Juba'. Available at https://radiotamazuj.org/en/news/article/foreign-minister-says-he-was-being-humiliated-in-juba (accessed: 21 May 2018).

Radio Tamazuj (2018). 'Kiir regrets sparing lives of Machar, Pagan's group'. Available at https://radiotamazuj.org/en/news/article/kiir-regrets-sparing-lives-of-machar-pagan-group#:~:text=President%20Kiir%20said%20he%20regretted,out%20 with%20them%20in%202013.&text=President%20Kiir%20arrested%20them%20 for,of%20them%20were%20eventually%20released (accessed: 24 November 2020).

Radio Tamazuj (2018). 'Kiir laments corruption: "I got people who know how to eat"'. Available at https://radiotamazuj.org/en/news/article/kiir-laments-corruption-i-got-people-who-know-how-to-eat (accessed: 27 November 2019).

Reno, W. (2002). 'Economies of war and their transformation: Sudan and the variable impact of natural resources on conflict', *Journal of Modern African Studies*, 40 (1), pp. 83–104.

Reno, W. (2007). 'Patronage politics and the behavior of armed groups', *Civil Wars*, 9 (4), pp. 324–42.

Republic of South Sudan (2011). 'Transitional Constitution of the Republic of South Sudan. Article 101/105'. Available at https://www.ilo.org/dyn/natlex/docs/MONOGRAPH/90704/116697/F762589088/SSD90704%202011C.pdf (accessed: 19 May 2018).

Reuters (2012). 'South Sudan officials have stolen $4 bln: President'. Available at https://www.reuters.com/article/uk-southsudan-corruption/south-sudan-officials-have-stolen-4-billion-president-idUKBRE8530RR20120604 (accessed: 24 November 2020).

Reuters (2014). 'U.N. says South Sudan army, rebels stealing humanitarian aid'. Available at https://www.reuters.com/article/us-southsudan-unrest-un-idUSBREA0E03M20140115.

Reuters (2017). 'Eight students die in Moi Girls School dormitory fire'. Available at https://www.reuters.com/article/us-kenya-school-fire/seven-kenyan-schoolgirls-die-in-dormitory-blaze-government-idUSKCN1BD0BS?utm_source=applenews (accessed: 24 November 2020).

Robin, Corey. (2006). *Fear: The History of a Political Idea*. Oxford: Oxford University Press.

Rogers, E. (1995). *The Diffusion of Innovations*. 4th edn. New York: Free Press.

Rolandsen, Ø. H., and Breidlid, I. M. (2013). 'What is youth violence in Jonglei', *PRIO Paper*, Oslo: Prio.

Rolandsen, Ø. H. (2015). 'Another civil war in South Sudan: The failure of guerrilla government?', *Journal of Eastern African Studies*, 9 (1), pp. 163–74.

Rolandsen, Ø. H., and Daly, M. W. (2016). *A History of South Sudan: From Slavery to Independence*. Cambridge: Cambridge University Press.

Rose-Ackerman, S. (1999). *Corruption and Government*. Cambridge: Cambridge University Press.

Rwakaringi, M. D. (2013). 'South Sudan to probe 'dura saga' grain swindle'. Available at https://www.voanews.com/africa/south-sudan-probe-dura-saga-grain-swindle (accessed: 24 November 2020).

SBS Dinka Radio (2017). 'Paul Malong: "Doctors need my DNA in order to identify the body of my daughter in Kenya but the presidency refused as per now"'. Available at https://www.sbs.com.au/language/english/audio/

paul-malong-doctors-need-my-dna-in-order-to-identify-the-body-of-my-daughter-in-kenya-but-the-presidency-refused-as-per-now.

Schomerus, M., and Taban, C. (2017). 'Arrow boys, armed groups and the SPLA: Intensifying insecurity in the Western Equatorian states', in Victoria Brereton (ed.). *Informal Armies: Community Defence Groups in South Sudan's Civil War*. Saferworld, pp. 6–16.

Schwartz, J. A., and Ariely, D. (2016). 'Life is a battlefield', *The Independent Review*, 20 (3), pp. 377–82.

Shleifer, A., and Vishny, R. W. (1993). 'Corruption', *Quarterly Journal of Economics*, 108 (3), pp. 599–617.

Small Arms Survey (2013). 'David Yau Yau's Rebellion'. Available at http://www.smallarmssurveysudan.org/fileadmin/docs/facts-figures/south-sudan/armed-groups/southern-dissident-militias/HSBA-Armed-Groups-Yau-Yau.pdf (accessed: 25 March 17).

Small Arms Survey (2014). 'The crisis in South Sudan: A podcast with HSBA consultant Joshua Craze' [Podcast]. 19 May.

Snyder, J., and Ballentine, K. (1996). 'Nationalism and the marketplace of ideas', *International Security*, 21 (2), pp. 5–40.

South Sudan (15 December 2013). 'National Conference of SPLA Board – President's Salva Kiir Speech'. Available at https://www.youtube.com/watch?v=5y3bp6Oehis (accessed: 28 November 2019).

Sudan Tribune (2011). 'Greater Equatoria demands federal system in South Sudan'. Available at http://www.sudantribune.com/spip.php?iframe&page=imprimable&id_article=38608 (accessed: 14 June 2017).

Sudan Tribune (2012). 'S. Sudan: Billions lost in fake contracts, inflated payrolls'. available at http://www.sudantribune.com/spip.php?article43293 (accessed: 7 April 2015).

Sudan Tribune (2012). 'SPLA top generals asked by anti-corruption to declare their assets'. Available at http://www.sudantribune.com/spip.php?article41727 (accessed: 13 April 2015).

Sudan Tribune (2013). 'Kiir threatens to dissolve parliament unless it supports Wani Igga's appointment'. Available at http://www.sudantribune.com/spip.php?article47776 (accessed: 14 June 2017).

Sudan Tribune (2013). 'S. Sudan police to arrest officials over cash stolen from presidency'. Available at http://www.sudantribune.com/spip.php?article46054 (accessed: 25 March 2015).

Sudan Tribune (2013). 'S. Sudan silent on $4.5bn loan obtained after oil shutdown'.
    Available at http://www.sudantribune.com/spip.php?article48903 (accessed:
    7 April 2015).

Sudan Tribune (2013). 'South Sudan president suspends two ministers for corruption
    probe'. Available at http://www.sudantribune.com/spip.php?article46997
    (accessed: 25 March 2015).

Sudan Tribune (2013). 'South Sudan's Kiir accuses army of corruption'. Available at
    http://www.sudantribune.com/spip.php?article48115 (accessed: 22 March 2015).

Sudan Tribune (2014). 'S. Sudan presidency warns finance officials over bribery'.
    Available at http://www.sudantribune.com/spip.php?article53080 (accessed:
    25 March 2015).

Sudan Tribune (2014). 'S. Sudanese rebels establish military command, create
    21 states'. Available at http://www.sudantribune.com/spip.php?article53509
    (accessed: 20 March 2017).

Sudan Tribune (2015). 'S. Sudan army chief rejects IGAD power-sharing proposal'.
    Available at http://sudantribune.com/spip.php?article55883 (accessed: 14
    June 2017).

Sudan Tribune (2015). 'S. Sudan justice minister acknowledges graft in government'.
    Available at http://www.sudantribune.com/spip.php?article57062 (accessed: 17
    November 2015).

Sudan Tribune (2017). 'Dinka Bor attack on Murle community leaves dozens dead,
    says Pibor commissioner'. Available at http://www.sudantribune.com/Dinka-Bor-
    attack-on-Murle,41548 (accessed: 20 March 2017).

Suliman, M. (1997). 'Civil war in Sudan: The impact of ecological degradation',
    Contributions in Black Studies, 15 (1), pp. 99–121.

Tang, S. (2008). 'Fear in international politics: Two positions', *International Studies
    Review*, 10 (3), pp. 451–71.

Tang, S. (2011). 'The security dilemma and ethnic conflict: Toward a dynamic and
    integrative theory of ethnic conflict', *Review of International Studies*, 37 (2),
    pp. 511–36.

Tang, S., Xiong, Y., and Li, H. (2017). 'Does oil cause ethnic war? Comparing
    evidence from process-tracing with quantitative results', Security Studies, 26 (3),
    pp. 359–90. doi: http://dx.doi.org/10.1080/09636412.2017.1306392.

The 211 Magazine (2019). 'President Salva Kiir donates 10,000 bags of rice to Bahr El
    Ghazal' [Online]. Available at https://www.youtube.com/watch?v=nEkJzbtvLao
    (accessed: 24 November 2020).

Thiong, D. A. (2014). 'How contracts are inflated in South Sudan'. Available at
    http://www.gurtong.net/ECM/Editorial/tabid/124/ctl/ArticleView/mid/519/

articleId/15309/How-Contracts-Are-Inflated-In-South-Sudan.aspx (accessed: 7 April 2015).

Thiong, D. A. (2018). 'How the politics of fear generated chaos in South Sudan', *African Affairs*, 117 (469), pp. 613–35. Available at https://doi.org/10.1093/afraf/ady031.

Thomas, E. (2015). *South Sudan: A Slow Liberation*. London: Zed Books.

United Nations Panel of Experts on South Sudan (2016). 'South Sudan's UN panel of experts report'. Available at https://www.undocs.org/S/2016/70; https://www.undocs.org/S/2016/793; https://www.undocs.org/S/2016/963 (accessed: 24 November 2020).

Van Oudenaren, D. 'Politicised humanitarian aid is fuelling South Sudan's civil war'. The New Humanitarian. Available at https://www.thenewhumanitarian.org/opinion/2017/02/27/politicised-humanitarian-aid-fuelling-south-sudan-s-civil-war.

Warner, L. A. (2016). 'The disintegration of the military integration process stability in South Sudan (2006–2013)', *Stability: International Journal of Security & Development*, 5 (1), pp. 1–20. doi: http://dx.doi.org/10.5334/sta.460.

Werve, J. (ed.) (2006). *The Corruption Notebooks*. Washington, DC: Global Integrity, pp. 231–2.

Williams, P. D. (2016). *War and Conflict in Africa*. Cambridge: Polity.

Wöndu, S. (2011). *From Bush to Bush: Journey to Liberty in South Sudan*. Nairobi, Kenya: Kenway.

Ylonen, A. (2005). 'Grievances and the roots of insurgencies: Southern Sudan and Darfur', *Peace, Conflict and Development: An Interdisciplinary Journal*, 7, pp. 99–134.

Yoshida, Y. (2013). 'Interethnic conflict in Jonglei State, South Sudan: Emerging ethnic hatred between the Lou Nuer and the Murle', *African Journal on Conflict Resolution*, 13 (2), p. 39.

Young, J. (2012). *The Fate of Sudan: Origins and Consequences of a Flawed Peace Process*. London: Zed Books.

Young, John. (2017). 'Isolation and endurance: Riek Machar and the SPLM-IO in 2016–2017'. Available at http://www.smallarmssurveysudan.org/fileadmin/docs/working-papers/HSBA-SPLM-IO-Update-Oct-2017.pdf (accessed: 28 November 2019).

Index

www.ingramcontent.com/pod-product-compliance
Lightning Source LLC
Chambersburg PA
CBHW050439280326
41932CB00013BA/2169